1975

P9-ARH-543

3 0301 00036953 4

This book may be kept

FOURTEEN DAY

A f

Tajos

'Costa del Sol they call this now; the hunger coast is what it used to be.'
Tajos countryman

'Creo que los que hicieron tantas cosas deben ser dueños de todas las cosas.'

'I believe that those who made so many things ought to be masters of everything.'

El Pueblo Pablo Neruda

Ronald Fraser

TAJOS

*The Story of a Village
on the Costa del Sol*

Pantheon Books
A Division of Random House, New York

LIBRARY
College of St. Francis

FIRST AMERICAN EDITION

Copyright © 1973 by Ronald Fraser

All rights reserved under International and Pan-American Copyright Conventions. Published in the United States by Pantheon Books, a division of Random House, New York. Originally published in Great Britain as *The Pueblo: A Mountain Village on the Costa del Sol* by Allen Lane, a division of Penguin Books, Ltd., London.

Library of Congress Cataloging in Publication Data
Fraser, Ronald, 1930-
Tajos; the story of a village on the Costa del Sol.
   1. Tajos, Spain—Social conditions.   2. Tajos, Spain—Economic conditions.
HN590.T3F7   1973   309.1'46'85   73-7010
ISBN 0-394-48002-3

Manufactured in the United States of America

914.685
F843

CONTENTS

	page
Glossary	ix
Introduction	1
The Old	9
Landowners: Three Sons	32
Men with Ideas	47
The Survivors: The Hungry Forties	71
Religion: Patron Saint and Parish Priest	109
New Men: The Ruling Group	119
Entrepreneurs	140
Men and Women: Engagement, Marriage and Parenthood	163
A Foreign Country	181
Foreigners: The Coming of Tourism	186
Youth: 'The Good Life'	201
Law and Order	233
Novios	235
Village School	244
Today . . . and Tomorrow?	256
Appendix A: Cost of Living and Wages in Tajos	261
Appendix B: The Land, Landowners and Farming	262
Appendix C: Some Aspects of Social Conditions in Rural Málaga, 1960–68	281
Acknowledgements	283
About the Author	287

69575

between pages 48 and 49

A water-driven corn mill in the countryside at the turn of the century

In the market: a fish-vendor today

'The thin white line separated into rows of low rectangular houses . . .' Tajos seen from the road up from the coast

The village lands reach to the sea; view over the roofs of the *barrio*

The main street, 1960

Tiles and concrete replace the old cobbles; a side street, 1970

Goatherd plaiting an esparto rope

On a mule track a small-holder makes his way to his farm

Acknowledgements

The photograph of the old corn mill is by courtesy of Mr V. T. Lees; those of other village scenes by courtesy of Fern Fraser and Berni Rich.

GLOSSARY

aguardiente, anise-flavoured spirit
alpargata, sandal usually made of esparto or hemp
bachillerato, matriculation
barrio, quarter or neighbourhood of village or town
buñuelo, doughnut, fritter
cacique, political boss
campo, the land; countryside
campiña, wheat-growing plains of the Andalusian interior
chiquillo, little one (endearment)
cochecito, little car (see *paseo* below)
colono, tenant farmer (either renter or sharecropper)
copita, small glass
Cortes, Spanish Parliament
cortijo, large farm
cuartilla, a quarter of an *arroba*
denuncia, information or charge laid against another person
feria, annual village fair in honour of patron saint
finca, land property; in Tajos usually a small farm
fonda, inn, pension
gazpacho, soup made traditionally of bread, oil, vinegar, tomatoes,
garlic and onion mixed with water
levante, east wind
mina, mine; as source of water, a gallery dug into mountain to
tap underground stream
novio, novia, boy-friend, girl-friend intending to marry
paseo, a walk; during revolution used in the sense of being 'taken
for a ride' in a *cochecito*, i.e. being shot
pueblo, village, the people

recovera, a person engaged in business of buying eggs in countryside to retail in town

señorito, master (applied to landlords, rich)

sindicato, trade union (today the corporate state-run trade union)

tortilla, omelette

vega, irrigated and fertile coastal plain

Weights, measures, money

arroba, weight of 11·5 kilos (25 lbs) or measure of about 4 gallons

duro, five-peseta piece

fanega, 0·6 of a hectare (i.e. 1·5 acres); as weight the amount of seed required to sow this area of land: wheat 46 kilos (101 lbs), barley 33 kilos (72 lbs)

hectare, 2·5 acres

peseta, approximately 166 pesetas to the pound sterling, 69 pesetas to the US dollar in 1971

For further details of cost-of-living and purchasing value of the peseta see Appendix A

Abbreviations

UGT Unión General de Trabajadores, socialist trade union

CNT Confederación Nacional del Trabajo, anarcho-syndicalist trades-union confederation

FAI Federación Anarquista Ibérica, semi-secret militant anarchist federation

CEDA Confederación Española de Derechas Autónomas, right-wing catholic party

Without the participation of all those in Tajos who gave of their time to talk to me this book could not have been written. I am grateful to them as I am to the many village friends who provided me with information, answered my questions and sought to put me straight on innumerable matters. To those who participated but do not appear in this book, I offer my apologies; space alone was the decisive factor.

Proud of their village, many Tajeños may wish that I had sought to draw a prettier picture; I apologize to their sensibilities but remain convinced that an unadorned portrait serves better to make this what it is: a record of their village; in fact *their* book.

My debt to a great number of people outside the village and to various books is also great. Rather than list them here, or inflict on the reader a great number of footnotes, I have indicated what I have drawn from them in a note of acknowledgement at the end, where their contributions can more appropriately be placed in context.

INTRODUCTION

Summer 1957

The dirt road wound upwards between narrow terraces of olives and wheat, circling on itself without destination. Grey-green agave lined the route. Somewhere above, out of sight in the folds of the mountain, lay the village at the head of the dry watercourses whose rocky beds were filled with flowering oleander. In the empty expanse of blue overhead the sun hung heavily, flattening the land.

The earth between the sparse stalks of wheat was powder-dry; behind the taxi a cloud of fine dust rose and hung in the motionless air. In its mineral silence the land seemed to have swallowed up movement; then, tumbling over the banks of the road, a flow of quicksilver broke the stillness. The water flowed on to a terrace in a geometrical pattern of furrows darkened by moisture under the splash of green maize. By the white farmstead a woman and children ran out to where, on the terrace, a man leant on his digging hoe: together they turned to watch the passing car.

Bumping round a curve, the village came into view, a thin white line carved into the grey and pine-green mountainside. As the road followed the watercourse cut deep in the land, the line separated into two rows of low rectangles whose whiteness was drained by the sun. Jutting out in front stood a promontory of rock with a sheer drop facing the road and, far below, Casas Nuevas and the Mediterranean.

From its flat surface, squat and fortress-like, rose the towers of the village church.

Skirting the rock the road climbed to enter the village on a level from the east. Immediately it plunged into a narrow, cobbled street which twisted and turned at the dictates of the terrain or the skills of the masons who, in the past, built the two-storied houses that ran in an unbroken white line on each side. The street was so narrow that only the sky was visible above. Figures in black stood in the doorways to watch the taxi's slow progress. Then a slight widening, a junction of two more streets, one of which dropped into a tree-shaded square of beaten earth surrounded by taller houses, the town hall and a couple of bars. From their cavernous ochre-coloured interiors, from the washing place by the fountain, from doorways people appeared to look and stare.

In the following weeks, which stretched into months, the realities of village life slowly unfolded for me. By chance 1957 was an opportune year to come to Tajos, in the province of Málaga, for the first time. The late 1950s were a watershed between old and new; a couple of years earlier things had 'got better' after the long post-civil war years. Ahead, over the horizon, lay a future no one foresaw as the lapping of tourism on the coast seven miles away turned into a tidal roar.

But then the village had not yet passed out of the old. Waiting for work, men stood or sat at empty tables in front of the bars; others staggered in from the sierra bent double under incredible burdens of firewood. On the land biblical implements continued to trace their ancient patterns over the earth. Cows pulled wooden, sometimes steel-shafted ploughs; wheat was threshed on circular cobbled floors by mules dragging a steel-runnered sledge on which a man stood; was winnowed by wooden pitchforks lofting it into the air and allowing the wind to separate grain from the chaff. The drought-seared earth echoed to digging hoes with a sound like wood being struck by an axe. In the evenings donkeys and mules brought produce up tracks from the country-side to sell by the basket in small front-room shops. Then, as the metallic heat declined at last, a few apparently better-off men appeared in pyjama tops to enjoy the cool and to talk to the priest and the Guardia Civil corporal; around them ran bare-bottomed children under the orange trees in the square. . . .

A heaviness lay over village and land. Nothing, it seemed, would change the secular routines of poverty. The rank, all-pervasive smell of bad olive oil cooking on fires kindled with rosemary and thyme – a pungent mixture of sour and sweet – hung heavily in the evening air. What, one wondered, had life been like in the past if now it was said to have improved?

The village lived from the land. Looking down from the rock with an eye accustomed to pattern, the immediate aspect was one of confusion. A random scattering of small, white, red-tiled farmsteads amidst random plantings of trees – olives, almonds, carobs, figs – along the edges of narrow terraces carved out of the hills. Each growing the same – wheat, barley, alfalfa, maize and a handful of vegetable crops; each apparently a small, self-sufficient world.

Only further off on the flat lands by the river four or five miles to the west was there any sign of ordered plantation in the serried ranks of olive groves. The river came down from Posadas to the north-west and ran at the foot of a range of red mountains before joining the sea near Casas Nuevas. Though its flow diminished in summer, the river never entirely dried up. Beyond it the view was blocked by the red mountains.

Covering in all over 140 square kilometres, the municipal area of Tajos extended to the crest of these mountains – and at one point a considerable distance beyond. Many of the best lands and biggest farms were not visible from the village itself. Those who worked on them lived closer to Posadas and Benamalí behind the mountains, and Casas Nuevas on the coast, than to Tajos.

This large municipal area in which some 7,500 people then lived – about 2,000 of them in the village itself – was a legacy of history and the village's strategic position. Occupied in turn by Phoenicians, Greeks, Romans, Visigoths and Moors, Tajos was captured after seven centuries of Islamic domination in 1485. Following the fall of Granada, Ferdinand and Isabella ordered Moorish land and property in a string of similarly-sited villages along this part of the Mediterranean coast to be distributed to Catholic settlers; in 1494 some seventy colonists received small-holdings in Tajos in return for agreeing to remain there a number of years. The aim was to create a defensive bulwark against possible Moorish invasion of the coast.

As a result, and also because most of the land was mountainous, Tajos did not, and was never to become a latifundist area as happened elsewhere during the Catholic reconquest of Andalusia. The land remained more equitably divided than in other parts, despite a steady erosion as first nobility and church, and later a new rural bourgeoisie, carved out large holdings of land.

From the mid-eighteenth to the first quarter of the twentieth century, one can estimate that never less than 49 percent of the land was held by more than 2·5 percent of all landowners; thereafter the proportions dropped to just over 1 percent owning 33 percent of the land. High as these figures may seem, they compare favourably with Málaga province where, as late as 1962, 1·8 percent of landowners controlled 55 percent of the land.

At the same time and at the other end of the scale 23 percent of the land was held by 82 percent of Tajos owners in mini- and small-holdings varying from a few hundred square metres to ten hectares in size. However, the proportion of small-holders was higher and that of mini-holders considerably lower than in the province as a whole; while the percentage of medium-sized landowners, holding between ten and fifty hectares on which they could hope to exist relatively well, was double that of Málaga overall.

Moreover, a higher proportion of Tajos land was irrigated than on average in the province. This, in the sub-tropical climate where irrigated land is at least twice as productive as dry land, and where lack of rainfall is always a threat, was of considerable importance.*

Comforting as the figures appeared, they did not expunge the poverty that was endemic; they led only to the conclusion that elsewhere the poverty must be still greater. True, the land in Tajos was only average to poor in quality; two-thirds of all landowners' holdings did not produce a taxable income of 5,000 pesetas (£45) a year. Nor did many large landowners display much enthusiasm to farm their own lands, preferring to split them up into small-holdings to rent or sharecrop. Sharecroppers were seven times more, landowners working their own land eight times less, numerous than in the province as a whole. Over 40 percent of the agricultural population owned no land at all.

Apart from the land there were few other resources; the sierra provided most that there were. Brushwood and pine cones for firewood; esparto, a tough grass used for plaiting paniers and harnesses; marble, desultorily quarried from the dolomite rock; and mica, which had been briefly exploited ten years before.

Between the majority who tilled the land and the few who lived by owning land, there was an exiguous stratum of self-employed: esparto-weavers, muleteers, fish-vendors, three barbers, a blacksmith, a taxidriver, a mason or two. The village had difficulty supporting these few.

In varying degrees the village was run by a handful of men: bureaucrats and professionals in the main. Town hall clerks, vet, doctor, secretaries of the Falange and the state-run *sindicato* (trade union), the commander of the Guardia

* For a fuller discussion of the land, property divisions and agriculture in Tajos see Appendix B.

Civil post and the priest formed the nucleus of the ruling group which was headed by a mayor appointed by the civil authorities in Málaga.

Despite the lack of employment, few seemed to leave Tajos. The village was, as it had appeared that first afternoon, a universe enclosed on itself. Endlessly circling the square in the Sunday evening *paseo*, the young couples, *novios* and *novias*, boys and girls walking round and round to look and be looked at mirrored this microcosm revolving slowly on itself. The *pueblo* was the focus of life; it had the 'urban' quality dear to the Andalusian of human concourse and discourse.

The strength of family life, immediately apparent, was its cement. Exaggeratedly, it appeared that everyone was related, that the village was one extended family. In fact the five most common surnames were borne by one-fifth of the population; the first ten names by over one-third.

To live and work in the countryside was to partake of a lesser destiny than to live in the village. When possible, most evenings the small-holder or tenant came to it from his farmstead; better, he lived in it and went out to his farmstead for the day; better still, he left the hard labour of the land when he could and found other work in the village. If obliged to migrate, it was of the village that he thought, to which one day he hoped to return.

If the land filled a man's stomach, which it did not always do, it seemed not to fill his heart. Tajeños lacked the ponderous solidity of peasants, the almost mystical northern devotion to the land. They were light of foot and quick of mind. Theirs was the world of the town and they looked on the land as little more than an inevitable, though regrettable, means of keeping alive.

Fourteen years later the waves of the Costa del Sol were beating against the walls of the village. Over the horizon Torremolinos, Marbella, Fuengirola raised tower blocks to the skies in worship of tourists who descended by the hundreds of thousands into an urban sprawl that had concreted the coast in just a decade.

Before this onslaught Casas Nuevas and the coast below Tajos had also bowed, though to a lesser extent. Tajos had surrendered much of its land to the foreigner in search of a private place in the sun; but the village held out. Its population had grown to just over 10,000, the bulk of the increase being in the countryside where, close to Casas Nuevas, a new village had sprung up to accommodate building workers on the coast. Progress and relative prosperity had come; but tourism had not, as it had on the coast, rendered it unrecognizable from the past.

A dozen years ago the project of describing Tajos through its inhabitants' experiences in the course of this century would have been more problematic. It is an irony perhaps that tourism, which has destroyed village life on the coast, has in a sense made my task easier in Tajos today. Perspective and comparison, which define the singularity and uniqueness of experience and place, were little in evidence in the enclosed community of those times. Change, the rupture with the past which has taken place in the last few years, has in the meantime provided much of the missing perspective. In the light of today the past can be more sharply seen.

In attempting to make articulate the experiences of people who, historically speaking, would otherwise remain inarticulate, the writer is midwife to others' history. It is their truth, not *the* truth that is his material. However, it is also the truth as he sees it which guides his investigation, orientates the questions he asks and provides the basis for the selection he finally makes.

A word about the underlying premises of this book may not, therefore, be out of place. Its guiding theme was to discover how Tajeños made their lives – and what was made of their lives – in the course of this century. Their work and the social conditions in which they lived were consequently the most important aspect. Thereafter, it was the attempt to recreate village history both vertically and horizontally: vertically in time to discern the changing patterns of society; horizontally through the different modes of making a living offered by this society. The investigation, carried out in 1971, was confined to people living in, or within a radius of a couple of miles of the village.

Because of its approach the reader will find some aspects of village life less prominently focused on than others. To mention but two: customs and folklore, which have been so admirably described for Andalusian village life in Gerald Brenan's *South from Granada* that little of worth could be added, are not central to this book. Also absent, though reluctantly, is the type of description which distinguishes *People of the Sierra* by J. A. Pitt-Rivers. Such social-anthropological observation is the privilege of the 'outsider' who 'sees' the village in a way it cannot see itself. Despite the new perspective created by change, Tajos remains too enclosed for villagers to reflect, as though they were outsiders, on how the village 'works'. The villagers lack the concepts, excepting only one, with which to articulate a view of the village's sociological framework. But the exception – a singular absence from Pitt-Rivers' book – is an important one: especially among those without land, but not only among them, there exists a class-consciousness, an understanding of exploitation and of the ruling group's power so marked that it is surprising that a social-anthropologist should entirely ignore it.

Tajos lies equidistant about fifty miles from each of the villages described in the above-mentioned books, the only two to have been written in English on Andalusian mountain life since the war. In a sense this book also lies between them, hopefully filling the space they have left.

THE OLD

'Called not so many years ago "Little Havana" for the wealth and variety of its agriculture, Tajos is presently suffering a crisis more terrible even than the rest of the province of Málaga, due mainly to the ravages of phylloxera in its formerly rich and extensive vineyards. . . .'

So ran the introduction to the land survey of Tajos carried out in 1899, part of a village by village tax assessment of the entire province. Not only Málaga but the entire Spanish economy had until recently been dependent on the vine: for the forty years to 1890 wine had been the main Spanish agricultural export and raisins had ranked between third and sixth – higher by far than olives or oranges.

In the 1880s and 1890s phylloxera, a type of plant lice, swept down from the north and virtually wiped out the vineyards of Málaga, which at their height had covered 112,000 hectares – a third planted with muscatel grapes from which the famous raisins exported mainly to England and the US were made.

Tajos was so hard-hit that 'large numbers of inhabitants have emigrated, leaving their houses deserted and in ruins'. On top of the phylloxera came a disease which struck the lemon groves, severely reducing production of another rich crop.

This exceedingly dire situation was aggravated by the size of land holding, lack of capital and the systems of land

9

tenure in use. 'The majority of landowners hold no more than small plots which, despite all the work put into them, do not bring in sufficient to meet their owners' most pressing needs. A contributory factor is that those owners who have extensive holdings split them up and lease them to share-croppers or renters who, from an economic viewpoint, are even worse off than the small-holder.'

The village, the report continued, was without communications. The old road to Málaga had fallen into such disrepair as to be impassable; the tracks to Casas Nuevas, Benamalí and Posadas were little more than mule tracks. With the exception of the olive, grape and lemon crops which were 'exported' to Málaga, the remainder of the agricultural produce was consumed locally.

By 1899 vineyards accounted for only 15 percent of the land cultivated. Wheat, barley and sweet potatoes took up the bulk. However, on the poorest dry lands, which made up 50 percent, wheat could be grown only once every four years, for the soil needed three years of fallow to produce wheat at all. On the better dry lands a crop could be had every second year, alternating with barley, while on irrigated land – which made up less than 10 percent of the total – two different crops a year could be grown.

The report showed a total of 805 rural dwelling places. Regrettably half the list is missing, but of the 400 still shown, fifteen were *cortijos* or large farms, sixty-seven were raisin-drying *lagares* and 119 were officially classified as hovels. It was in these that lived, on land which was not theirs to till, the scores of day-labourers who were out of work for anything up to five or six months of the year.

Some of the vineyards were being replanted with phyl-loxera-resistant American stock; but these vines, the report stated, were 'expensive, slow to produce and require more labour and greater care than the indigenous vines which produced in the poorest soils'. It went on to show that viticulture had become the most cost-intensive agricultural sector, requiring an outlay between three and seven times higher per hectare of irrigated land for a return barely double that of other crops (and in the case of lemons, under half).

There was little improvement in the next twenty-five years. Population figures, an index of emigration and the flight from the land, show that after the initial blow labourers and small-holders held out in hope: from 1900 to 1910 the village population rose by 10 percent. In the next decade the despair is manifest: the population showed a net fall of 6 percent while in the province as a whole it rose by the same percentage. This is all the more striking because for half that decade, thanks to the First World War, Spain experienced an economic boom, and overseas emigration showed its first serious fall since the turn of the century.

Few of the other figures available give a happier picture of rural life. Almost half the people who worked the land were landless day-labourers; the other half were more or less equally divided between small-holders and *colonos* – renters and sharecroppers. Only half a dozen or so of the nineteen large landowners worked their land directly – and these were mainly the new owners who had moved in after the phylloxera to replant the vineyards.

When he found work, a day-labourer earned at the turn of the century 1·50 pesetas a day; at that time employees' income nationally averaged four pesetas. In the 1920s day-wages of two and later three pesetas were being paid; by then inflation had pushed the national average to ten pesetas; at the start of the 1930s a day-labourer earned 3·50 pesetas with the national average standing at nine.

Because of inflation and increased unemployment labourers were, if anything, worse off in 1930 than they had been at the turn of the century. Nor were the wage differentials compensated for by lower prices in the villages. Though rents were cheaper, food costs were almost always higher than in the towns.

In 1900 80 percent of the rural provincial population was illiterate. There was barely a change until 1930 when the figure officially fell to 66 percent – reflecting the school-building programme of the Primo de Rivera dictatorship (1923–30) which engaged in extensive public works. Remembered by many Tajeños as a 'golden age' because it brought work, the dictatorship also brought to an end the two-party parliamentary system, if not all its abuses, and towards its close saw the rise of trade unionism among the farm-hands in the village.

Today, looking back, the old recall the hardships and poverty. For fifty-two years Jaime Naranjo worked in the town hall, taking over the town clerkship, sometimes for as long as two years, between the departure and arrival of the state-appointed clerks. Now retired, he sits – a small, grey-haired man – looking out of the window of his house in the square. His working life has spanned monarchy and dictatorship, republic, revolution, civil war and the Franco regime. Beneath the dry manner of one who has spent a lifetime among dusty documents in a place where only a few could read, one senses a nervous caution as though, in the past, he has had to steer a careful course through the troubled seas of village politics.

JAIME NARANJO   *Seventy-three*

Town hall official

I was born in 1898, a disastrous year for Spain. It was that year the nation lost its last colonies. Cuba, Puerto Rico and the Philippines. 'The generation of '98,' they say, a famous generation, yes. A disaster all the same.

My father was clerk to the Justice of the Peace. His father was a bloodletter who came to Tajos from Montilla, in the province of Córdoba, when an uncle of his was appointed priest here. Medicine was very rudimentary in my youth, injections weren't known and bloodletting was common. There was only one doctor and he was old. There was no chemist and the doctor mixed all his own prescriptions in a mortar and pestle. A bit of this and a bit of that. The people called him 'floor tile' because, when it wasn't bleeding, that was his usual prescription: a hot tile placed on the chest.

I went to school in the village. There were three schools then, two for boys and one for girls. Less than half the village children attended. There was apathy and lack of interest among the parents, the fathers would send their children to collect firewood or to look after goats as soon as they were old enough. But even so, there was room in the three schools for only eighty boys and forty girls. Schooling was very deficient then.

I was lucky, I had a master who was in love with his profession. My father was a man of some learning and his poetry won prizes in Málaga on more than one occasion. I wanted to become an elementary school teacher. After leaving school at fourteen, I studied on my own. I had passed my first year's examinations in Málaga and had only one more year to do when the Minister of Education changed the whole system. There were no more two-year elementary teachers, one had to study for a minimum of four years. Our economic situation was always precarious and my father hadn't the means to let me continue studying, so he got me a job as secretary to the town clerk.

It was 1916 and my salary was 750 pesetas a year. The village was very poor in those days, poorer than Benamalí or Posadas where more people owned their own land than here. Most of the rich landowners had left the village by then and had moved to Casas Nuevas which was beginning to grow and was a more desirable, less isolated place for them to live. Their absence meant that there were very few people left here with money to spend. More important from the point of view of the village budget, they paid only half the taxes due from a landowner who lived in the village. These landowners, natives of Tajos, saved themselves money by living on the coast. Even today a good portion of the land belongs to owners living in Casas Nuevas.

After the phylloxera many small-holders' farms were bought by vineyard owners from Vélez-Málaga who had the money to replant with American vines. But they didn't come to live in the village either.

The majority of the 1,800 people living in the village were

poor: day-labourers, fish-vendors, esparto gatherers, goatherds and the like. I don't suppose there were more than forty or fifty men living in the village itself who worked their own land. There were twenty or thirty artisans, shoemakers, masons, barbers – perhaps not even that many. And of the privileged, the rich – eight or ten, no more. The top part of the village backing on to the sierra was the poorest. It was almost all hovels, one room or two at most, with thatched roofs.

Things weren't much better in the countryside where about 3,300 people lived. 500 of these were labourers. Those who had a bit of land to work were better off. The majority of the *colonos* were sharecroppers – not that sharecropping is a bad system because it gives work and food to a whole family. The trouble was there wasn't enough work for everyone. Why? I don't know, how can one explain it?

I remember the waves of emigration between 1910 and 1915. The majority who went were labourers and those who no longer had any land to work. They emigrated to Brazil and Argentina. In Rio de Janeiro there is a *barrio* or neighbourhood made up of Tajeños they say. And then at the end of the First World War there was the 'flu epidemic. In the month of November 1918 fifty people died of it; in all there must have been close on seventy deaths.

At that time to get to Málaga one had to walk or ride down to Casas Nuevas to pick up the diligence which left there at eight a.m. It reached Málaga at one p.m. after changing horses in Arroyo de la Reina. So to get anything done in Málaga meant a trip of two days – imagine that! Today it's an hour by car!

We were under the monarchy then. The two parties, conservative and liberal, took turns in office. When one party had to resign or it was time for elections, the king gave the other party the task of organizing them. The civil governors of the provinces were changed and they named new village mayors. The latter were usually the *caciques* – the persons who held power, one might say. The *cacique* organized the election – well, he manipulated it through pressures of all sorts, some friendly and others not so friendly. The *cacique* was always one of the rich men, someone a bit wider awake than the rest. He ordered things the way he saw fit, even if it was outside the law. 'Dressing up the doll' we used to call it, to make things look legal.

The conservative *cacique* of Málaga owned a lot of land in Tajos. Most of the time the village remained in conservative hands. One of the big landowners was *cacique* and he became mayor while I was still young. The last time he had himself appointed mayor was in 1935 under the Republic; by then he had become a republican. Before that he hadn't been above changing his shirt and becoming a liberal. The *pueblo* didn't understand these things. Only a few people knew what was really going on.

I wasn't anything, I had no political bent. It made no difference, no one could oppose the *cacique*; it was he who commanded. Even if one knew he was breaking the law what could one do? One would have lost one's job if one had tried to do something. No doubt at all. No one protested – to whom could one protest? The *caciques* were backed up by the provincial authorities, by the deputies to the Cortes. . . .

No, one had to put up with things as the *cacique* wanted them. I suppose he and his people helped themselves to what they could from village funds. I don't believe they were puritanical enough not to have done so. Not that there was much money to 'eat'. When I started work the village budget didn't run to more than 70,000 pesetas a year. And of that only about 40,000 to 50,000 pesetas was ever collected in taxes because the labourers couldn't pay. The state didn't help villages – on the contrary it levied subsidies to provide for the provincial government and the judiciary. That amounted to 15,000 pesetas a year, so that only 25,000 pesetas were left. There wasn't much that could be done with so small an amount except pay the wages of the town hall staff and the doctor who got 2,000 pesetas a year for attending to the poor. So if anything was 'eaten' it was only a few pesetas in reality.

Of course it wasn't a democratic system, not by a long way, and I wasn't sorry when it was replaced by the dictatorship of Primo de Rivera. I wasn't sorry at all, one could begin to breathe again.

Everything improved in those seven years. My old school-master was appointed mayor and he saw to it that five new schools were built in the countryside where there was great need for them, and another girls' school added to the existing one in the village. The Guardia Civil barracks were built then, and the coast road asphalted.

Those were a few very good years. They lasted too short a time. When the Republic came in things started to go down. Then the civil war came and we were under the reds – things got really bad then. A time of fear; I don't like to think about it. . . .

But under the dictatorship people had work, earned money and lived better. I got married then, in 1925 to be precise. I was earning 208·33 pesetas a month and on that I could live better than I do today on 8,000 pesetas a month pension. I rented a house in the square here for twenty-two pesetas a month, a kilo of bread cost forty-five centimos and a pair of children's *alpargatas*, which were what was mainly worn then, fifty-five centimos. We ate meat and fish often enough. Not that often to grow fat from over-eating, oh no – but enough!

He chuckles, the memory overlaying bitterness about the scale of his pension; today it is less than a bricklayer's wage. Then his eyes grow vacant, staring into the square where, in the afternoon sun, a group of men are standing in front of the town hall. Black-suited and hatted, the figure of Francisco Avila towers over them. Cautiously, as though excusing himself, Jaime Naranjo's voice murmurs, 'Others can tell you better than I. . . .' He turns slowly in the chair. 'Yes, there are so many things in a life. . . .'

FRANCISCO AVILA   *Seventy-six*

Small-holder

Under the black hat he wears indoors and out, master of himself and his house, Francisco's face is well-preserved: sun, wind and hunger have not ravaged his features in a lifetime spent working the land. In 1898, when he was three, eight men carried his dying father in a litter to Málaga; the trip took twelve hours. After his father's death, Francisco was brought up by his paternal grandfather who sent him to school in the village. When his grandfather died, he and his mother moved on to the grandfather's farmstead where, at the age of thirteen, Francisco began to work the three and a half hectares of land he had inherited.

Small plots, poor land and not enough water – that's the way it has always been here as long as I've known it. Lack of money and insufficient preparation of the land – in those conditions there was no means of going forward. Where there's little production there's little surplus. Most of the small-holders had to go out at some time or another looking for work as day-labourers. At wages so low that a man could barely live on them. That was the life in those days, the life of Spain formerly. There were twenty million people and nineteen million of them went hungry so that one million could eat to their heart's content.

I was a bit luckier than the majority. For one reason only – we were a small family. Just my mother and sister and I after my father died. At least we ate every day and that was saying a lot. We were among the better-off of the poor.

I planted a bit of everything on the land – vegetables, wheat, maize, vetch, barley. Almost everything was for our own use, the wheat especially. Like everyone else in the country we made our own bread. Sometimes if there was some wheat left over I'd sell it to buy something else. I've known plenty of small-holders who have had to sell their wheat at ten or eleven pesetas the *fanega* in order to buy maize at 7·50. They'd live on maize bread and maize soup in order to get by. Meat was cheap in those days – but money was dear; fish was cheap but money was dearer. In the country-side we had to live on what we produced – bread, potatoes, cabbage, lettuce, chard. . . .

No one grew more because there wasn't water enough to irrigate. The little I got from the old *mina* in the village dried up every other year. All one could do was to let the crop wither and die. It's happened to me more times than I can tell – and to all those who've worked the land here.

The years of drought I've known, they're too numerous for me to remember. Ruinous years. And they've come, one after another without break. About twenty years ago, it must have been, the drought was so long and so severe that even some olive trees on my cousin's plot next to mine dried up and died.

I remember better the times when it rained. It's the month of

April that makes the land here. If it rains then the earth will produce. In all my seventy-six years I've known only three good years of April rains: 1906 when I was still a kid, 1923 and 1936. The wheat crops were good those years. With the poor earth we have it makes no difference how much you fertilize, the wheat won't grow unless you get the April rain.

1906 I remember especially. The year before the drought had been so severe that nothing was harvested. The land was dry as a bone. 1906 started the same way. The wheat came up a little way and stopped growing. Then, on St. Joseph's day it started to rain and it didn't stop all April. The wheat suddenly began growing – not very high but the ears were large. That year there was more grain than straw. But the year before – ozu! There was hunger, near starvation. Thanks to God I didn't go hungry but I knew plenty of people who did.

How else could it be when everyone was so poor? A man and his family couldn't live on a day wage of 1·50 pesetas, even if that had been the money he earned. But in reality it wasn't. His real wage was closer to fifty centimos, since two-thirds of the year he was out of work. What could he and his family eat? They didn't, and that was that.

Yes, a day-labourer's life was abysmal – but a small-holder had to work even harder. Twice as hard, I'd say. From before light until long past nightfall. A day-labourer works his fixed hours, but there are no hours for a small farmer. It had to be that way to win any sort of living from the earth. I had no money to pay labourers to help me – but even if I had had, I would have been working in the fields for four hours of a morning before they arrived and gone on long after they'd left at night. Just speaking for myself, I can tell you there have been more times than I can remember when I've worked a day and a night through without rest and gone on the next day working the same. I'd be busy digging or ploughing the terraces all day, at night the water would come and I'd irrigate by the light of an oil lamp, and the next day I'd go on digging. In those times the only rest was work. One's body had to be stronger and put up with more than a pack animal's.

When I was young we had neither artificial fertilizers nor steel ploughs. Then for every *fanega* of wheat sown I'd hope to harvest four to six *fanegas*. More often than not the crop was under rather than over those figures. But with the introduction of artificial fertilizers during the First World War, I think, the yields increased to between seven and eight for every one sown. Ten for one would have been exceptional. The steel plough cut down the work of ploughing because the old wood ones just scratched the surface and one had to go over the land four or five times in different directions. The steel plough lifted all the earth it moved and with one ploughing the land was better worked than after four or five times with the old one.

This isn't land for growing wheat, it's too poor. And yet we had to grow it to have bread. It's a crop that requires a great deal of work from winter until mid-summer. You've got to prepare the land twice – the earth has to be bribed if it is going to produce anything here – then sown, fertilized, weeded once if not twice before reaping, threshing, winnowing the crop. And what did you get for it in those days? Sixty or seventy pesetas for a *fanega* of land sown!

It wasn't much different with any of the crops or animals you raised. Sell a calf in those days and you'd get a couple of pesetas a kilo, seventy-five to a hundred pesetas in all. That was the price when I was young and it was still the price in about 1930. You don't have to ask whether people ran to the bank with the money they made out of the land – even if there had been a bank!

Everything came down to that, everything we wanted and needed came down to saying, we haven't got the money. What's worse than not having money? I'll tell you: not having brains. We had no money then, but we didn't think that we'd have no money tomorrow either unless we did something about it. The people didn't have the brains to think of the future. This soil is good for late apricots, the big ones. There ought to have been enough trees planted here to produce twenty million kilos of fruit a year. Why weren't there? Because the people didn't care. We're slow-witted – that's it in a word. Anyone with a thought in his head would have planted 500 apricot trees on his land and made a pile of money. Instead they planted one or two to eat for themselves and that was that.

I suppose you can say I had enough sense to think of the future. Not that I ever planted the trees either. But I was always thinking how things should be done, I was always ready to put more into my land than the others. I wasn't able to make a lot of money in the end, but enough to buy my uncle's plot next to mine and now to be living as I am. And despite all the hardships, I enjoyed living in the countryside. Life was quieter and better then on the land than in the village. One had a good time on very little. Simple amusements they were, tranquil and moderate and all done in good faith. Going to a neighbour's farmstead for a game of cards; fiestas with dances to the sound of guitars and castanets at maize-harvest time when all the neighbours gathered of an evening to help each other out. There'd be oil lamps on bamboo canes and a big stewpot full of sweet potatoes, and wine and *aguardiente*; and the people stripped the cobs of their outer husks as someone sang and played the guitar. From one neighbour's to the next as the maize crop was picked, the fiestas went on all summer. In my opinion, people got more pleasure out of these simple amusements than they do out of all the complicated things they've got today. It was more pleasurable and a lot healthier too.

I'm not discontented with my life or my work. My wife and I got by on the land we had. But then we had no children to support. It's in old age that you notice their absence most. It's the reward for a life of hard work to have children to look after one when you've reached our age. No one can give one the company and support that children do at this time of life. So here we are now, not lonely but alone. . . .

He falls silent. His wife, a small figure in black, looks at him. Even lost in regret he sits on the hard upright chair with the pose and authority of one who has known a lifetime of self-confidence in his skills. The two-storeyed village house, to which he retired eleven years ago, is large and cool – evidence of his mastery in winning a living from the earth. His wife, Maria, two years younger than he, looks up, hesitates. Then she says:

It is a sad thing not to have children, yes. I used to pray to bear a child. But when one didn't come I thought also of the suffering we were spared. To have children and to see them suffering, to be missing an eye, to be lame, to be without an arm – what greater affliction can there be? I've seen too many mothers suffer through their children's misfortunes to believe that children are all a blessing. Even if they're healthy, not to be able to give them what they need, to see them go hungry – that is a most terrible thing. So I thought, if God doesn't want us to have children it must be for a reason, it must be as He willed.

I was one of nine children myself, the youngest. My father rented a farm where one year in four the water didn't dry up. Three and a half hectares of land on which, three years out of four, we could hardly grow anything. With so large a family we hardly ever had enough wheat to last us through the year. It was a fine thing if my father had twenty-five pesetas put away at any one time to buy a sack of flour.

The farmstead was three or four kilometres outside the village. Except for the couple of years when I went to the village school, we never came to Tajos all year except for Holy Week, the *feria*, Corpus Christi. Our house had two rooms, a kitchen and a store-room above. My parents slept in one room, the three of us girls in one bed in the other, the six boys in the storeroom in a couple of beds.

My brothers had to go out to work as day-labourers because the farm didn't produce enough. I was ten when I started to work helping my mother wash the floor, whitewash, clean the dishes – not that there were too many of them. We all ate out of the same bowl, we didn't have plates. No one could put their spoon into the bowl until the parents had taken the first dip.

In the mornings before work we had coffee. Barley coffee, we couldn't afford the real thing. And with that, if we were lucky, we'd have a sweet potato. If not, nothing. At noon we'd eat soup, with a bit of dried cod if it was a good day, a piece of bread and a dried fig. After lunch it was straight back to work.

Because my brothers were always out looking for a day's work, we women had to work the land. Weeding was our job and it was hard, bent over double with the short weeding hoe. So was reaping and carrying in the sheaves. We never made enough for us to buy any clothes to speak of. Two dresses, one for best and one for working in, that was all. The men were as badly off if not worse. If they had trousers they'd be lacking a jacket, if they had a shirt they'd be without a waistcoat. It was a life of misery, a life of want; it was a thousand times harder than I can tell.

Yet my father thought he was lucky to have a farm to rent. He had been a day-labourer earning seventy-five centimos a day in his youth and had known more hunger than any of us – and we knew enough, I can tell you. When he killed a pig, and we had quite a few, we couldn't afford to eat it ourselves, we had to sell it. We didn't know the colour of meat and that's the truth.

After a few years on the farm we couldn't go on with it. It wasn't producing enough to keep us alive. My father was fortunate to get another *finca* to rent. It cost 250 pesetas a year, and I remember very well the trouble he had getting that much money together.

I had to go out to work for a day wage too. I was sixteen and one evening coming back from a day's picking beans on a farm near Paco's he started to talk to me. It was several days before I agreed to become his *novia*. You couldn't be too long or too quick about it in those days. The people began to talk about you if you didn't accept or reject a suitor. At the same time you couldn't say yes straight away because that wouldn't have been right.

We were *novios* eleven years before getting married. It was partly because we became *novios* very young, but more because my mother had a stroke and her whole left side was paralysed. I had to look after her. Things had been bad enough before but now they were worse. Not having the money to look after her properly, not being able to buy the things she needed – it was horrible, I suffer still thinking of it.

When I could I had to go out olive-picking to earn money to buy the linen and kitchen things I had to provide to get married. Olive-picking was a job only women did. We got paid seventy-five centimos for a *fanega* of olives and it took a day to pick that many. They called it a *fanega* but it was a basket that held more than that. They cheated us even there! If you said anything there'd be another in your place the next day; there were only too many women who wanted the work.

I got married in 1924. I wore a dress I'd bought for the *feria* five or six years before and the only pair of shoes I had, which my cousin, who was a shoemaker, let me have cheap. Paco wore the suit he'd bought when he went for his military service. That was how the poor lived in those days.

Life was a bit easier for me after we married. My husband's farm was good and he worked very hard. So did I. We were able to eat a bit better than most, we had fish more often and every year we killed a pig. From that I cured a couple of legs of *serrano* ham, made sausages, mortadello, black puddings.

When you slaughtered a pig it smelled good for a mile around, not like today when pigs are fattened on artificial foods and garbage and stuff of that sort. Then they were fattened on figs, sweet potatoes, groundnuts, green stuff, and they tasted delicious.

There was little else but work in the *campo*. The country people saw the world through the eye of a needle, they knew only what was going on right round them, among their neighbours. Even if there had been newspapers, when would there have been the time to read them? We worked from before dawn until late at night, we worked every day of the year. I hardly ever went to the village, though it was only three kilometres away. It wasn't the distance. Time off was time spent away from working the land, time off was money spent and nothing earned. You couldn't afford that. There were people who lived and died without having seen Málaga – what am I saying? – who lived and died without knowing where Málaga was. They thought what they saw in front of them was the world.

What more can I tell you? It wouldn't matter, I couldn't describe even one-tenth of how bad things were in those times. We didn't realize it then perhaps the way we do now looking back when things have changed, now when we've already got one foot in the grave. We can't have done, can we?

JUAN CORTES   *Seventy-three*

Water mayor and rural guard

I was ten when my father started to teach me his job as water mayor. There were two sources of water here then, one from the fountain of the seven spouts in the village, the other on the road to Castillejo. They were both *minas*.

The one in the village dried up very often and there was always a shortage. There were more fights about water than about anything else. And in a year of drought even more still. I've known men come to blows with digging hoes. There was so much poverty, so much misery; no one had a peseta to his name and the crops were worth hardly anything. An *arroba* of dried figs fetched a peseta, imagine that! For twenty-five centimos men would have words. During a drought the people would have to go looking for a landowner who had water and would let them plant a terrace or two for the season. Sharecropping it was, they'd have to give the owner half the crop.

The water from here irrigates all the way down to Casas Nuevas. From sunrise to sunset it irrigates around here; at sunset it is cut off and sent down to Casas Nuevas. Each farm gets so many hours of water which belong to the owner, depending on what he has acquired or bought. The water goes round each of the farms in turn. That can take nine or ten days, depending on how many hours everyone owns. A water mayor has to know each farm's rights, he has to control the time when a farmer begins and ends irrigating, he has to make sure no one is taking water that is not his.

When I was sixteen I took over from my father as night water mayor. I was one of nine children and my father's small-holding of five hectares couldn't support us. We all had to go out looking for work.

In the four or five irrigation months of summer I was up and down the water channels all night. I didn't trust the people; if they didn't see me patrolling anything might have happened. When I found a place where a little water was being taken off by a farm which had no right to it, I'd take my hoe and block it off with a scoop of earth. The next day I'd warn the small-holder or sharecropper or whoever it was. But when there was a large flow being taken I'd go and knock on the man's door or find him where he was sleeping on the threshing floor. 'What's this?' '*Hombre*, I've got to irrigate a terrace of maize. . . .' 'That maize isn't worth what the fine will cost you,' I'd say. 'The next time I'll have to denounce you and it'll cost you dear. Don't do it again.'

The people respected me. I only had to denounce a few people in all the years I was water mayor. This business of water carries heavy fines – up to three times the value of the water stolen; and that in those days when there was no money about was a great deal. A fine could be as much as 3,000 pesetas.

The water channels were never properly kept up. They were dug out of the earth and a lot of water was lost. Still is, come to that. For the water to reach the *vega* of Casas Nuevas it had to pass for more than three kilometres along the bed of the watercourse. At least half the water was lost in the sand, it just filtered away. It was a shame so much was wasted. Those who had money then didn't want to spend it and those who hadn't couldn't. For everyone who had money and plenty of land there were fifteen who had only a small plot. The rich didn't want to pay for the poor and so everyone lost.

I got paid for my work in maize. From 1915 to 1930 I got four *arrobas* from each of the twenty-four owners of water on the *vega*. After 1930, when the Republic came in, the landlords down there started to let their vines go. The labourers were demanding too high wages – no, not too high, they were asking what they needed – but the landlords said it was too much. The export of raisins had fallen off. Where they didn't tear up the vines, the landlords tried ploughing them. But that's no good, the plough cuts through the main roots and the vines die. They have to be worked by hand.

I had to ask for an increase too. Ten *arrobas* of maize for each owner's night of water, or I wouldn't continue, I told them. They paid me. I was worth it to them.

It was about this time that I became a rural guard. Four people in the village had to sign the papers on my behalf before they could be sent to Madrid for a licence from the War Ministry to carry arms. A two-barrelled gun, one barrel mounted on top of the other which cost 1,500 pesetas. I, and the other guards, said we weren't going to buy any firearms unless the government paid for them. 'Nothing will happen,' I said, 'I haven't carried a firearm for the past twenty years. . . .'

There's nothing but problems for a rural guard, that's what he's there for. One of the major ones here was boundary lines. There were no markers between one plot and another. So there would be fights over who owned a tree, for example. The neighbours would call me, saying there was trouble, and I'd arrive on my horse to find the men on the ground fighting. To separate men who are enraged you've got to go in with good words, not arrogantly, otherwise you only add fuel to the fire. When I'd managed to separate them I'd say, 'What's this? Just for a carob tree! If that's the problem, then cut it down and make charcoal out of it and divide the charcoal. Or firewood if you want. It's not worth all this, a court case will cost you a lot more than the

69575

LIBRARY
College of St. Francis
JOLIET, ILL.

wood's worth.' Or else I'd suggest that one year one of them collect the fruit and the next the other. The best thing always was to try to split the difference, especially in boundary disputes. There were so many fights over this sort of thing that little by little I came to mark out a large part of the countryside, and today everyone knows what is his and what belongs to his neighbour. The people always obeyed me.

From an early age I had a taste for the countryside, an understanding of the land. There aren't many round here who have either; for every hundred perhaps only seven or eight. Without that liking for the land a man can't get anywhere. There are some who can't even plant a fig tree properly – and that's not very difficult since all that's needed is a small branch. There were plenty of farms that weren't worked as they should have been. By working the land I mean knowing how to graft, how to cultivate the vines, dry raisins, select them, pack them, estimate crops. . . .

By the age of fourteen I could estimate crops. One day I said to my father, 'Papa, you'll have to get more tarpaulins for the raisins this year.' 'Why?' 'Because all the grapes won't fit under the ones you've got.' I was right. After that the neighbours used to send for me. I was the only one round there with an eye for it, and they wanted the estimates so that they could go to the shops and ask for credit on the crop to come.

Soon I was in demand on inheritances, dividing up land among heirs. In this broken and mountainous land you've got to know a lot because it's not a matter of dividing the land into so many plots of equal size. It's a question of dividing it into plots of equal production. A plot without water will have to be larger than an irrigated plot or a plot with fruit-bearing trees, so that each heir will get the same benefit from his inheritance. When the land has been divided, each plot gets a number and the numbers go into a hat; the heirs draw lots. There's always trouble with inheritances, the heirs never agree. More bad feeling is caused by this than by anything else. But I never made an enemy in all my life, there's no one here who won't speak to me.

I couldn't live only on being a rural guard, I had to work the land, too. Two small-holdings I sharecropped, one of them belonging to a retired colonial official who lived here. Sharecropping brought the landlords a great deal more than renting, especially since the time under the Republic when landlords couldn't raise rents at will. Most of the landowners mistreated their sharecroppers, they gave them their half share of seed and fertilizers and that was that until harvest time when they took half the crop.

But don Salvador wasn't like that. If a day's labour was needed for weeding the wheat he would pay for it. When we fattened pigs he always gave me one for myself and often he didn't want to take his half share of the crop, or else gave it to my wife to buy clothes for the children.

But the other landlords were hard. Too hard. There was too much abuse of those who worked the land – that's why what happened later came about. During the revolution they shot six landlords, including don Salvador. He was the first they shot – they went wild, the brutes.

PEDRO PEREZ *Sixty-eight*

Day-labourer

The year began for us in December, the work year. That was when the vines were pruned. There was work then up to Christmas; after that there was no work until mid-January when the vine-yards were dug. We had to be down on the land by first light for the digging. It was an hour and a half's walk in the dark and we had to be up by half past four, sometimes earlier. We were thankful to have work for a month and a half. The vineyards – that's all there was here then! That and the sierra.

We went down the tracks to Casas Nuevas with esparto torches burning. And we came back with them too. The work day started when the light showed on the summit of the sierra; 'in the name of God', the foreman said and we began digging. The day ended when the last light left the sierra and the foreman said 'Ave Maria'. Then we began the walk back. It took longer than going down and we'd get back so tired at nine or ten we hadn't the strength to eat. All one wanted to do was lie down and sleep to be able to get up again the next morning.

The digging lasted about six weeks. After that there was no more work for a month or more. We had to go to the sierra for esparto or leave the village to work in the sugar-cane plantations round Málaga.

In April there was a little work here, digging holes for the new vines, and a bit later picking off the new shoots and covering the young fruit so it wouldn't burn in the sun. But it didn't give work to many. From then until the harvest began towards the end of August hundreds of us left the village to reap the wheat harvest in the *campiña* of Cadiz. From August to October we had work here, bringing in the grapes and drying them – and then there was nothing more until December. Four or five months of the year there was no work for us in Tajos. That was how we lived in those days – bitterly.

When there was work in the vineyards there was plenty of it. Too much you could say for what we were paid. 1·75 pesetas a day, two pesetas if things were good, 1·50 when things were bad. I'm talking of 1920 and thereabouts. It was hard work. The landlords and their foremen had a trick. They put two or three of their own men in the digging line, one at each end and the other in the middle. They got paid twenty-five centimos a day more. It was their job to force the rest to keep up the pace. Their own companions, who had no other livelihood, they'd force like that for twenty-five centimos a day!

There were plenty of foremen who expected a worker to break his back digging. They were always after you shouting if you dropped behind the vineyard men. If I couldn't keep up I let them go on. I knew I was working as hard as was right; I was fulfilling my obligation. 'If they push, let them go,' some of us would say to each other. 'We'll work at the proper pace. If they say anything we'll tell them, "It's enough".' There's time enough in this life to kill oneself digging. At sunset I and those who thought like me would say to the foreman, 'Tomorrow, if you want, and if not we'll leave.' They couldn't rightly force one to leave because everyone knew why they had the vineyard men there.

But there were other foremen who had pity and said, 'ech! How can one drive half-starved men to work like mules?' For that's how it was, we were always half-starved.

We walked to the vineyards on empty stomachs and worked for an hour before eating a bit of the food we took with us: a pot of bread soup, the sort we make here, a *tortilla*, a few dried figs when we were in luck – that was all we had to eat from dawn until late at night. No one had more. At noon we had an hour off and ate the rest of our food. In the afternoon we had two cigarette breaks. From sunrise to sunset we had just a couple of hours' rest. I was always hungry – one couldn't get rid of it.

We talked about it among ourselves, we protested to one another. But there was nothing we could say, nothing we could do to change anything. If you talked too loud, the landowners threatened you, wouldn't give you work. There was a lot of fear because there was so little work. You had to keep your mouth shut and put up with it.

I joined the 'society', as we called the union, in 1918 when it was first formed. 'Triumph of Labour' was the slogan we chose. Each village had its own. 'Defence of Labour' was what they adopted in Casas Nuevas, 'Hope of Labour' in Benamalí.

Being a member made one a lot of difficulties. Most of the landlords hated the union and they looked for ways of making trouble for us. We had a strike almost immediately. It was over the day-wage. They were paying us 1·50 pesetas for bringing the grape harvest in – and after a man had been working forty days they dropped the wage by twenty-five centimos. We demanded three or four pesetas a day. Two thousand workers from here, Casas Nuevas and from outside who had come for the harvest, gathered outside the *cacique's* farm down by the river. We had to force some of the outsiders to join us, threaten them a bit. We didn't object to their working here as long as they didn't take jobs under the going rate; but we couldn't allow them to go on working while we went on strike.

As we made our way to the *cacique's* house – he was mayor at the time – even the Guardia Civil didn't try to hold us back. 'Go by the path of truth and no one will get in your way,' they said. When we were all gathered, the union president said, 'I'll take care of this. I'm going to talk to the mayor, we'll sign new agreements straight away.' When he came out he told us we could all go home, the agreements were going to be signed.

The next day the village and countryside were swarming with *guardia*. That was the agreement that had been signed! I don't know what the landlords did to buy off the union president. We stayed out four days anyway and then had to go back to work on their conditions – a rise of fifty centimos a day.

A bunch of traitors they were in charge of the society; they sold themselves to the *caciques* and bosses. We held an assembly and sacked the president. But we had no more strikes. Five years later when the Primo de Rivera dictatorship came in the union was banned. I never held any official position because I can't read or write; I never went to school, my father sent me out herding goats when I was nine. . . .

When there was no work I went for esparto or sat at home. What was the good of going out to hang about in the street with no money to spend? If it hadn't been for the shops we would have died of hunger. They gave us credit, they'd let us buy for a month or two without paying. No longer. Because if it took a man longer to get a job they knew he wasn't going to get one. When you got work most of the money went to pay off what you'd had to spend to stay alive the rest of the time.

I've been as far as Granada and Córdoba to pick esparto. To tell the truth, that's as far as I've been in my life, with the exception of military service in Tetuan. Going for esparto meant sleeping out under a tree in the sierra until it got too cold around Christmas time. We'd spend nearly three months there, coming back here by train for a day or two every month. At the end of it all we'd have 300 or 400 pesetas saved. Saved by not eating because the man who had the business made all the profit. But with that sort of money in our pockets we felt as rich as a marquis, we were millionaires! The women went mad when we gave them the money. We were all accustomed to living on so little in those days. . . .

I've walked as far as San Roque by Gibraltar looking for work. Five days I and two companions were walking, asking for work at every farm and *cortijo*. At last we had to ask for alms. We were nearly starving, there was no work anywhere and we had to come back without a thing in our hands.

It took me five years to get together 4,000 pesetas to buy the furniture to get married. Five years! And most of them spent away from home to be able to earn a bit more. Those 4,000 pesetas were the most I was ever able to save until a couple of years ago.

I've never had any land nor my father before me. Our class had no possessions or wealth of any sort. My father was out of work eight or nine months of the year. Things were even worse for him than they were for me. And yet there's plenty of land in Spain, plenty. Enough for everyone to have a plot. There are many, many *cortijos* out there, *fanegas* and *fanegas* of land that's not worked, that's lost. If all that had been divided up. . . . Yes, señor, we would have been worth something, Spain then would have been worth a great deal more.

For the past forty years, until he was made a street sweeper a few years ago, Pedro worked the land as a labourer when he could find work; picking esparto when he couldn't. The deep brown skin is stretched tight across his cheeks to the mouth where three or four teeth are all that remain. He has the shrunken, intense look of a man who has never eaten enough, for whom, as he says, 'prosperity has come too late. The young today can earn money and save. That was something we could never do.'

LANDOWNERS

Three sons

In the 1920s nineteen individual landowners – 2 percent of the village's landowning population – owned just under half the land of Tajos. Their holdings were all over a hundred hectares in size. The immediate families of six of these large owners, and another five families, none of whose individual members owned as much as a hundred hectares, together held a further 10 percent. In all, 58 percent of privately-owned land in Tajos was in the hands of some 35 individuals, many of whom were inter-related by birth or marriage, thus concentrating their control.

More significant than the total extent of their holdings – of which the large landowners left two-thirds untilled as pasture and scrubland – was the fact that they owned more than 50 percent of the irrigated land and the best vineyards.

By the time of the First World War only three big land-owners and their families lived in the village itself. Some, like the two noble owners and the vine-growers who had moved in after the phylloxera, had never lived there; the others had already moved to Casas Nuevas or Málaga.

Of the three who remained only one family was native to Tajos: the Tejadas. Antonio Tejada and his five younger brothers and sisters between them owned nearly 500 hectares, most of which they had inherited from their father. The largest *cortijo* in Tajos by the river belonged to them. From the turn of the century until the civil war, don

Antonio, a tall commanding figure, was the *cacique* of Tajos.

Over the years marriage united the three principal families. Don Antonio married Maria, the eldest daughter of Juan Saenz, a Castilian who had set up a cloth shop in the village in the 1880s and who had, in the course of time, accumulated over a hundred hectares of land. Saenz's younger son married into a large Tajos landowning family who lived in Casas Nuevas. The son of this union, José, in turn married the eldest daughter of the remaining large landowner, Gil Lopez.

Don Gil, as he is still called locally (to distinguish him from his son who is called simply Gil), left his native village in the north at 14. He went to seek his fortune in Grazalema, a village in the province of Cadiz famous in the last century for its cloth manufacture. From there he was brought to Tajos in 1899 by Juan Saenz to serve in his cloth shop. Some ten years later he had opened his own cloth shop and had bought his first land. By the time he died, in 1934, he had become the biggest landowner living in Tajos, owning over forty farms and 230 hectares of land.

Don Gil made a smart match by marrying the eldest daughter of the liberal *cacique* who had held power before don Antonio. Though he wore it seldom, his father-in-law's mantle fell on him. He did not often dispute don Antonio's rule in the village; it was not given to many to do so. However, once in a while, 'out of sense of duty' his sons say, and under pressure from the provincial Liberal Party bosses, he became 'leader' of the party locally. (*Cacique* is today a derogatory word.) Otherwise he concentrated on his business which increasingly became dominated by his accumulation of land.

Village lore which, unsolicited, every Tajeño except don Gil's sons will relate, has it that he built up his land-holdings by extending credit to small-holders to buy in his shop. As security he held the title deeds of their farms. When they were unable to pay he foreclosed on them, snapping up their land at very low prices. The fact that most of the land he acquired consisted of small-holdings lends credence to the story. However, it is true that he also bought land from a nobleman who, being an absentee owner with far bigger interests elsewhere, was willing to sell most of his land after the First World War.

Don Gil's sons are today the only heirs of the three big Tajos landowners still living in the village. The rest have gone. Some, like don Antonio, lost their lives in the revolution of 1936; others followed the earlier pattern and moved to Casas Nuevas before the civil war; yet others found their holdings dwindling through inheritance. No Tejadas or Saenzs live in the village today.

LAZARO LOPEZ   *Sixty-one*

Eldest son

My father was very hard-working, a good businessman. He wanted me to study and make a career for myself. When I was eleven he sent me to an Augustine school in Málaga. There were only two other boys of my generation who left here to study and neither of them were native Tajeños. Not that there weren't boys clever enough to have gone on to study; there were several who were a lot cleverer than me. But their parents hadn't the means. It cost my father a lot to send me to school, about 3,000 pesetas a term what with board, books and fees.

The two others who went to Málaga with me succeeded; but I gave up. I passed my *bachillerato* and went to Granada university to study medicine. I didn't like studying, I liked dancing and girls and having a good time – the things of one's youth! So my father told me to come home and help in the shop or with the running of his farms. I was seventeen when I came back.

I had no intention of helping him either in the shop or on the land. I was more rebellious than anyone I know. My father couldn't do anything with me. He'd tell me to do something and I'd stay at it for ten minutes or half an hour until he was gone; and then I'd be gone too!

I spent my time doing nothing – and that's what I've done ever since. To begin with I used to get rather bored, it was monotonous. But one gets used to it in the end.

In those days I'd get up at nine, have my coffee and then go for a walk round the village and out to that little area by the Virgin's chapel. I'd sit there with a book and talk to the girls until it was lunchtime. After lunch the same routine. Sometimes I'd go to a friend's house or to a bar which I enjoyed a lot. And that's the way the day – and the evenings – went by, all exactly the same.

I could live easily on a peseta a day. A coffee cost only ten or fifteen centimos and for another five you could get a *copita* of rum or anis. My mother used to give me the money and if she didn't I'd take it from the till in the shop. My father would tell me off if he found out but I made sure that most of the time he didn't.

My father didn't like my way of life, but what could he do? Of course, in not obeying him I was lacking the respect a son should show for his father. Sometimes he'd be sitting with friends at the door of the tavern when I came by. I always wore a suit and a tie. He'd look at me and say to his friends, 'Huh! there's my son putting on the airs of a grandee. . . .' I just used to laugh.

I liked reading but I seldom had the patience to finish a book. I read the lives of a lot of the saints and of Jesus Christ. I've always liked religion and religious functions. When I was seven I asked the priest to allow me to become an acolyte and, because I had a good voice, I was soon singing in church. Later I learned plain chant and at school in Málaga I was first baritone in the choir. I've sung in the cathedrals of Málaga and Granada. Plain chant, I loved that above all else! The true flamenco *cante jondo* I've never enjoyed.

When my father died my five brothers and sisters and I inherited half his wealth. The other half went automatically to my mother. I got eight farms and four houses, the best in the village, and 200,000 pesetas in cash.

All the farms were good land, not very large, between three and six hectares each. They didn't earn a thing, a thousand or two thousand pesetas a year in all. They were all being sharecropped and often I didn't even bother to have the sharecroppers bring my half of the crops to my house. I'd tell them to sell it and give me the money. The produce of the land was worth nothing in those days.

I couldn't live on that sort of money. It wasn't enough for a month, let alone a year. Forty to fifty thousand pesetas was more like the figure I needed a year.

I kept three of my four houses empty and with a bed in each. Depending on where I happened to find myself in the village I'd decide where to spend the night. Whichever house was the closest! I had a woman who came to make the bed and clean the houses, but I never ate in any of them. I'd go to my sister's or to the *fonda* in the square. I didn't want to be tied down anywhere. I wanted to live adventurously, to travel and see the world – and that's what I did after my father died.

I bought my first motorbike. I was a great one for motorbikes, I had over thirty in a few years. I'd buy a five horse-power BSA which cost 4,950 pesetas. Then, if a new model came in which took my fancy a few weeks later, I'd turn it in and give a thousand or two thousand pesetas to take the new one.

I used to go to Gibraltar a lot on my motorbikes. You didn't need a passport to get in and you could spend the night at the Hotel Royal for only ten pesetas. It took me about four hours to get there because the road, though asphalted by then, was full of potholes. There wasn't much traffic, that's for sure. One time I skidded and the bike fell on top of me; I lay there a couple of hours before a lorry came by and the driver lifted it off me.

I went to Madrid three or four times and to visit my father's home village in Logroño. To get there I rode up the coast to Almeria, Alicante and Castellon and then across to Cuenca. I've seen a few places in my time – but you can hardly call it seeing the world.

The money I inherited I left in the bank and drew out what I needed when I needed it. All the same I had to sell some of my farms and houses and livestock – cows, goats and sheep – to keep in funds.

One of my farms I swapped for a horse. That was in 1934. The horse was worth a couple of thousand pesetas, I suppose. I preferred having a horse to owning a farm. I could ride the horse along the road at least.

The Republic had come in by then. There was a great deal of disorder. I joined Lerroux's Radical party when a branch was formed in the village. Not that I had any idea what it was all about, I've never liked politics. But when everyone joined I joined too. I became a municipal councillor in 1934; not that I ever attended meetings; what was the point? The mayor and the town clerk decided everything between them; it made no difference what a councillor said.

I was here when the civil war started. I got out after a month, I was frightened the people would kill me or put me in jail. That's what they were doing to the rich and those who were on the right. Not that things were as bad here as elsewhere, not by a long way. The people of Tajos aren't bad. I don't believe anyone envied me because I was rich – on the contrary, the people always showed great affection for me. But one always has enemies. . . .

I went to Málaga; things were much worse there, so I jumped on my motorbike and made for Jaen where I had friends and wasn't well known. After a short time I was called up in the republican army and served as a dispatch rider on the Córdoba front. I was wounded in the arm in 1937 and invalided out. I spent the rest of the war in the republican zone. The day the war ended I made my way back here. The authorities naturally checked up on what I had been doing during the war. But nothing happened to me because I hadn't done anything.

His arm remains crippled from his war wound; and in the past year glaucoma has taken the sight of one eye and threatens the other. A lifelong bachelor, he sold his remaining land and all but one of his houses, mainly to his brothers and sisters. The loss of the land and property, which at today's prices would have made him a considerable fortune, seems to trouble him little. He laughs. 'I'll tell you a funny story. That farm I swapped for a horse – well, four years ago I bought it back for a million pesetas. Three months later I sold it for three and a half millions to some English people. On behalf of some friends of mine I bought it back a week ago for seven and a half millions. The English did all right out of the deal and so will my friends. They're going to add it to some land they've got alongside and develop it. They'll make plenty of money from it still.'

GIL LOPEZ   *Fifty-eight*

Second son

He stands outside his shop on the narrow pavement or sits on
the doorstep, his massive head on the heavy frame watching
the slow progression along the street. Behind him, through
the door over which a blanket is folded back, one glimpses in
the dim light shelves piled with different cloths and boxes,
jackets and trousers hanging from a line above the counter.
The shop has neither display window nor sign to differentiate
it from the other houses. It is don Gil's shop, unchanged
since he started it in 1910 in the front room of this house
where his son works and lives today.

Gil is one of the richest men in the village. He wears a suit
from which his corpulence seems in constant flight, and an
open-necked shirt. His booming voice is often heard in the
square of a summer evening, holding forth on any subject
that moves him, especially the state of the nation. His
opinions – provocatively, in the view of the villagers –
suggest a nostalgia for the 'freedoms' of the monarchical
Spain of his youth. He has few friends and, despite his
wealth, is not one of the village's ruling group.

Now, with a yardstick in his hand which he uses to
emphasize his points, he stands behind the counter from
which he has been serving for the past forty-six years. His
eyes are sharp; as he talks he watches the people passing by
the door.

I started work at twelve in this shop. My father didn't offer me
the chance of a career. My brother Lazaro had been given the
opportunity and had thrown it up, and my father never said
anything to me about studying. I never thought about it. I'd done
my four years in the village school and learned to read and write.
Everything in those days depended on what one's parents decided
for one.

My father was a very quick-witted man, with enormous business agility. He worked from eight every morning until midnight, writing letters and keeping accounts. Once a week he went to Málaga on business. He never had a holiday in his life, not even to return to his native village where those of his brothers who hadn't emigrated to South America still lived working the vines. He set up this business and in twenty years became the biggest landowner here, after starting with nothing.

It took him ten years of saving before he could make a start dealing in grapes and raisins. Then he got the shop and little by little began to buy land. Of course, land was a lot cheaper then than it is today. Fifty thousand pesetas was the highest he ever paid, and that was for a farm of eighty-five hectares by the river, of which twenty-five hectares was irrigated land. Still, that was a fortune when you think that an eight horse-power Ford cost 6,000 pesetas then.

When he bought a small-holder's farm he used to leave the owner on it as a sharecropper or renter. He had about as many sharecroppers as renters in the end. There were no laws regulating the contract a landowner made with a *colono*. That came in only under the Republic when tenant farmers were given some rights; before that it was completely free. There were plenty of men who wanted land and by giving them a farm and the implements to sharecrop it they had the means to live and raise their children. Naturally, sharecropping produces more for the owner, but he has to invest in livestock, fertilizers, implements and the like to set the *colono* up until he can begin to pay off. That's a considerable investment. Also, my father broke a lot of new land and terraced it. Especially the land he bought from the marquis of Valdeverde whose family had owned it since the time when the Moors were thrown out. The marquis lived in Madrid and had enormous landholdings in Granada, Jaen and Badajoz and never came here. One of the farms my father bought from him, *El Verdegal*, had nothing, not even a house, on it until my father took it over.

His farms came to interest him more than his shop which assistants attended to. It was exactly as it is today, he sold what I sell. But sales were a lot smaller then. A yard of cloth – it was sold by the yard not the metre – was worth fifteen centimos whereas today a metre of any sort of cloth costs a hundred pesetas. Drills and corduroys were the cloths he sold most of. Before the First

World War a labourer couldn't afford to buy a suit more than once a year for the *feria*, if that. And, as like as not, he'd have to go into debt to buy it and pay off little by little. *Si,* señor. As long as my father knew he would pay he'd give him credit. But if not, he'd say, 'well, I can't serve you.'

He made a lot of money, but we didn't live any differently from anyone else. In our house we ate what everyone in Andalusia eats – bread and tomato soup made with oil and water, fried fish, fried potatoes, pimientos – whatever the land produced. We had money enough to buy meat but we hardly ever ate it. The Catalans and Basques say they can't understand how the Andalusians have the energy to work eating only 'bread and water'. That's what they call the soups we eat here. But you go to the largest, wealthiest *cortijo* and that's what you'll find being eaten there.

We all went to the village school like everyone else. There were poor and rich alike and we played together and called each other *tu*. And go on doing so. There was no discrimination of any sort in those times of the monarchy which was totally liberal. The rich were a bit better dressed perhaps, but everyone went to the dances and bullfights together. We were all equal.

I hadn't been working long for my father when he went blind. He had cataracts in both eyes. That was one of the reasons he needed me to be here. I had to stand in for him, go down to the farms on his behalf, give instructions, weigh the olives as they were brought into the mill he had built. I worked in the shop too and took him about as much as he wanted to go. At the age of sixty-eight he was operated on by an excellent surgeon in Granada and recovered his sight. It was a miracle, but it came too late for he was already close to the end of his life.

When he died all the property was divided up equally in terms of its value, of course. I wanted the shop and the house because they had a cash value. Not that it did me much good later. But anyway, I inherited no land until my mother died in 1947.

Before the civil war I used to like to keep up with politics. I liked the discussions it involved. In the early 1930s, under the Republic, I joined *Acción Popular*, Gil Robles' party, which stood for the defence of religion, order and property. It wanted a democratic monarchy with elections every four years, like in England, or a right-wing Republic.

I don't consider myself very religious, about average, I'd say; I haven't been to communion or confession for the past ten years. But I consider religion the backbone of a nation, it's important that people believe in and fear God so they don't rob and kill one another. That's the only thing that prevents them – and the same is true of me.

Under the Republic there were only two political sides – the left and the right. Socialists, Communists and Anarchists on the one hand, the CEDA, of which *Acción Popular* was the most important party, and the Monarchists on the other. The civil war would never have happened if the right had won. But the left won the elections of 1936 by a narrow margin; and then, after the assassination of the right-wing leader Calvo Sotelo, the army rose to restore order. Before that it had been a time of total disorder. I and everyone else in the village who belonged to *Acción Popular* was locked up in jail here for forty-eight hours without blankets or anything to sleep on, without tobacco, after a bomb incident in Madrid. It was terrible and I was badly frightened.

But the civil war was worse. Awful! Forty million times worse than the world war. On top of all the disasters a war brings to the civilian population, the hunger and hardships, a civil war is a struggle between brothers. One was on the nationalist side and one's brother was on the red side and you never knew if it wasn't your brother you were shooting at. It happened to me – I served in the nationalist army; it happened to the majority of Andalusians. What can be worse than thinking: 'Am I shooting my brother?' Almost everyone had someone on the other side; the immense majority didn't want to fight for one side or the other, I believe.

I was an ordinary soldier in a shock division, I didn't want responsibilities of any kind. I fought on the Madrid front, in Extremadura, on the Córdoba front and the Ebro. The Ebro was the worst, a terrible, bloody battle. The reds were very courageous fighters; the whole war was so bloody because they always resisted. They were Spanish and the Spanish are like that, they resist. But they lacked discipline, that was their trouble. . . .

After the war I came back here. I run the shop and work the land in the same way as my father. The farms I inherited are let out to renters. One of them produces at least 200,000 pesetas a year because it's good land with lemons, oranges, plums. And I get 7,100 pesetas a year in rent. That's what I was getting in 1947 and that's what I get today when 7,100 pesetas isn't worth a tenth of what it was in 1947. The law forbids me to raise the rent. If I wanted to get the tenant out he'd ask for 200,000 pesetas compensation or more. This is why so much building is going on in Spain. No one wants to invest in farming because you can't get a decent return, especially on land as poor as this is here. On an apartment building you can make 12 percent or 14 percent whereas the land doesn't make you even 2 percent.

I have to work harder than I used to because I have a girl and a boy of twelve and eleven studying in Málaga. Nowadays I sell a lot more ready-made clothes than my father; it's only the old who still stick to their ways and buy cloth to make their own clothes.

I don't expect either of my children will keep this shop. When I die they can do what they want with it; until then I shall go on working here. What's the point of retiring? To spend all day in the cafe and become a slacker? No, I have no intention of doing that. . . .

EUGENIO LOPEZ   *Fifty-four*

Third son

I have a nostalgia for the times of my youth. People say I'm romantic but I'm sure life was more natural, simpler in those days. The evilness of today didn't exist here then. Sometimes I go out into the countryside with a loaf and some lard and a penknife to slice the bread the way the people used to. It reminds me of my childhood and the way everyone lived.

How well I remember it! The barley coffee and *buñuelos* before going to school when the men and women took down the *aguardiente* bottle from the dresser to drink a *copita* to start the day off. The 'viva Jesús' I always called it. The women drank too, there were some who liked the bottle a bit too much. One I remember, she has only just died. After the war she used to stand in front of Franco's picture and address it: 'Franco, Franco, Lord of the Armies. . . .' It was her way of thanking Franco for having granted her husband a pension!

Then off through the cobbled streets to school. At mid-day we came home, but in those times lunch wasn't the main meal of the day. That came at seven. In the summer we children would have our dinner on the steps leading down into the patio and as we ate the big African swallows swooped overhead like aeroplanes in and around the church tower. Watching them was amusement enough in those days.

At ten we had supper. Between dinner and supper my father offered himself his only luxury. He went to the cafe to drink his *moreno*. Those of his political persuasion had a room reserved for them in one of the cafes; those of a different persuasion went to a room in the other cafe. And there they discussed the political events of the day – I don't know what, I know nothing about politics – and played cards and drank their black coffee with the sugar lumps soaked in rum which they burnt before adding it to the coffee. That was a *moreno* and it cost fifteen centimos and it was a luxury!

We children would often run from the house to fetch our father in the cafe because he, like all the other men, had to be home by ten. That was the rule, at ten the doors were shut and we ate supper. We had little spirit lamps on which the camomile tea or the chocolate was heated up, and some people added a little anis or cinnamon to their tea, while others poured in a drop or two of *aguardiente* to warm them up. And with that we ate toasted bread.

My father was a generous man and he often invited people who had come in from the countryside to stay for a meal. They might have had to leave their farmstead the night before to get to Tajos to do business worth only a hundred pesetas. My father knew this and invited them to stay. And so we ate like everyone else in the village, without distinction. A chicken – why we'd eat one only on some special fiesta, the Day of Our Lord for example. It was a luxury to eat an egg!

There weren't more than half a dozen privileged families in the village. And they weren't what you can call rich. The rich in Spain were the counts and marquises, the people like the Dukes of Alba. The rest had to live from their labour, whatever it was: the land, esparto, palmetto weaving. Any little things the village women bought came from the money they made selling eggs to the *recoveras*. The latter, I remember well, kept their accounts by making a stroke for each peseta and when there were five making a cross. That's how they added up what they bought and sold – and there are people here who still do the same.

People worked harder in those days, they had to. Without thought of hours. Our shop, with its four young boys as assistants, opened at six in the morning and closed at midnight. Mass was at six and everyone attended before going to work in the fields; and the shops opened then so that the old women could buy a centimo's worth of coffee and sugar, and a few dried figs, for their husbands before they went to work.

Men were machines – and yet there was more closeness among people than there is today. People shared their joys and their sorrows; in spite of the servitude, the village was more one family. Today, thanks to God, everyone is equal, but this style of life in which everyone is chasing money, everyone is on the make – as though we had all become Catalans – that didn't exist. And just as well, because – unlike the Catalans – once someone here has got two pesetas together he believes he's as important as a *capitan-general*.

The village was poorer, of course; there was less food, fewer clothes, less sanitation. Food measures poverty. I remember there were many children who used to come to our house to play, and at meal-times my parents saw to it that they didn't see us eating. As a child I didn't understand why, but today I see it was so as not to humiliate them, not to show that we were more privileged than they.

Twice a week the servant or one of my aunts heated up water, grabbed us and scrubbed our heads. That was the only way to rid us of what we had picked up playing with the children from the top of the village, the poorest of the poor, who were always in and out of our house. My father never objected to their coming to play. There were other houses more 'elegant' than ours in that respect, but not many.

Yes, there was poverty, but with it went something that has been lost today. An innocence perhaps. I'll tell you a story I often tell my pupils. Every Sunday we children would play outside the church before going to mass, and we'd say to each other: 'After mass, let's go to the Cross at the entrance to the village and from there see if we can make a hole and get up to heaven. . . .'

Yes, at the age of twelve I still believed that! We were so trusting, so credulous! Our parents wouldn't even let us go alone the few yards out of the village along the road to where the mulberry trees grow to collect leaves for our silkworms. They told us blood-suckers would catch us if we did!

When I was small a priest whose ideas were very different from those we had been living by was appointed here. Most of the priests in those days were men who, by their position, expected to rule the village. They were into everything and, because they were priests, everyone kept quiet. But this priest had ideas about charity we hadn't known before. At Christmas he got the children of the privileged families to dress up as shepherds and angels to take part in the midnight mass and the procession afterwards. We enjoyed that, he made the mass symbolic of Christ's birth. But for Epiphany, which is when we give presents here, he demanded from each of us either a kid or a lamb, money or eggs for a meal for the poor. It was held in the town hall and it was we, the sons of the more wealthy and powerful, who served as waiters.

Before, he had gone round to our parents for gifts of blankets and food to be distributed to the poor. On Holy Thursday and for the fiestas in honour of the patron saint, he did the same thing. He was a priest from Málaga who was well connected with the aristocracy there who sent him great quantities of gifts. He kept nothing for himself, everything was given to the poor. This was the atmosphere in which I was brought up.

There was a great deal more devotion then than there is today. During Holy Week the processions were full of penitents who went barefoot or with their arms attached to a pole in the form of a cross or on their knees through the streets. When they got up their knees were bloodied and torn. Another form of penitence which was typical of Holy Week was for a man to put on a white or black habit and, with his arms outstretched in the form of a cross, to run through the village without stopping for anyone. When he reached the door of the church or the cemetery gate he kissed the earth and prayed; then, still with arms outstretched, he ran through the streets to his home. These *aspados*, as they're called, had usually taken a vow to make this penance if they or someone close to them recovered from illness. I remember they used to frighten us kids as they ran through the streets. . . .

When my father gave me the chance of studying in Málaga I accepted it gladly. I was thirteen. I finished my studies just as the

civil war and revolution broke out. It was a terrible time, terrible.
I stayed with one of my sisters here. Every day the militiamen came
and took things away until at last we no longer cared. They took
everything from my brother's shop. I stayed indoors, in bed much
of the time, covered with all the blankets there were, I was so cold
with fear. I think I hardly slept at all.

It was the lack of education and culture that was responsible for
the horrors. When the houses of the priest and don Salvador, the
retired civil servant, were sacked the people burnt all the furniture
and food they found. Imagine that – people whose children were
sleeping on the floor at home for want of a bed and lacking food
could think of nothing better than burning what they could have
used.

When it was all over it was like taking a warm bath after seven
months of not washing.

Eugenio served three years in the nationalist army. As an
ex-combatant after the war he had the right to a university
place. But at the university of Granada he realized that six
years of study would be necessary for a degree; through the
father of one of his sister's husbands, who had a post at the
university, he was able to apply to take a three-month
intensive training course to become a schoolteacher which
he has been ever since.

After some years in a small village in the province of
Málaga and again in the north of Spain – from both of which
posts he asked to be relieved – he was appointed to the school
in Tajos.

Concerned for the education of his five children, he decided
in the early 1960s to sell off all his inherited land to raise the
money for their schooling in Málaga. More open, less
shrewd perhaps than his brother Gil, he sold the land
relatively cheaply to a foreigner, Avery Mark.

Very recently Gil finally overcame his reluctance to pay his
tenants compensation and sold one of his farms to a foreign
construction concern for fifteen million pesetas (about
£90,000).

MEN WITH IDEAS

This is the expression the labourers use to designate those among them who have and expound definite political ideals.

Labourers and Landowners in Southern Spain, Juan Martinez-Alier

From the late nineteenth century the 'idea' in most of Andalusia, including Málaga, was the anarchist one of libertarian communism. But here and there, for reasons it is now only possible to guess (distance from main anarchist centres, higher proportions of small-holders and tenants than landless labourers) the majority of workers in certain villages rejected anarchism in favour of socialism. Such was the case of Tajos among others.

The difference between the two political creeds was naturally great. But if the aims were different, a similar awareness of the realities of rural exploitation, a similar class-consciousness, inspired both movements. To take but one small example: in Tajos, as throughout rural Andalusia, popular language recognizes only two principal classes – *obreros* and *señoritos,* workers and masters. Though words for peasant and labourer, tenant and sharecropper exist, they are almost never used; everyone who works the land is a worker; every landowner who does not work the land with

47

his own hands is a *señorito*, a word which moreover has a derogatory connotation.*

Closed down at local level by the Primo dictatorship, the socialist trade union resurfaced in Tajos in 1931. By then not only had the dictatorship fallen but the monarchy with it. In Tajos as in every Andalusian *pueblo* hope was alive that under the new Republic poverty, unemployment and the rule of *caciques* was a thing of the past. Land reform was promised; all landless labourers and a proportion of small-holders and tenants (between 20 percent and 40 percent of the total in Málaga province) were eligible for resettlement. Bogged down in legalities, the reform hardly got off the ground; in Tajos, specifically, nothing happened.

Villagers from Almárgen marched twenty-eight hours to reach Málaga to protest that local landlords were refusing to employ labourers and leaving their land unworked. In Tajos the vineyard owners followed the same pattern. Elsewhere there were reports of hungry labourers invading estates to shoot game because there was no work – 'only hunger and children begging for bread'.

The situation worsened when a right-wing government came to power in 1933. Wages were depressed to pre-Republic levels; labour unrest and militancy increased. In the elections of February 1936 a Popular Front government was brought to power. Five months later the military rose, expecting to overthrow the new government in a matter of days. They counted without the populace. In riposte, the masses rose in a revolution the likes of which had not been seen in western Europe for nearly a century. The result, only too well known, was a civil war which lasted nearly three years.

In every village and town not immediately captured by the military, revolutionary committees were formed. As every-

---

* Because there are important differences between labourers, tenants and small-holders I have tended not to follow popular idiom; however, in talking it was always necessary to ask people to say what type of worker they were referring to. They might then reply *colono* which in Tajos refers equally to a renter or a sharecropper between whom, as the reader will see, there are also important differences.

A water-driven corn mill in the countryside
at the turn of the century

In the market: a fish-vendor to-day

'The thin white line separated into rows of low rectangular houses . . .'
Tajos seen from the road up from the coast

The village lands reach to the sea; view over the roofs of the *barrio*

The main street, 1960

Tiles and concrete replace the old cobbles; a side street, 1970

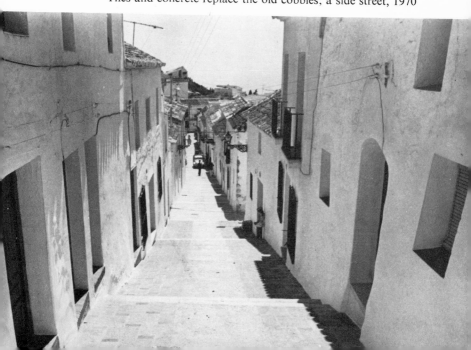

Goatherd plaiting an esparto rope

On a mule track a small-holder makes his way to his farm

where, the revolution in Tajos had its moments of violence and terror. Equally its many, perhaps more, moments of compassion and mercy. Those seven months until Málaga fell to the Franco forces early in 1937 are something most people today talk about with reluctance. An old share-cropper breaks down in tears as he remembers being jailed. Militiamen from Málaga arrived 'to take care of the fascists'. One of them asked him where he had been arrested. '*Compañero*, I was digging potatoes on the land. . . .' 'So you're a slave of the landlords, working at night, eh?' 'I have calluses on my hands, *compañero*.' Through the bars the militiaman felt for his hand. 'Nothing will happen to you, I'll see to that.' Shortly afterwards the sharecropper was released. The militiaman had a *novia* in Tajos and had come to the village specially when he heard what was happening. 'He wanted to do what he could to prevent any killings. He saved a number of people, including the doctor.'

Not everyone waited on chance to intervene. Dressed in a militiaman's overalls, Gil Lopez immediately fled the village by night. He was hidden first by a sharecropper in his straw-loft, later in a secret recess his mother enlisted a mason's help to build in the roof of their village house to which he secretly returned. 'The red militia searched for me on many occasions but they never discovered me. It was for my political beliefs, not because I was rich that they were after me. . . .'

Had he been found he might have been shot. 'It wasn't the socialists who were dangerous. They were moderates concerned with the defence of the working class; they hardly took part in the killings. It was the FAI. In Málaga and some of the other villages, though not here, the anarchists were very strong; if they hadn't been there would have been hardly any deaths because the people here didn't want to kill. What I feared – after my earlier experience of being jailed – was that I'd be locked up and a FAI patrol would come and liquidate me as they did the others. . . .'

Six people were shot; their names and the dates of their

deaths are inscribed on a plaque in the town hall. The first was not killed until five weeks after the start of the uprising: Salvador Jimenez, the former colonial official, who had been prominent under the Primo dictatorship. The remainder, including Antonio Tejada and two of his brothers, were killed in the following weeks. With the exception of Jimenez, all are said to have been killed by anarchist patrols.

The killings did not take place in the fury of the first few days. Would they have taken place at all if the news had not started to come through of the repression in areas controlled by the military? Possibly they would have; but it is also indisputable that these reports, augmented later by refugees' own accounts, inflamed passions. In Seville, 9,000 people were reported executed in the first weeks of the military regime; in Badajoz some 2,000 slaughtered after the city was captured on 14 August. Every night General Queipo de Llano, conqueror of Seville, bellowed threats over the radio: for every person killed by the revolution his troops would kill eight.

When Málaga fell this threat was proven to be no idle boast. 'There ensued the most ferocious proscription that had occurred in Spain since the fall of Badajoz,' Hugh Thomas comments in *The Spanish Civil War*. The exact numbers executed may never be known; they were so great that the Italian government ordered its ambassador to take up the matter directly with its Spanish nationalist allies as a 'moral question affecting the reputation of both Spain and Italy'. (Gabriel Jackson, *The Spanish Republic and the Civil War*.)

Estimates of those executed from Tajos and its countryside vary widely. It is certain, however, that in the first months the figure was more than fifty shot and twice that number imprisoned. Six 'reds' were shot out of hand in a watercourse outside the village by the local gentry before nationalist troops arrived to take the village. Many claim that in all at least a hundred were executed in the first six months.

The repression continued until 1941. At the end of the civil war in April 1939, it was again intensified. Each day from mid-April to September the Málaga falangist paper ran a column under the unvarying headline: *Arrest of Outstanding Marxist Elements.* The majority came not from the capital but from the villages; frequently the arrests in one village occupied the column for the day. Sixteen arrests were reported in Tajos. Undoubtedly this figure understates the reality, for at least nine men were shot at the time, none of whose names appeared on the list.

Local denunciation formed the basis of the charges at the accuseds' courts-martial in Málaga. Such *denuncias* allowed villagers to settle old scores. Thirty years later the memories have not died.

The 'men with ideas' who survived the repression deplore much of what happened during the *movimiento.** They were and remain moderates; had they not been it is unlikely that they would be alive today. Without denying their beliefs, they – even less than others – wish to recall those times. In their eyes there is the pale glimmer of fear; their voices often drop to a whisper. Their pasts are known and in the village they are not shunned. But there is something lonely about them, as though their memories, their hopes for a new and different world in the past, kept them apart. 'In my youth there was much more singing and dancing than there is in the village today. It was the war that ended it; there's been a sadness ever since.'

JUAN MORENO   *Sixty-four*

Shoemaker

My father lost his shop, his livelihood and in the end his life due to a *cacique.* He voted for a candidate opposed to the ruling *cacique*

* A word of ambiguous usage. The military rising is officially called the *Movimiento Nacional*; but the men with ideas use it – safely – to refer to the revolution. 'Uprising' best translates both usages.

and when the latter won he avenged himself. He got my father's licence taken away and had the shop made over to one of his supporters. My father was the victim of a parliamentary system which in the end led us all to tragedy.

That was in 1917 when I was about ten. My father had to do what he had never done before – work the land. My mother had inherited two or three plots and he tried to provide for us by working them. But he couldn't manage. One day he went to the sierra and returned ill. A cerebral congestion from which he died, leaving my mother to look after us.

Politics at that time was the exclusive privilege of those of property. At elections the *caciques* put on a great show. They laid on *paellas* and wine and cigars for the country people who were hardly ever able to eat a good meal. Those who could afford to wear boots could afford to buy votes. That was what *caciquismo* meant.

The ruling classes conceded universal suffrage only as long as they could manipulate it. Little by little the people began to wake up, we began to know that a nation called England and another called France existed; we were starting to read and learn something. But in a rather exotic way, without proper schools or education, so that we were only able to guess the value of the vote. When we discovered it, they took it away and brought in the dictatorship of Primo de Rivera which lasted seven years.

After my father died I became an acolyte in the church. The priest had taken a liking to me at school and he paid me 2·50 pesetas a month. The other acolytes were all sons of the rich. They didn't toll the church bell as I did. At that time infant mortality, especially in summer, was enormous. Babies of six months, a year, died by the score. I earned a lot of money tolling the funeral bell – twenty-five centimos for each chime. The child's godfather by tradition paid for the funeral and the bells. 'What a fine godfather that child had,' the people used to say, 'the bell has tolled forty chimes.'

Christianity had a powerful effect on me. I don't know whether it was more that than my father's death that started me thinking about social justice. To act not for personal gain, to do injury to no one – I seem to have had those ideals since childhood. My ideas became clearer after reading Pope Leo XIII's *Rerum Novarum*. This encyclical was the church's response to Marxism, not to combat it but to show that the church was on the side of the poor. Very few people in Spain paid heed to it. The big land-owners thought Jesus Christ descended on earth for them alone. I used to ask the priest why, when there was this marvellous encyclical, things remained as they were; either he wouldn't answer or said there was nothing he could do about it. Given all this I began to move to the other side.

When I was twelve I was apprenticed to a shoemaker in Casas Nuevas. After three years there working for my board and lodging alone, I got a job with a shoemaker in Posadas. He paid me 400 pesetas a year. In my spare time I read a lot and took drawing lessons. I wanted to go to art school, but the way was barred without a *bachillerato*.

In Madrid where I did my military service I used to go often to the library of the *Heraldo* newspaper. As an ordinary soldier without education I wanted to find a place where I could learn something instead of spending my time in bars with the other recruits. In the library I met Professor Besteiros. He was a moderate Marxist, one of the leaders of the socialist party and later president of the UGT. I think he was impressed that an Andalusian went to a library to study; most Andalusians are too light-hearted to want to learn and above all when they're in Madrid where there's a different atmosphere, a sexual life....
It was in the library that my ideas really started to form, combining Besteiro's with my own Christianity.

I had returned here when the Republic was declared in 1931. The monarchy overthrown without bloodshed – think of what that meant! It seemed like the start of a new era. There was great popular rejoicing. The *cacique* forbade demonstrations of any sort but that made no difference, his reign had come to an end.

But later I came to believe that the monarchy fell too easily. Power was given on a plate. Instead of being seized. That was one moment when socialist power could have been achieved. It might even have been unnecessary to cause bloodshed; democratic means like those of Allende in Chile today might have sufficed. And even if some blood had been spilled – would it not have saved the lives of one million people later, during and after the civil war? But the socialists were too naive, they thought a coalition with the republicans was necessary....

Between the dozen or so of us here who were really politically aware – there weren't any more – we created a branch of the socialist party and of the union, the UGT. The latter grew very quickly for any worker could join; but the party was restricted to militants whose task was to provide political guidance for the union which saw itself – locally, at any rate – concerned mainly with wage demands. In truth it was never able to do very much. It got wages raised and reduced working hours, but the landowners retaliated and started to tear up the vines. What could the union do? It was working within a capitalist system and the holders of capital, of land, were more powerful. The Republican government tried to correct some of the abuses of capitalism but its leaders were politically naive in my view. They were intellectuals of the famous generation of '98, but for all their intelligence they didn't know the *pueblo*, the people. You have to understand the people in all their grandeur and pettiness to be a successful politician. And to change Spain, above all else, you have to control the state first.

The Republic controlled the state in appearance only. It failed to reform either the army or the church properly. As for agrarian reform, it looked all right on paper. But the politicians let it be sabotaged by the very landowners against whom it was directed. I used to write to some of the Republican leaders to try to show them how the laws they had passed, which appeared so fine on paper, really looked from the perspective of a village like this. Take the law of municipal districts for example. It was meant to prevent landowners taking on labourers from other areas than their own as a measure against local unemployment. It looked fine but in practice it didn't work. The labourers of Tajos and Casas Nuevas were constantly at each other's throats because Casas Nuevas had as many labourers as Tajos but a very much smaller municipal territory. Were they to be deprived of their livelihood simply because they had no municipal district in which to work? No. The law should have been conceived within a national framework, not in terms of individual villages. I had often to intercede with the labourers of both villages, telling them they were all workers and must have the right to work where they could.

Those of us with a bit of education here wanted socialism from the top downwards. The rest wanted it from the bottom up. They were often good enough people, but they had only a vague notion of socialism. It was they who were at the throats of their fellow union members in Casas Nuevas about who had the right to work. And when the time came for them to die – as I know from experience – they didn't know what they were dying for, they had so little real ideology in them.

A revolution isn't made without understanding the nature of the state and of power, and seizing it. That's what I believe. And that's why the revolution here, if you can call it that, failed. It was necessary for the socialists to take power centrally. They had a second chance after the Popular Front's electoral victory in 1936 but they refused it. To seize power requires *cabeza, corazon y cojones* – brains, heart and balls to put it bluntly. It requires great intellectual capacity, political understanding, determination.

What revolution has ever been made without intellectuals as leaders? The French, the Russian, the Chinese, the Cuban.... We had no intellectuals in the socialist party who were good politicians. Caballero was an able man and intelligent – but that's not the same as being an intellectual. Prieto was very clever, an astute politician but no intellectual. Besteiros, De los Rios – good theoreticians but not politicians. There was no Lenin in Spain. It's a difficult thing being an intellectual. A painter, a musician, creates and sees his finished product because his effort is that of a single individual. But a great thinker works with collectivities; his work depends on society and people. If he acts individualistically what can one expect of him?

I know – if the socialists had seized power it would have led to a period of totalitarianism. I say that even though I'm a believer in democracy. I've always wanted a human socialism. To harm another is to harm the ideals of socialism. If someone does me harm my ideals can remain unharmed; but if I do personal injury to another my ideal of socialism is injured at the same time. There is a universality in socialism which is to do good to one's fellow men. It is to create a better, more just society in which everyone can live humanly and not damage the other. So I would not have welcomed any form of totalitarianism, except in as far as I believe it would have led to something better. The transition period is the hardest of all – look at Cuba today. When we talked about it later we were always grateful that the Russian experience existed to help us through such a period. The Russian model with all the lessons one can draw from it.

But the socialists, like the republicans, were ingenuous. They were like the rabbits in that fable who see a dog coming in the distance. One says, 'that's a hunting dog,' and the others say, 'no, no, it's an ordinary dog' – and while they argue about the nature of the dog it comes and gobbles them up.

The leaders weren't prepared. Everything was fragmented. For the revolution to have succeeded the UGT and the anarchist CNT would have had to be unified as a proletarian force. They were of about equal strength then. But of course they weren't united. *Pueblo dividido es pueblo perdido* (a people divided is a people lost).

The CNT was apolitical, it wanted to achieve libertarian communism without participating in politics and without leaders. But without a leader where do you go? Nowhere in my opinion. Only the socialist party, as founded by Pablo Iglesias, united the social *and* the political. The anarchists didn't; not to speak of that exotic and anachronistic excrescence the FAI – for what else can one call it? Apart from some Latin American countries the wind has blown this anarchist phenomenon away.

When the military rose and the revolution started we in the socialist party were overwhelmed. What could we do? The people who took over thought only of violence. We were the strongest party here and yet we were helpless. We hardly ever met, to tell the truth. Those who took power had so little political consciousness that they robbed small-holders and others of the little they had and themselves refused to work. A revolution isn't made like that. It requires discipline and sacrifice – more sacrifice than ever before. The mass of the people here wasn't willing to make that sacrifice. The proof is that we had a food shortage in the end. At the beginning as much food as anyone could eat was handed out; later that food was lacking.

The revolutionary committee itself didn't govern the village. It couldn't govern the ungovernable, the extremists who were willing to do anything. They were the ones who ruled. These sort of people come up in every revolution and in Russia Lenin knew how to deal with them.

I never served on the committee. When the food shortage got serious I was put on the provisions committee in order to try to regulate supplies. From that I know what the extremists were like. They did what they wanted and no one could say a thing to them.

When they gutted the church I protested. Though I'm reserved by nature I was never a coward. They did harm to the revolution, nothing else. The church was a veritable religious museum with its altars, sculptures, paintings and reliquaries; the accumulation of centuries – and they burnt the lot. For what? For nothing. I told anyone who would listen what I thought; but who wanted to listen?

And the killings. . . . They occurred at night when our backs were turned. People from other villages, from Casas Nuevas and Benamalí came for them; there were very few here who joined them in their dirty work.

Discipline and sacrifice. . . . The Republic could have won. Perhaps they existed elsewhere but here, where the front was so close and we were almost trapped in a pocket, no one thought from the first day that we stood a chance. That's one of the reasons the people didn't want to work.

It didn't last long, seven months in all. On 7 February 1937, the nationalist army sealed off this pocket and captured us. It was the end of the first part of the tragi-comedy of my life!

A tragi-comedy whose full dimensions remained to be revealed. Arrested in Tajos when the nationalists took the village, Juan was jailed locally and then kept under house arrest. Later he was called up to serve in the nationalist army to fight against his own side. At the end of the war, on his return to the village, he was denounced by certain locals for having served on the provisions committee during the revolution. Arrested again, he was sentenced by a nationalist court-martial to twenty years and a day in prison. After serving two years of his sentence an amnesty was declared and he was released. He returned to the village and took up his old trade which, solitarily, he continues to ply.

SALVADOR TORRES   *Seventy*

Day-labourer

Born into a family of day-labourers, Salvador started work
at the age of ten; his first job was shifting stones in an olive
grove for which he was paid thirty-five centimos a day. At
fifteen he was going with his father to the plains to reap.
Every year thereafter he spent many months out of the
village looking for work. In 1918 he joined the union; and
when it was reformed in 1931 he became its treasurer for
two years.

It was hard work having a union post. You'd come up in the dark
tired out after a day's digging the vines, eat whatever there was –
more or less bad, depending on the day – and then have to do
union work. We weren't paid, no one was, either in the union or
the party. Everything had to be done at the cost of self-
sacrifice. *Unión General de Trabajadores* – what a beautiful
name! Union and unity of all workers – that's what it was!

It was a strong union, much stronger than it was the first time.
We had close on 1,500 members by the end, by the time the civil
war started. The landowners didn't like it, they tried to boycott
us. Not only tearing up the vines but refusing work to those of us
who were prominent members. I was one of those refused. I went
round all the vineyards asking for work, telling the foremen my
specialities: classifying grapes, packing raisins. Everywhere I got
the same answer: 'We've taken on all the men we need.' I and the
others had to leave in the end. We found work for the summer
and autumn in the maize and bean harvests in the province of
Cadiz where earlier we had had to go to reap wheat.

Reaping – uh! That was hard work. Even harder the way we did
it: the *manijero* in charge of the gang contracted a flat rate for the
job, so it was up to us to get it done as quick as possible and move
on to the next farm. As soon as the sky was beginning to lighten
we were at work. We slept in the fields, under a lean-to if we were
lucky, in the open otherwise. Lying down drenched in sweat,

some with their shirts still on and others with them off to dry overnight.

It can get so hot out on the plains in summer that I remember a gang of men passing out once. Even the birds were dropping out of the sky with their wings spread out. Yes, even the birds. We had to pull the men under some cork trees and fan them with our hats and put damp cloths on their necks to revive them.

There weren't hours in the clock to count how much we worked. We always had a young boy with us who brought us water in the fields and cooked. He had to get up at two or three in the morning to start preparing a soup. We'd eat that at seven, for by then we had been working two or three hours. At noon a *gazpacho* – and then back to work until six. By then the boy had prepared a stew of chick peas and potatoes. We ate and returned to work until nightfall. At the end of the day's work we'd eat more *gazpacho*. For three or four months we'd be going from farm to farm out on the plains.

Even before the union there was always difficulty getting work here. During the Primo dictatorship, when they were building the Guardia Civil barracks, a friend of mine who was working on it said he'd get me a job. The next day he came to my house: 'I can get you work but you'll have to join the *Unión Patriotica*.' That was the dictator's party. The power of the *cacique*! Don Salvador, the colonial official it was. I wasn't having any of that; I was a member of the UGT. So I went to the *vega* of Málaga looking for work.

I was digging the vines there when a funeral passed on the way to Málaga. I said to my brother-in-law, 'Juan, everyone from here to Málaga with a fat belly ought to die.' The foreman had a belly as fat as you've ever seen. He made off for the farmhouse and immediately was on his way back. 'Which of you was it who said that about fat bellies dying?' I looked and saw he had a revolver in his hand. I had to keep quiet because he was capable of shooting me. That evening, when we were eating our *truchas* – hot water and bread, that's what that is – I said I wanted to be paid. 'Yes,' the foreman said, 'and you can call your mates.' He lined us up with two or three guards who were employed there and told them: 'Get this lot off the *cortijo* and don't let them set foot on this land again.' That night we had to sleep in a ditch, there was nowhere else to go. The following day we returned to Tajos.

But a few days later we had to go back to the Máiaga *vega*, though to another *cortijo*, because there was no work here.

There were some real brutes of foremen then. One in particular in the vineyards here. He went round behind us saying: 'There are all those fine lads walking the roads looking for work when what I've got here is a bunch of lazy dogs.' Then he'd pull his revolver out and shout: 'If I see your arse out of line I'll shoot it off.' We were frightened because he was a mad brute who might have shot anyone. It wasn't long before the civil war. He was killed during the uprising later. The people set fire to his brother's *cortijo* near Málaga where he was working. Scorched and wounded, he escaped and made for safety here. Someone saw him in the mountains. The people went after him and set fire to the brush. He was hiding among the rocks and when a man saw him raise his head he blew his brains out with a musket.

Before the war the *señoritos* had their club in Casas Nuevas and the smaller owners used to meet them there. That's where they organized their boycott of the union. We had to organize in return to make the owners take on men by force. Working *al tope*, it was called. The union drew up lists and, depending on the size of the farms, sent so many men down to each of them. 'We don't need any labourers here,' the owners would say. 'The vines can rot for all we care.' 'All right, if you don't need any labourers to work you're going to have to pay us for doing nothing.' If they didn't pay our day's wage they knew they'd have to pay double in the end. Before that, when as was the custom here, men went round to the farms on their own looking for work, the landlords just turned them away. 'Go and ask the Republic for work, that's what you wanted. . . .' But now when they saw four or five labourers coming they began to think twice about not giving them work.

None of us liked this system; we all preferred to get jobs without force. But as the owners didn't want us freely or under pressure, what could we do?

By 1936 we had got the minimum wage up to seven pesetas a day. That was double what it had been before the Republic came in. And working hours were shorter, no longer from sunrise to sunset. We started at nine and ended at six, with a twenty-minute break every couple of hours and an hour for lunch.

When the uprising started I was no longer union treasurer. I became a member of the livestock committee. We had to make sure all the livestock wasn't slaughtered.

There were many extremists who wanted to jail the rich, if not worse, and expropriate everyone who had land. I used to speak out then: '*Hombre*, no, communism hasn't come yet. When it comes, I believe each of us will get a plot of land or we'll work the land collectively. But it will be organized properly by a central body. . . .' And they'd have at me and say, 'You're always against us, you're on the other side. . . .'

Because of the extremists we had to protect the rich. We had seventeen of them under guard for several nights in case a *cochecito* came for them. Anarchists from Benamalí or Casas Nuevas. Once my uncle asked me to stand guard for another rich man; and for many nights I did so behind the bars of the window in his house. My father and he were second cousins, though their economic situations were very different. I did it out of respect for my uncle and his orders; and out of friendship too.

I helped save a couple of landlords who had been arrested in Casas Nuevas. I knew them, had worked in their vineyards. A relative came and said they were in the prison ship in Málaga and going to be shot. I and some others went to the Committee of Public Safety in Málaga and signed guarantees on their behalf. We took them to the house of one of their sisters and told them to stay there lest the people in Casas Nuevas got to know they had been released.

I didn't want to see anyone killed – what good does that do? A man isn't made in a couple of days. Expropriation is the biggest punishment you can inflict on a person. If you come and take my twenty-five pesetas that's a lot worse than giving me a beating. A beating I can get over but the twenty-five pesetas is gone for ever. It should have been done in the first weeks but it never was. So many things were done badly or not done at all; it drives you mad to think about them today. . . .

Though he does not say it immediately, and then only painfully, the experience marked him in other ways. Arrested, he was released through the intervention of the landlords he had helped save and to whom his mother appealed. He was given a safe-conduct and told to leave the village for his own safety. After a seven-month absence he returned to a cousin's farm in the countryside from which he came to see his wife in the village. One night he was caught, arrested and a *denuncia* prepared. At his court-martial the death sentence was demanded. He was accused of the armed robbery of two landlords during the revolution. The landlords named, a Saenz and a Lopez, testified on his behalf; his military defence succeeded in getting a sentence of twelve years and a day. He served nearly four years in different prisons and was released on conditional freedom when a review of his case reduced the sentence to three years. He returned to the village where, until he retired, he made a living as a lime-burner.

JAIME ALARCON   *Seventy*

Marblecutter

We were at work in the quarry as normal that Saturday morning. We had a dog there which never barked, but that day, about eleven, it started to yap. 'Is that the *señorito* coming?' we said. It was. He called us and said, 'I've come to pay you – you don't know what is happening in Spain.'

'What's happening?' we asked, 'we don't know anything.'

'The revolution has broken out. I've come to pay you and take my cousins away.'

At noon we went down to the village to eat and all the radios were at full blast. The military had risen in Morocco.

The people went wild, they were in the streets, everyone was shouting and talking. Soon all the workers started to come back from the fields. Many of them were working in the Málaga *vega* at the time and they poured in. Some wanted arms. Others didn't know what to do. There weren't any arms anyway, other than a few shotguns the people had.

Have you ever known a revolution in your country? No? Well, it was very hard here. I was in agreement with it, but things weren't

done as they should have been. Everything was salt and water –
here and everywhere else. One flag, another flag, flags all over:
UGT, CNT-FAI, Communists – all those parties! *Hombre*, what
could come of all that? There wasn't *unión* enough. That's what
was needed. The government itself didn't know what was going
on.

I was in the UGT myself. I'd been in it in 1918 and I joined
again when it was restarted. Not straight away. A friend of mine
had started a branch of the radical socialists. One day I went for
a shave. As I sat in the chair, Juan the barber said: 'What are you
doing here?' 'What am I doing? I've come for a shave as usual.'
'You're not being attended to here.' 'But I've been shaved all my
life in your shop.' 'Not any more, not until you join the union.'
I went and put my name down then. I realized that if my friends
were going to boycott me like that I wouldn't be able to find work.
And that was right, what was needed was more *unión*, not less.
The UGT – that's where all the workers were. The CNT didn't
have many members, it never caught on here.

I wasn't an extremist. No, señor. I remember during the strike
we had in 1918 I was sent with a message from one of the union
committee down to Casas Nuevas. When he gave me the letter he
tucked it inside my hatband. I didn't know what it said, I can't
read or write. A little way out of the village the *guardias* stopped
and searched me. Then another pair stopped me again. What a
good job none of them thought of looking at my hat! When I got
to Casas Nuevas and they read the letter out I wanted to die. It
was all about how the priest should be killed and the *cacique*
caught and his head chopped off. If the Guardia Civil had found
it on me, I would have been killed. I wasn't in agreement with
things like that, either in 1918 or in 1936.

I didn't have any position in the union or the revolutionary
committee. I didn't have the education for that. Not that those on
the committee understood very much. There were some on it who
were there for their personal advantage. That's not the way a
revolution ought to be, to my mind. One man in particular, a real
reactionary whom the committee trusted, I don't know why. I
came home one day from bringing in the grape crop – three weeks
I'd been away – and I heard it said that my wife had come away
with a basket of rations although I hadn't been working. I went
home. 'Have you touched the food they gave you?' I said to my

wife. 'No.' I picked up the basket, the kilo of bread, the oil, a bit of rice and chickpeas – and took it back.

'Ea, here's all the food you gave my wife, take it back. From now on those who don't work aren't going to get food, because it's going to be my pleasure to stay here to watch it.'

The man denied he had made the remark, denied everything. 'Are you going to deny it now, you piece of lard. Well, I'll tell you. . . .'

I wasn't wrong. As soon as the village was taken he turned his coat and became an even bigger grafter than before. A rich man, rich enough to leave the village and set up in Málaga.

There were a few like him. They thought the revolution meant eating and drinking without working. But not many. The majority knew that the revolution meant working harder than before so as to produce more. And that's what they did.

The landowners should have been expropriated. Of course they should. It's sad and painful that a person should own half the world when I've got nowhere to place a foot. Why should it be so? Aren't we all born the same? With the difference that the one's father has left him a bit of land and my poor father left me nothing because he had nothing to leave.

But nothing was expropriated. We worked the land the owners had abandoned to bring in the crop. The union organized that. All the produce came to the village to be distributed among the people, and we got our wages in food.

I worked the land like everyone else. We stopped quarrying marble, there was nowhere to sell it. One day we got a letter from the owner, he sent it to the foreman and we took it up to the quarry to read. It said that if we wanted our wages we should go to a certain street in Málaga where he was. 'Nothing will happen if you come.'

I was delegated to go. When I got down from the lorry I was suspicious. Two militiamen from the village had come on the lorry. 'I'm going to my sister's house,' I said. As I went down the street I saw they were following me. It didn't smell good. I turned back. 'Aren't you going to your sister's?' they said. 'Ech, just for a meal – what's the good? I'll eat round here or if not I'll go without.' I knew by then that if I went to the owner's house as like as not I'd get shot. There were one or two people in the village who wanted to know where he was hiding because he was a reactionary and if they could get him they'd take over the quarry for themselves. Someone had informed on me, that's why the militiamen had come.

I'd worked on the land often enough. The quarry only provided work four or five months of the year. As soon as the sales stopped we were out of a job.

Once, before the war, we asked for a rise. The half dozen of us agreed. I said I'd speak to the owner. I overheard the other men saying they didn't trust me to do it. I went over to the boss that afternoon and told him straight out what we wanted. I've always believed in speaking my mind. He said he'd have to talk to the foreman. The next day we went to see the foreman. 'Who wants a rise? You? Stand over here then. Who else?' One other man came to stand beside me. The rest wouldn't move. That Saturday the two of us were sacked. Just like that. I had to go to the *vega* of Málaga to look for work. The shopkeeper refused my wife any more credit 'because of what happened today in the quarry'.

There wasn't the *unión* there ought to have been. Hadn't we all agreed to ask for the rise? But when it came to it. . . .

On the land none of us would go to work for less than the minimum. Never, however hungry we were. The landlords would always try what they could, and there were always some who bent their necks and worked for less. We called them *arrastrados*, grovellers. I was digging the vines one time and the land was thick mud from the rain. We had to work barefoot or lose our *alpargatas* in the mud. The next day the foreman shifted us to lighter, sandier soil. Then he said we'd be earning three pesetas instead of the 3·50 of the previous day. I and one other said we wouldn't work at that rate and walked out. But the others stayed.

I had my troubles during the revolution. One day I was summoned by the committee president. 'Go and bring in so-and-so,' he said. I didn't want to go but the militia chief warned me there'd be trouble for me if I didn't. At the end of the village there was a militiaman on duty. 'Take my shotgun in case he doesn't want to come.' 'I don't want any gun.' 'Here, take it just in case,' and he pulled out some cartridges. I had to take the gun. When I got to the small-holder's farm I shouted out his name. He heard me and called out: 'What do you say today? *Buenos dias* or *salud*?'*

* *Salud* was the form of salutation used by the revolutionaries; *buenos dias* is the customary good morning.

'Whatever you want. . . .' 'Good, *buenos dias* then.' I told him he was wanted by the committee and he came with me. I don't know what they wanted him for, but certainly nothing happened to him. Of that I'm sure because he lived to denounce me six months after the village fell. . . .

The military prosecutor asked for a sentence of life imprisonment. 'A known leftist since 1918, a professional gunman who made three arrests and assassinated two men.' Relatives of the two landlords he was alleged to have killed testified on his behalf. He was sentenced to twelve years and a day. He served two and a half years in prison and a further two years in a labour camp. After being amnestied he went to live in Posadas where his wife had relatives and a plot of land.

JOSE RUIZ   *Sixty-three*

Day-labourer

I had been president of the union for three or four months when the uprising started. The military rose in Málaga but were quickly defeated by the workers. We had to organize as quickly as we could; when the revolutionary committee was created I was elected to it by my union. Once the committee was in being I was named its president.

It was called the revolutionary committee though in truth the revolution was being made by the other side, not by the working class; the workers hadn't prepared sufficiently for it.

On the committee there were two UGT members, one from the socialist party, and one each from the two republican parties. The committee took over the running of village affairs. Every Saturday there was an assembly of the UGT to discuss and approve the decisions the committee had made. Later, after I left, I believe the committee was elected by popular assembly.

We met two or three times a week. The rest of the time we had to go on working at our usual jobs. None of us on the committee or in the militia got paid. Each of us had a particular function: supplies, militia, requisitions. . . . We had disarmed the Guardia Civil and had them sent to Málaga; in their place we had to organize our own militia. They patrolled the countryside in pairs as the Guardia had done before, but they were workers, men from the UGT mainly.

The committee took over the produce of the land, but it didn't expropriate the land itself, nor the owners' rents, at least while I was here. No orders came from the government to expropriate land. The government, it's true, was weak at that moment. I believed the land should have been expropriated and distributed individually, a man has more interest in the land and works harder when he has his own plot. We had had experience of that because two years before a number of landlords handed over their vineyards to the union to run. They said the rise in wages had cut down their profits – huh! the profits with which before that they had bought cars and land on the backs of the workers. The union parcelled the vineyards into about 500 plots of a *fanega* each and they were drawn for by lot. Every worker in a family was entitled to one and the produce from it. They were worked individually – and a lot better too, as I know from experience because I had one.

During the uprising the committee took them over because there was so much more land that the owners had abandoned and which had to be worked.

If the government had organized a proper land reform at the start of the revolution it would have brought whole-hearted support for the revolution from the *colonos* and everyone working the land. As it was, many of these people – the sharecroppers especially – continued to cling to their landlords. They were a middle class really, these tenants, and many of them were hostile to the revolution.

A lot of sharecroppers said the committee was bad in taking the landowner's half share. Why, when the owner's share was distributed to the people? Obviously the committee couldn't leave the sharecroppers with the whole of their crop. If we had they alone would have benefited from the revolution. We expropriated the owner's share so that the revolution would benefit the working class as a whole.

A revolution isn't made by shooting off revolvers, by violence and nothing else. And yet a lot of people thought that was what

it was. It was the worst problem I faced. There was too much freedom, everyone had his own idea of what should be done, of what
could be done. If people had had discipline, if they had listened. . . .

Some of these extremists accused me of favouring the rich. More
than once I was threatened. Yet I'd known as much suffering as
any of them. I was eleven when I had to support my mother and
two younger brothers on seventy-five centimos a day weeding
wheat after my father died. At fourteen I was working alongside
the men digging the vines. I've known what it is to have to beg a
bit of bread from a *cortijo* after walking three or four days looking
for work. I've waited at little country stores for friends who had
got a day's job to ask them for a bite of bread when they came
from the fields. My youth was one of hunger and suffering, for
that was all the working class here knew at that time. Men out of
work stuck to the sides of the houses like flies and as white as the
walls with hunger. I didn't have to be told.

But for all that I couldn't let the extremists do things with which I
didn't agree, especially since they wanted to resolve everything by
brute force. I had to be in the middle trying to reconcile both sides.

I was eating supper one night, a fried egg, I remember it well,
when some people came running and told me that one of the landlords – a woman – was being maltreated in her home by some
labourers from Casas Nuevas who had come for day-wages they
claimed from her. I ran to the house. The men were armed and the
woman was in a terrible state. She hadn't the money to pay. I
managed to get the men out and she said that one of her tenants
might be able to pay his rent in advance so that she could pay the
men. I went to see the tenant, collected the money and gave it
to them.

Another day I was warned that a large group of labourers was
coming up from Casas Nuevas to claim sixty or more days' wages
from don Cristóbal Saenz. They said they were going to set fire
to his house unless he paid on the spot. I went in to see him. 'Don
Cristóbal, these men are claiming wages from you, I don't know
if their claim is just. . . .' 'Yes, the work was done but I'm not
paying them.' 'They're outside now. If their claim is just I suggest
you pay them or I can't take responsibility for what may happen.'
'Ah,' he said, 'you're forcing me to pay.' 'No, don Cristóbal, I'm
not forcing you, I'm saying that the blame won't rest on my
shoulders if you don't.' 'If you're forcing me to pay, I'll pay.'

'No, I'm not forcing you. . . .' In the end he paid, but not on the spot. I had to take the money down to Casas Nuevas myself. I don't know what would have happened if he hadn't paid.

The rich went in fear. Some of them wouldn't leave their houses to collect the rations they, like everyone else, were entitled to. I, and others too, used to leave food for them at their doors. One of them came one evening to my house. 'Don José,' he said to me, 'they've ordered me to report to you.'

'I'm not don, call me *tu* as you've always done,' I answered. As president of the committee I neither got nor wanted any signs of respect. I was a *compañero* like everyone else. 'But don José . . .' 'Speak to me as you've always done. I say *Usted* to you out of respect and you say *tu* to me.' At last he used the usual form. Then I told him I hadn't sent for him and told him to return home. As he went out I saw the militiamen bringing in another man from the country. 'Who gave the orders to bring him in?' 'We're just detaining him,' the militiamen said. 'Let him go home, no one has ordered his arrest.'

The militia took things into their own hands. They'd go into a shop or a house and requisition goods, saying the order came from me. And I wouldn't know anything about it until it had been done. I had often to oppose them. We on the committee couldn't throw them out – we might have had to shoot them. In some places it was necessary to shoot militiamen and the like who assassinated people or looted. But they were too strong here, they had all the arms. When the people came from outside look-ing for landlords to shoot, the militiamen handed them over. That's what happened with the *señoritos* who died here.

Things got to the state where the workers began to threaten me. The committee organized several donations for hospitals for the wounded in Málaga. For one of them we decided to make a donation of chickens. The rich who had twenty chickens should give five and a worker with say ten should give one. As I came out of the town hall that day a labourer pulled a pistol on me. He said the workers shouldn't have to give any chickens. I looked him in the eyes. 'Put that pistol away.' I knew he hadn't the courage to shoot.

It happened again. I came back from Málaga one evening and found all the notables and a number of small-holders in jail – a dozen or more. I got my pistol, stuck it in my waistband and ordered the jail opened. As the men went through the square, which was full of people, a worker came up pointing a shotgun at me. Loudly, to make sure he heard, I told him to move away fast before I shot him.

A friend of mine in the militia told me the militiamen had met and decided to call me out one night. I told my friend not to come with them if they did. 'As soon as I hear them I'll come out shooting.' The way some of them were going they'd have ended up shooting everyone, including me.

I had wanted no more for some time than to be able to leave. When the Republic began calling up men I joined the army. I was president of the committee less than two months.

Denounced on his return to the village at the end of the war, a sentence of life imprisonment was demanded at his court-martial. 'When the prosecutor rose the *guardia* who was next to me said, "Don't worry, you'll be out of here in three or four days". And that's what happened. They released me, I was free. I'd spent about a year in prison waiting for the court-martial, that's all. It's a sign for sure that I never did anything bad.'

His two successors as presidents of the committee were less fortunate: they were shot.

Looking back on the past, José says: 'I was twenty-seven then. When one's that age one has all sorts of hopes for the future, one's ready to launch into it. Not that I was ever political; I was in the union to defend the workers' interests, that's all. Those who were political, those with more culture than me, were in the socialist party. I never read books or newspapers, I didn't bother about that much then. All I've learned to read I've had to teach myself.

'Today I know more than I did then. Like everyone else I believed that capitalism should be overthrown, that we should have a proper agrarian reform. The one the Republic brought in was sabotaged by the capitalists, you see. But now all these things don't matter to me any more. Life here has changed so much – nearly 100 percent – because today everyone can earn a good wage.'

THE SURVIVORS

The Hungry Forties

'Amidst immense rejoicing, celebrations in honour of the triumph of the nationalist armies were held in Tajos on Sunday 9 April. The virtuous Sr. Benavente Olgado, parish priest, magisterially extolled the glories of the Virgin and her constant predilection for the Spanish Nation. . . . In the afternoon a procession was organized. At its conclusion our fervent mayor, Sr. Saenz, addressed the crowd, concluding his eloquent oration with the following words: "Let us rise to the heights, the highest of heights, to the region of the stars where *they* reside, our heroes and martyrs, whose precious blood like holy seed has made possible the salvation of Spain. Let them, so that they should feel proud of their sacrifice, let them hear us shout with all the fervour of our hearts, with all the force of our souls, with all the strength of our lungs until we are hoarse: Spain for ever! Long live Generalissimo Franco! Long live our allies! Long live the glorious Spanish army! Long live the bravest of the brave, General Queipo de Llano! Long live honest labour! Spain for ever!"

'At nightfall, in affirmation of the traditional catholic faith of Tajos, our patron saint was brought out in procession. The parish priest from the pulpit brought this unforgettable day to a close by expressing his pride at ministering to the souls of a people who had so amply demonstrated their unblemished catholicism.'

Sur, the Málaga falangist newspaper, April 1939

71

For the next ten years and more Tajos suffered the fortunes of peace. Its fate was that of the nation. Famine, unemployment and pauperization for the mass of the people; for the few, fortunes made out of low wages, speculation and blackmarketeering.

Figures speak better than words. Not until 1953 did *per capita* income again reach the level of 1936; not until 1959 did *per capita* agricultural production attain that of the 1931–35 average. In 1942 total agricultural production was under half, by 1945 it was not yet three-quarters of the pre-war average.

To the ravages of the civil war were added natural disaster – drought – and the upheavals of the Second World War. But the main thrust of the burden came from the new regime.

Wages were controlled by state decree; strikes were prohibited and repressed by force if they took place. The old trade unions were smashed, the old political parties proscribed. Hundreds of thousands of militants, workers and party members languished in jail or in labour camps; 200,000 were executed or died, the American historian Gabriel Jackson has estimated – as many again as had been killed in the nationalist repression during the war.

The new state was built on the armed forces, the Falange, the corporate state-run trade union, the church.

While wages were fixed, prices rose steadily. Between 1940 and 1955 agricultural and industrial wages increased by 100 percent; in the same period the cost of living rose by 240 percent. This meant a loss in purchasing power for the working classes of 50 percent in fifteen years.

Looking more specifically at agriculture, prices quintupled in the twenty years 1939–59; wages by contrast rose just over two and a half times, the bulk of the increase coming after 1955.

'Never has such poverty been known before,' a Málaga falangista admitted to an English writer as late as 1949.

The repression, the extreme exploitation, was not an

arbitrary event; it was a matter of policy. The goal pursued was that of cowing the working class into submission and permitting the new bourgeoisie a high rate of capital accumulation at its expense: an accumulation which, in the early 1960s, funded the beginnings of Spain's industrial take-off.

Little wonder that under these post-war conditions the survivors in Tajos were those who had kept, and continued to keep their heads down. 'De politica nada' is the common refrain. To know nothing about politics is a safety precaution; it exorcizes past implications, obviates present ones, even represses temptation of the forbidden. 'Politics' is a dirty word. But this non-politics is also a form of politics: that of the regime which, to maintain the *status quo*, attempts to repress all political activity other than its own.

The gravity of the situation in Tajos, where the 1940 census showed nearly 200 people 'missing' – an indication of the ravages of the war and repression – was in part palliated by public works. For two or three years most of the village unemployed were given work planting pines in the sierra as part of a provincial afforestation campaign.

In return, the unemployed lost the right to one of their traditional forms of livelihood: esparto-picking. During the post-war shortage and under the government's policy of autarchy, it was decided that esparto, which covers 10,000 hectares of Málaga province, could replace other raw materials. The concessions to pick were sold to private businessmen who put guards in the sierra.

A quarter of a century later, when the Málaga businessman who had controlled the Tajos esparto stood in the limited elections to the Cortes* of 1971, Tajeños remembered. Some went as far as to tear up his propaganda in public; on the day of the poll he received only 200 of the 3,000 votes cast.

* Since 1967 two deputies from each province have been elected to the Cortes by heads of families and married women. These 'family representatives' are the only directly elected deputies to the Cortes.

In the late 1940s the discovery of mica by a local man brought a brief moment of prosperity; thereafter the village stagnated again until the mid-1950s. 1955 is the date commonly given as the year when 'things started to get a little better'.

ANTONIO ALARCON   *Fifty*

Sometime sacristan, ambulant country teacher and housepainter

Two years before the outbreak of the civil war, when Antonio was thirteen, the local priest got him a scholarship to a Franciscan school in Antequera. His father, a mason, knew how to read and write, and ensured that his children, in particular Antonio who had been born with a deformed foot, went to school. Antonio had done well at his studies and was an acolyte in the church.

A week before the outbreak of the war his parents sent for him. 'Things were beginning to look bad. I was sorry to come back but it was just as well. During the revolution the reds killed the director of the school and about a dozen of the monks.'

I don't know anything about politics. I don't want to know because I don't like it. I'm poor and I've got to work to live and I can get on with the blues, the yellows or the reds; they're all one to me.

During the revolution I and a number of boys my age joined the socialist youth. I don't deny it! We hadn't an idea what it was all about, and we joined because we could go to the cinema free. And there they taught us to sing the International and all sorts of revolutionary songs. Long live the Red Army, long live the Soviet Union! There was a man in charge of the trench-diggers here who had been sent from Málaga for the defence of the village and he made me one of the youth leaders. You'd hardly believe it – he turned out to be a leading falangista when the nationalists entered!

Nothing much happened here. It wasn't like Casas Nuevas. They called that 'little Russia' in those days. I remember militia-women coming up from there in their overalls with revolvers stuck in their belts. But Tajos is different, we're almost a family here and there was more respect – more *unión*, more simplicity – than in Casas Nuevas.

I went down there one day with my father and as we were wait-ing we heard shots. We thought it was nationalist planes come to bomb, but then we saw fifty or sixty men coming into the square. They were dragging a corpse. 'Come on, boy,' my father said, 'we're going home.' We left without waiting to collect his pay.

I was in the square the day the people sacked don Salvador's house. They threw all the furniture out the window and set light to it. Then they went up to the church and set fire to the saints and a beautiful organ and the altar piece. But a lot didn't burn and the people rescued what they could. There was a fine statue of a Nazarene penitent by Mena, a beautiful thing. Don Pedro Jimena saved it and put it in his house. A few days later some of the men heard where it was and went for it. As they came down the street José Ruiz, the committee president, tried to stop them. '*Hombre, hombre*, what are you going to do with that? It's time to leave off burning things.' But the others said, 'Come on, this one has got to burn too,' and there was nothing Ruiz could do about it.

From the street at the top of the village where I lived we could see the churches burning in Casas Nuevas. It scared me, I was reminded of the burnings when the Republic came in in 1931.

Although I've got no interest in politics, I'll say straight out that there's only one person for me: General Franco. He's called Franco and he's lived up to his name of being frank with the nation. Our regime is going ahead well, as I see it, and it's due to him. Though I was young, I can remember what things were like under the monarchy. Four or five landowners here, another few in Casas Nuevas, a handful in Posadas and Benamalí. Everyone else lived under their yoke. That should never have been allowed, he who has should succour the poor, that's what I say. That's why there was a revolution. For that and because of the priests. Yes, too many priests – though not all – were mixed up in politics on the side of the rich.

There are plenty of anecdotes in *Don Quixote* about that. Do you know them? The one where don Quixote says to Sancho Panza, 'Sancho, we've run up against the church. . . .' Well, that's how it used to be here.

A lot of the priests were arrogant. Not all, I've known some good ones. There was one, a real saint, who lived on next to nothing and gave everything he had to the poor and the sick. Don Tomas, he was called, and he was here when I was a boy. For some reason, I don't know why, Sr. Antonio Tejada and Sr. Salvador Jimenez didn't get on with him. Perhaps it was because he wanted things done as religion commands and not for the few to boss the others around. One day he told the congregation he was going to Málaga for a few days. After a couple of weeks he sent a message saying he was returning. The whole village turned out to welcome him back. The car arrived – the only one in the village then – and he wasn't in it. The people were crying, on my honour. Well, he never returned. Rumour had it that don Antonio and don Salvador had got rid of him. Later, as I know because I've seen his grave, he was shot by the reds in Antequera.

Then there was don Francisco. It was under him that I became an acolyte. What a fine man! Uncle of our present mayor. He would go to the trade union centre and give talks there. Not about religion but to tell the workers what the proletariat really was. 'I don't deny my ecclesiastical vestments, you can see me in them,' he would say. 'Don't you deny either the Republic or the left and what it is doing for you. Go on working as you should. . . .' He was an authentic man, he had no fear and the workers respected him. I've seen the union president and the secretary in the front pew listening to his sermons. He was a fine orator, talking always of real things, and the women when they heard him would be in tears . . . .

I'll tell you a story about him. During Holy Week, when he preached a lot, he used to send me to a tavern to buy a few bottles of Málaga wine. As he went up to the pulpit I followed him with a bottle in my pocket. I stood on the steps below and each time he knelt down I poured him out a drop or two in a jar. 'Come on, Antonio, have a drop too!' During a long sermon we'd get through a bottle; all the pious old women in the congregation hadn't the faintest idea! A fine man, really fine. He had no money, everything he got he shared out with the poor.

In about 1934 or 1935 he decided to leave the priesthood and became a schoolmaster in Málaga. Though I don't really know, I suppose that being an intelligent man, he saw around him these rich, egotistical *señoritos* who gave nothing to the workers nor helped them at all. He inclined to the left, though he didn't renounce his religion. Not at all. He observed all the rites and went to mass every morning before the day's teaching – it was just that he no longer wanted to be a priest. He got married, I believe, and had a child.

When the uprising started he came to take the village priest away from here to spare him any hardship. Perhaps, who knows, he saved his life.

When Málaga fell to the nationalists don Francisco was arrested; then he was shot. When the people heard he had been executed there were plenty like me who cried.

At the end of the war, in 1940 to be exact, there was a year of terrible hunger everywhere. Spain was destroyed. There were no crops, no bread, no oil, nothing. The people ate anything they could find: thistles and weeds of all different sorts. And that's how it went on, though not quite so bad, for the next seven or eight years.

During those 'hunger years' I was the sacristan here. The village was dead. No one was earning money and nor was I. A first-class funeral cost 250 pesetas and I'd get a percentage because I was also the cantor; and I still couldn't make enough. There weren't that many first-class funerals, you see. Once, when the priest was away, I conducted a few funeral services in his place. One had to earn what one could.

I had some funny times with this priest, don Fernando. One day I'd been having a few *coñacs* in the tavern to warm me up because it was winter and cold. I saw Barnabé there; he told me he had to go to the priest's because he was getting married shortly. 'Tell me how to answer his questions,' he said, 'because I don't know. . . .' 'You just keep quiet,' I said. 'I'll come with you and when the priest asks the questions you watch my hand under the table. When I put up one finger you answer "one", and when I put up three you answer "three".' We had a few more drinks and went to the priest's.

He was sitting by his brazier with his sister beside him. He entered Barnabé's name in the register and then he said: 'Well, let's see. Do you know how to pray?' 'Look, don Fernando,' I said, 'Barnabé is from the country and he doesn't know how to pray.'

'All right,' said don Fernando. 'Let's see. How many Gods are there?' Under the table I put up one finger. 'One,' says Barnabé. 'Good,' says don Fernando. 'And how many in the Trinity?' 'Three,' says Barnabé. The priest looked at me through his glasses. 'Very good, very good. And where do the blessed go after death?' I looked at Barnabé and mouthed the word. 'Heaven,' he says. 'And the wicked, where do they go?' asks the priest.

I don't know what got into me then. I whispered to Barnabé and he repeated my words: 'To Casas Nuevas.' The priest threw down his pen, his sister leapt up and I ran out of the house. When I saw don Fernando later he burst out laughing. 'Antonio, *chiquillo*, what got into you?' 'I don't know, don Fernando, it just came out and what could I do?'

Everyone was so poor in those years we hardly ever left the village. Once in a long while we'd get to Málaga if there was a good bullfight or a circus. And a visit to a whorehouse beforehand! There was a woman in the village who had turned whore and we used to go with her, even the young kids. Sometimes we didn't even pay her. She'd start to cry, 'Ay! please a peseta. . . .' Other times if we had any money we'd throw her a peseta or two. There were married women who went in for a bit of whoring because they liked it or their husbands were away. I had one who had a small child and I used to give her four or five pesetas a time. Otherwise it was Málaga, that was the only place.

The priests I've known weren't above it, either, come to that. There's been more than one who came here with a 'sister' or a 'niece' to look after his house. Well, they're men, it's normal, isn't it?

Don Fernando wasn't like that, though. He was a good priest and he did a lot to help the poor. He used to get them out of jail when they were arrested in the hunger years for picking esparto. Everyone has his own way of making a living, hasn't he? So I'll tell you what happened. All the esparto that was confiscated from the poor men and women bringing it from the sierra ended up in the then mayor's house and he used it for his own business. A scandal it was. Don Fernando would go to the Guardia barracks to get the people released, until at last a new commander of the post put an end to the whole business by refusing to arrest anyone.

I couldn't go on scraping by on a sacristan's earnings so I had to look for something else. '*Chiquillo*, the times are so bad. What are we going to do?' a friend of mine said. He'd been out of the village and had had to come back. After a few drinks he came up with this idea. We'd set ourselves up as sewing-machine mechanics. He knew a little – very little – about being a mechanic. 'Look, Juan,' I said, 'the people don't know you in the country-side. You put on a fine accent as though you're a Singer repre-sentative from Barcelona and I'll say I'm taking you around.'

We bought a large bottle of paraffin and put it into small bottles so it looked like some special oil; and off we set.

What a time! Juan broke more machines than he repaired. A couple of weeks after he'd gone over them with paraffin they'd seize up. All the time I had my eye out for only one thing – a farmstead where smoke was coming out the chimney. 'That's where we'll eat today,' I'd say to Juan. We were hungrier than church mice. I'd introduce my companion and he'd put on his accent and start to take the machine apart. They'd be laying the table for dinner and ask us to eat. 'No, no,' Juan would say, 'we have a long way to go yet, señora, to see if we can earn our day's keep.' All that in his fine accent; half the time I had to keep myself from bursting out laughing. Then the woman of the house would insist and after a bit more persuading we'd give in and accept the meal.

If they hadn't got money we'd take payment in eggs, chickens, whatever they had. Seventy-five pesetas for an hour's overhaul of their machines, that's what we charged. How hard-faced and shameless one had to be in those years! Once at a farmstead we had dinner, supper and breakfast, as well as bed and tobacco, because Juan didn't realize he'd got the needle working in reverse. A nearly new machine it was, too. He couldn't fix it. At last, when no one was about, he said: 'I'm going to tell them it needs a new piece which I'll bring from Barcelona where I'm going tomorrow.' And that's what he did, and we took off and never went near that place again.

We could do three or four operations a day. We were at it several months, living all the time on the farmsteads. After that we ran out of new farms to go to. So I gave up sewing-machines and became an ambulant teacher. In the countryside at least there was always something to eat.

I went from farmstead to farmstead giving lessons. Because I knew the lie of the land I could rely on getting a meal in a different house every day. I never went hungry and I was better off out there than here in the village.

After a while I had a regular round of a dozen or so farmsteads, and I'd do an hour a day at each with the children. And not only children – young men of seventeen, eighteen, twenty. There was only one school in the country then and that was too far away for most of them to go to. I earned about twelve pesetas per pupil a month and my food. It wasn't much money but I kept alive.

I did that for a year and a half and then I bought the brushes and things I needed and set out to become a housepainter, white-washing mainly. Things were beginning slowly to get a bit better by then. And that, except for a short time teaching in a school on a *cortijo*, is what I've done ever since.

PACO MORENO   *Thirty-eight*

Building labourer

I was four when they took my father to jail. My brother was just over a year old. It was in 1937. My father was denounced for a stupidity – what else could one call it? I've only heard about it from men of his generation because my mother would never talk about it. They say that he told someone that a Russian boat had arrived off the coast somewhere here. Two women whom he trusted had told him about it. When the Guardia Civil went to question the women they denied it. So my father went to jail.

I believe those women did it deliberately to get him into trouble. My father was a day-labourer and a man of the left but he never did anything bad. He was a man of *cojones*, firm in his ideals. Right or wrong, he wouldn't betray them, that's what his friends have told me. I hardly knew him, you see.

He was given three death sentences at first. Two of them were lifted almost immediately. Then the last one was commuted to thirty years and a day in jail. In 1943, after six years in prisons all over the country, he was amnestied. He came out of jail in the north and he didn't have the money to get back here. He had been out only three or four days trying to find a job to get the money together when he fell sick and died. The prison people sent us a telegram giving us the news.

While he was in prison we were thrown out of our house. My mother rented it from a man who lived upstairs. One day he came down and they started to talk, then to row. I was there, I remember it perfectly. Suddenly the man pulled a knife on my mother and *pssst* he slashed her face. She ran screaming out of the house and my brother and I after her. She ran straight to the doctor and he had to put in twenty-six stitches, that's how big the wound was.

The man did it because my father was in jail and he wanted to get us out of the house. My mother denounced him for attacking her but nothing happened, his contacts were too good. There was an old *guardia* here, a very fine man, who said to my mother: 'My house is yours for the night, bring your children and sleep there.' He was the only person in the village who was capable of generosity and justice.

For the next month or two we stayed with my mother's cousin, the three of us sleeping in one bed in the attic. My mother was out all day whitewashing, scrubbing floors, cleaning houses. I can remember her hands when she came back at night – they were bleeding from having to work so hard and so long. No one here suffered as much as she. And she never had a better life, for as soon as she had raised us and we were a bit better off – not much, but a bit – she died.

I started work at seven. At eleven I was working with the men planting pines in the sierra while the afforestation was going on. Everyone who could get a job wanted work. At night when we all came back to the village it sounded like a donkey train in the streets. To make our *alpargatas* last longer we attached horseshoes to the soles. I earned 8·40 pesetas a day digging holes to plant the cones. Later they raised my wage and towards the end I was earning thirteen pesetas if I remember right. The money helped my mother a bit; I gave it all to her, of course.

Before that we were lucky if we ate twice a day. I remember once we went nine days without tasting bread, any sort of bread, black or white. No one had white, but we didn't even have black. Some days we had nothing to eat at all. My brother and I would be crying with hunger and there was nothing anyone could do about it. Sometimes friends would give us something but they couldn't be handing out food every day, they needed it themselves.

Our skin burst open with ulcers. From not having enough to eat, from not washing. There wasn't any soap. We were covered in fleas. Uf! It was terrible, we were so under-nourished.

I don't think anyone in Tajos went through a worse youth than my brother and I. The others at least had a father who could earn something. We didn't even have clothes of our own. For many years all I wore were hand-me-downs of the present mayor. For my first communion I went to church in a patched pair of his trousers, a pair of *alpargatas* and a white shirt. Whatever his mother was ready to throw away she gave to my mother. His parents always had plenty of money and he and I became friends when we went to school together. Not that he wanted to go to school much! He often came to my house to play because his grandmother lived almost next door and we were good friends. And still are. He's a good man, a very fine mayor. Ask him a favour and he's always willing to help.

My mother was very proud of my father, very proud. But, as I've said, she wouldn't talk to me about him. Nor would my aunt, though I often asked her. All I know is from the older men. And everything I've heard makes me respect him. He was a man of courage and guts.

CRISTOBAL GONZALEZ — *Sixty-two*

Sharecropper

'On top of the hunger there was the drought. For three years running I wasn't able to plant anything because there was no water to irrigate. I don't know how I would have got by if my brother hadn't taken me with him to work in the lead mines where he had a job. Uf! – those were bad years. I haven't known worse.'

On his return from the nationalist army at the end of the war, Cristóbal took over *El Verdegal*, the farmstead his father had been sharecropping since 1907 when old Gil Lopez bought it from the marquis. Cristóbal was born on the farmstead; in all, first with his father, then alone, he spent over fifty years sharecropping *El Verdegal* for the Lopezs. When don Gil died, his eldest daughter Rosalia inherited the farm; since her death in the mid-1960s, Gil has been administering it on her heirs' behalf.

His face deeply lined, Cristóbal speaks in the deliberate manner of one whose life has revolved endlessly through the same seasonal tasks; even bitterness comes slow-moving to the surface.

El Verdegal was one of don Gil's best farms, not as good as some he had along the river, but not bad at all. About three and a half hectares of land there are.

If it had been ours we could have lived off it. There were seven of us in the family and as it was even my father had to go out to work. My mother had to do a lot of the labour on the farm. I remember her carrying as many as seven sheaves of wheat on her back from the bottom terraces up to the threshing floor. When she wasn't working on the land she'd be cleaning out the cowstall, cutting cane and brush for the bedding. She had to work very hard – too hard.

Half of everything we grew or raised went to the *señorito*. He put in half the seed – only for the wheat, barley and vetch for fodder – and half the fertilizer. Everything else, including the work, we had to provide. When we planted a terrace of tomatoes, pimientos, onions or whatever from seeds we had saved, half went to him. If the seeds failed and a friend gave us plants he had over – or if I had to buy the plants – the *señorito* took half and paid nothing.

The owner's half we had to take up to his house. There it was weighed and then we had to carry the sacks up to the attic. With only one mule we lost the best part of a day's work making the several trips. And it wasn't as though there was time to spare.

The señorita Rosalia inherited the farm when she was twenty-three or twenty-four, a few years before the war. She said she was going to put her *colonos* through the eye of a needle. And that's what she tried in the end to do with me. She was very hard, much harder than her father.

The times were getting bad; my father was too old to be able to work the land and I stayed with him. He gave me a share of his part of the crop in place of a wage. Sometimes I still had to go out to work; one day I was digging some almonds on another of the señorita's farms when two of the workers' delegates arrived. It was just before the uprising. 'What are you doing here?' they said to me and the nephew I had working with me. 'Are you union members?' 'No,' I said, 'I haven't signed up yet.' I was frightened. 'All right, sign up tonight or you won't get any more work.' That night I went to the village and joined the UGT; I was one of the very last. I wouldn't join the communists or the anarchists, they were too dangerous. The socialists were more moderate.

The delegates came back the next day and started to dig the almonds with us. One of them worked alongside me, the other next to my nephew. They were appointed by the workers themselves and one had to work at their pace. 'How long have you been digging here?' they asked. I told them three days. 'Well, you've done a lot,' they replied. If they'd known that we'd been at it only a day – uf! With them alongside us it took another eight days to finish; the two of us alone could have had it done in a couple of days. The señorita had to pay their wages but I never got mine. She never offered and I never asked.

They were on at me all the time, these delegates, asking what I worked on the señorita's farm for. I told them my father was old and instead of hiring a labourer he hired me. 'Does the señorita pay you?' 'Yes,' I said. Of course she didn't but you had to tell them that to keep them quiet. 'Ah, we thought it was your father. You be sure it's the señorita who pays, not your father.'

Then the uprising happened. I was frightened a lot of the time. We had been close to the señorita and her father for so many years; for the slightest thing the workers would say we were fascists and ought to be taken for a *paseo*: shot. They didn't give you the time to breathe. They threatened people, they'd say so-and-so was a fascist and had to be watched, that we had to be careful not to work with fascists but that we had to go on working the land properly. All that sort of thing. So many things that we were frightened. But they never touched us.

The committee sent down two or three youths with shotguns. 'Are the crops divided?' My father said no. 'Well, we'll divide them now and the señorita's share we'll take with us for the committee.' They took a pig and a calf, too, which were the señorita's. But my father's share they didn't touch. Nor did they get nasty; it was just as though they had taken over the land. They used to tell my father that the farm was his now, that instead of giving half to the señorita he had to share it with them. But they usually left us the better half if they could.

I had a friend who worked a very poor bit of land his father had left him. Juana the *recovera*'s husband, he was. He signed on in one of the other lot, the communist one. He had some sort of job in it and was always after me to join him. 'I'm getting ten pesetas a day and my food,' he said, 'and I don't have to work much.' I was earning a lot less but I didn't want to leave my father. What a good thing I didn't! He was shot for being a member of that bad union when our forces took the village. They were all shot, my wife's brother-in-law too. He had been something in the militia.

It was a relief when it was all over. Then I had to go into the nationalist army, but I was lucky. I never had to fire a shot.

When I came back at the end of the war the señorita gave her permission for me to take over from my father. We were of the same age and I had known her since we were children; her father often brought her to the farm with him and we played together. *El Verdegal* was her favourite of all her father's farms. From childhood we always said *tu* to each other, always – except when there were people of social standing about; then naturally I said *Usted* to her.

To begin with, though the times were terrible in those hunger years, I didn't have too much to complain about from her. Not that she ever helped me any more than she had to.

I had to work very hard because my children were young and I had no help. In summer time I'd work day and night. During daylight I'd have to irrigate, plough, sow maize, potatoes, tomatoes, groundnuts, sweet potatoes ... and at night bring in the wheat for threshing. That was the only time left for the job. In summer, if I slept at all, it was out on the threshing floor, never in bed. Like that, as soon as the *levante* started to blow, I would be winnowing with the wind. Many a time I've had the threshing floor winnowed by dawn. I was used to it because that's how my father had worked, but it was a hard life. One worked a lot and ate very little.

The señorita used to say that work was healthy. She said it so often that one day I answered, 'Yes, work is very good for the body, but if you had to eat the little I eat you wouldn't say that. Look, Rosalia, a thin soup and a bit of onion salad with a little dried cod – and on that hoeing all day from before light until dark. That doesn't bring health. That harms the body rather than anything else.' But all she said was that that was nourishment enough. 'Yes,' I said, 'nourishment enough it may be. Put on a pair of trousers and come and work with me for a week – not even a week, a couple of days – and then see if you say the same. This work doesn't bring health, it kills you. . . .'

One *feria* she didn't send her administrator to divide the early crops and fetch her share. After working so much the rest of the year one likes a few days off in the village during the festivities. I asked the administrator to come down because I didn't want the responsibility of having her share in the house while we were out in case something was stolen. But the administrator said he couldn't come, he didn't have any sacks. So there the crop stayed.

A week later, when the señorita arrived from Málaga where she was living, she came straight down with her pencil and note-book. I was working on a terrace below the house and my wife called me. The señorita had gone up to the attic to search through what was there. I came up to the house and asked what she was doing. 'Who are you to enter my house and search without my permission?' 'This house is mine,' she replied. 'All right, it's yours but I live here. I'm giving you twenty-four hours to take all your produce out of the house.' From that time forward we didn't get on.

The next year when I took her up the account of the wheat I had threshed she said she didn't agree with the amount. 'There's wheat missing,' she said. 'Ah! How much wheat is missing then?' 'I'm missing eight *fanegas*.' Forty-two had been threshed and she thought there ought to be fifty. She had been down to *El Verdegal* during the reaping and had made her calculations in her book.

'Well, if they're missing they must be somewhere. Get the

Guardia Civil and search my house. If you find more than my share of the crop there – if you find a *cuartilla* more – I'll pay you eight *fanegas* – the four that belong to me and your four.'

She went very quiet then. At last she said: 'I'm not saying you've eaten them, only that someone has taken them from you.'

'Yes,' I answered, 'while I was out every night in the bars getting drunk someone stole them from the threshing floor. No! No one has taken a grain. Because when there's wheat to be threshed I sleep on the threshing floor. Forty-two *fanegas* is what was produced this year.' She didn't say any more, she could see I was serious.

She wanted the land to produce more, always more; but she never put any money into it. She wanted it all to come out of me. So as to make more I went out to plough; I was paid, as is the custom in summer, in fodder for the cattle, half of which were hers. She didn't pay me for the fodder I earned for her. Even that wasn't enough. I asked her for fodder for the calves we were fattening. 'They've got to eat what the *finca* produces,' she answered.

When, after threshing, the straw was divided she took her half share. I had to buy it back from her to have fodder for the cattle. She wouldn't pay for anything – but when the calves were sold she took half the money. And I had to borrow money to pay our debts in the shops; we had to buy rice and sugar and things like that. With young children we couldn't give them maize soup, dried figs and sweet potatoes all the time. I borrowed the money from her, never more than 2,000 pesetas a time. And on that I'd have to pay her back 2,500 or 3,000 pesetas.

The poorer one was the more she wanted. I can count the years on the fingers of one hand when I ended up with some money put aside. And then it was only because we had sold a calf. In all my years of work I managed to save only 35,000 pesetas. I wouldn't have saved that if my son hadn't insisted I put something aside for old age. Instead of getting help I worked even harder myself.

The farm was producing about 100,000 pesetas a year towards the end. Half of that was clear to the señorita after she'd paid her share of seed and fertilizer. But I had to pay not only half the seed and fertilizer, I had to pay for fodder, tools, labourers when I needed them – not to speak of food and clothes for the family. She never once paid anyone to help me on the farm.

I thought of looking for another farm; but in those times it was impossible. There were so many people just waiting for a farm to fall vacant, so many people without land or work. So I stayed; I didn't protest – not until she tried to put her foot on my throat and push me under for ever.

She started coming to the farm and searching the house again. She told her administrator – she wouldn't tell me direct – that I was giving my son-in-law some of the crops to sell behind her back. I heard what she was saying in the village. That I was selling fertilizer and irrigation water. She wanted to put a guard on me at night. 'Let her send down seven guards,' I told the administrator. 'She knows I've never stolen a thing of hers, not a *cuartilla* of grain, not an olive. I've made new terraces and I've planted trees, like my father before me. I'll tell it to her face if she likes – and if she doesn't.'

So I spent my 35,000 pesetas on building a small house in the village. She thought the money was stolen from her, she said so behind my back. By then I had worked it out; I was earning about thirty pesetas a day when the basic minimum was already twice that amount. The 35,000 pesetas was gone before the roof was on. I borrowed another 10,000 pesetas and finished it, with my son and son-in-law helping me. Then, after twenty-seven years share-cropping for her, I left the farm.

JUANA CUEVAS   *Fifty-eight*

Recovera

Six months pregnant and with a twenty-two-month-old daughter, Juana was left a widow in 1937 when her husband – as Cristóbal Gonzalez has related – was shot for his participation in the revolution. Juana refuses to talk about those times. 'While he was alive I was happy. Ever since I've been unhappy and I'll never be happy again as long as I live.' With these words, and in her silences, she seals off the past, speaking only of her struggle to keep alive in the years afterwards as a *recovera*. As the widow of a 'red' she was not entitled to a pension for her husband – such was reserved only for those who died on the nationalist side – but she did receive the normal subsidies for her children.

The profession of *recoveria*, traditional in many villages, consists in buying eggs from the farmsteads for sale in the city. There the *recovera* purchases cloth, soap and domestic articles for sale on the farmsteads in return for the eggs. Although predominantly a woman's business – chickens on the farmsteads being the woman's domain and the proceeds from the sale of eggs going to her – there are also men in the trade.

I was too ashamed the first time to go on my own asking for eggs. I made my sister come with me. Most of the people had their own *recoveras* already, so at each farmstead I had to explain what had happened and most of them took pity on me for my misfortune. I was born here and the people knew me. So one sold me a couple of dozen eggs and another three dozen. After walking all day I came back with a basket of thirteen dozen. A lot of them turned out to be rotten after all that.

I had a hundred pesetas. I sold the apricots on my husband's land and that's what they fetched. I became a *recovera* because there was nothing else I could do to provide for my daughters. Without my husband what could I do with the plot of land?

I walked down to Casas Nuevas with my basket and got a lift on a lorry to Málaga. I went to the place by the market where all the Tajeños always go. My brother-in-law and I counted the eggs, he two by two and I by the half dozen. There were fewer than I had started with. 'They've stolen some,' my brother-in-law said. 'That's how they are in Málaga.'

That first time I managed to sell all my eggs because there was a shortage. I made fifteen pesetas; I wouldn't have made that if my brother-in-law hadn't paid my bus-fare back to Casas Nuevas.

With some of the money I bought cups and jugs. I sold them for a profit of five or ten centimos each at the farmsteads. I bought cloth too. There was such a shortage that people were wearing old bits of tarpaulin and sacking. I could sell all the cloth I could buy in Málaga where I knew a man who worked in a factory and who, once in a while, let me have rolls twenty metres long.

The people paid in eggs, that was the custom. No one ate them except during Holy Week. I'd go out twice a week collecting. I had to leave early in the morning and I wouldn't get back until nightfall with a couple of baskets so heavy I was worn out. Fifteen kilometres or more I'd walk in a day. Once a week I'd walk down to Casas Nuevas to try to get to Málaga. Often the bus was too crowded to let me on with my baskets and more than once I spent the day there trying to get to Málaga.

Other times I and another *recovera* walked to Arroyo de la Reina to catch the bus from there. It left early in the morning so we'd walk there the evening before and sleep in the bus to be sure of a seat in the morning.

During the hunger years there were such terrible shortages that the government controlled the sale of eggs. The price they fixed was less than we had to pay for them. The only way to make any money was to smuggle eggs into the city. At first I thought of putting them in wooden crates and the crates in sacks. The first lot I took on the village lorry arrived without the police finding them. Then the man who was unloading picked up a sack and said, 'Huy! this weighs a lot,' and threw it on the pavement. Twenty dozen eggs smashed! My companion began to cry at the sight but I only laughed.

I decided we had to take the eggs ourselves, there was no other way. My brother had a mule and he agreed to cart them. We left at ten every night and walked through the night until we got to a friend's house on the outskirts of the city the next morning at eight. But we still had to get the eggs into town. We pretended we were fisherwomen and walked along the beach with small shopping baskets covered with napkins. Back and forth, back and forth all day – and we still had to walk round the town to the private houses where we knew they would buy the eggs. On top of walking all night! It was a hard life. Two years it went on like that.

When the chickens weren't laying we turned to other things. Slaughtering pigs and making black pudding which had to be smuggled into Málaga too. We packed them to look like raisins or dried figs so as not to be caught.

Early in the morning, late at night until my eyes shut with tiredness, I wove esparto plaits. For all that it took me six or seven years to save 1,000 pesetas because I had my children to provide for. When I was out in the countryside they stayed with my mother in the tumbledown house she had at the end of the village. At night I brought them back to the house I had rented and which cost me seven pesetas a month.

Just when I had managed to save a little, my older daughter fell ill with lung trouble. Three years she was here with the doctor trying to cure her and all my savings going on medicine and his charges. 'Put me on the poor list,' I used to beg him. 'How am I going to pay your bills?' 'You'll pay them in the end,' he said, and though it sometimes took me a year, I always did. But she wasn't cured until she went to the sanatorium in Málaga where, because of the doctor's recommendation, her cure cost me nothing. Eight months she was there and I often used to walk to see her.

All through those bad years my children never went hungry. I had my sack of flour, my sack of noodles saved up. Not that I could use the flour for bread because if the people had heard I had flour – ay! Even the bakers didn't eat white bread. Maize bread was all anyone had in the village. On the farms it was different – there people would sometimes give me little bits of white bread for my children. Often it would be seven or eight days old; but it was bread. No, thanks to God, we never went hungry despite all the other misfortunes we went through.

MANUEL GUTIERREZ and his son SALVADOR
Sixty-nine
Forty-one

Renter

A small man with a twinkle in his eye and one tooth in his head, Manuel was born on the farm his father rented from one of the large landowners who had moved to Málaga at the turn of the century. At the age of twenty-five, he took over from his father. The rent was 500 pesetas a year. 'Where am I going to get that money? I thought. It seemed impossible. Then a cow calved and I sold the calf for 525 pesetas. There was the rent! I took it to Málaga to pay the owner and I've stayed with the farm ever since.'

The farmstead has about three and a half hectares of land, half of which are cultivable. Early this century Manuel's father bought the adjoining two-hectare plot – of which approximately one hectare can be tilled – for 750 pesetas. The money, as Manuel laughingly relates, came out of a stocking in which his mother kept her savings from the figs and charcoal she sold in the village.

Manuel's son Salvador began work at six looking after the animals and, by the age of twelve – during the famine years – was working alongside his father. He never went to school and he got no wages. 'My father bought my clothes and fed me. When the *feria* came round he gave me twenty-five pesetas and that was that. It was the same for everyone of my age on the land then.'

Locally the Gutierrezs are considered a fairly prosperous family.

MANUEL It was a hard and bad life when I was young. I hope those times never return. And they weren't as bad for me as they were for the labourers and people who had to go to the sierra. Uf! If you knew the number of people who used to come begging food. Half-starved they were, the labourers, they'd beg work just to be able to get something to eat. A bit of bread, a handful of dried figs – anything. If it wasn't the fathers it was the children who came. My father always found them something to eat and I did the same.

Between the two farms we always had enough to eat. The land had its own spring and with water from the *mina* in the village there was irrigation enough. Though there were seven of us in the family we didn't have to go out looking for work. My father never wanted us to go as day-labourers digging the vines.

We grew mainly grain crops before the war but we sold hardly anything of what we produced. A few carobs, lemons, figs, a bit of charcoal – that was about all. The wheat was for bread and the straw for the cows, maize for bread and soup – we never fed the cattle on wheat or maize – and a few vegetables. When I started the land would have been producing about 4,000 to 5,000 pesetas a year so in fact the rent wasn't dear.

The owners hardly ever came to look at the land. When the daughter inherited, her husband, a colonel, used to come once in a while to shoot pigeons. But he didn't trouble about the land or how we lived. When I told him the roof of the house was falling in he said: 'Oh, I don't want to have anything to do with that. If I repair it I'll have to raise your rent.' So I had to make the repairs out of my pocket.

But how hard one had to work in those times! I've walked to Málaga and back night after night with hardly any rest. I'd leave here of an evening to load raisins and lemons in the village and lead the three mules to Málaga. I'd be back by three or four the next afternoon. If there was someone to load the mules I'd get a couple of hours sleep; if not, I'd set off again. And all that to make three or four pesetas – that's what it came to. And I'd be delighted to make them!

SALVADOR After the war, in those hunger years, the farm didn't provide for the six of us. It wasn't only that there was no money: it didn't rain. In summer everything was burned dry. In those years it rained a lot less than it does now.

We had to find land to sharecrop. The land was fifteen kilometres from here and it took us three hours to get there and three hours back every day. We sowed wheat and for every *fanega* of land we had to give the owner a *fanega* of wheat.

The land was so bad no one would plant it today. We thought ourselves lucky to have it then. At threshing time we slept down there on the threshing floor. One of us always stayed awake, more to be sure the others woke before dawn than to keep guard. All the wheat and straw had to be brought to our farm and that meant loading day and night; we rarely got more than two or three hours sleep during that time.

But thanks to that we always had flour for white bread. The people in the village were starving. I remember once I was cooking up sweet potatoes to give to my hunting dogs when two lads a little older than me came up. When they saw me giving the food to my dogs they began to cry. They were so hungry that I took the food and gave it to them.

You'd plant a terrace of potatoes and in the morning there

wouldn't be a potato left in the ground. The people came at night and dug them up. To protect the crop one had to build a shack on the terrace and stay there all night. But what could the people do? There was famine and they had to find something to eat. I know of two brothers who died as a result of their hunger. They stole broad beans from a farm and ate them raw. Their fathers were firewood gatherers in the sierra and they had nothing to eat. The beans blew up their stomachs and they got sick and died. A lot of others died like that, not directly of starvation, but from eating only cabbage leaves and things; they'd get diarrhoea and, since they were already half-starved, some complication would set in that killed them.

To get by you had to be prepared to do anything. Working all day and ploughing by moonlight all night, carrying contraband tobacco, looking for something to make you a peseta or two.

I went once with my father's mare, the best in Tajos, to meet a smuggler's boat from Gibraltar. There were ten or twelve of us down there with horses. One of the men from the village was the chief and he knew the boat was coming in. For 500 pesetas each of us had to make three trips from the boat to a farmstead not far away where the tobacco was hidden and later distributed to the different villages.

It was dangerous work, the Guardia Civil were always on the lookout. Once in a while they caught someone or shot his horse from under him. But that night there was no trouble. We had sentries posted on the main road, passwords and signals. If we heard a handful of gravel fall on the road we knew we had to scatter and ride as fast as we could.

When my father heard that I'd gone he gave me such a telling-off that I never went again. But there were always plenty who did because there was a lot of smuggling then.

When the worst of the drought years ended we started growing tomatoes in quantity. We couldn't sell them here, there wasn't the market. So I took them to Posadas with the mare. As soon as I was out of sight of my father I emptied the mare's fodder sack and picked up smuggled tobacco in the village to sell in Posadas. I'd get seventy-five pesetas, a hundred pesetas a time, and very soon I had 2,000 pesetas saved. I thought I was rich, I'd tell myself I had become someone with that sort of money!

On the way to Posadas I often met the outlaws. As many as eight in one group I've seen together, but there were twenty-five or more in all, I believe. They stopped me once and asked where I was going and what I was carrying. I gave them some of the tobacco I was carrying. They always went armed with rifles and shotguns. They'd lie in hiding and you'd hear a voice: '*Oyez! oyez!* where are you going?' I'd stop then because I knew who it was. If I'd been one of those who turned straight round and reported them to the Guardia Civil, no doubt they'd have done something to me the next time. They had spies everywhere. But I just played the idiot. . . .

MANUEL Reds who'd escaped after our forces took this region, that's who they were. Fled into the sierra. Men from Posadas, Benamalí, Arroyo de la Reina and one or two from here.

The day before the nationalists arrived all the reds fled as fast as they could. They tried to steal my mare for the second time but I outwitted them. By that time I wasn't frightened any longer because I knew their time had ended. But before that – ozu!

A bunch of thieves they were, the lot of them. They told me I hadn't to pay the rent to the landlord any more. 'Good,' I said, and the day it took my fancy I went to Málaga and paid the landowner's widow. 'Here is the rent,' I said, 'and don't say I came to pay it.' 'Ay! God will repay you, son,' she said. 'Times are terrible. I haven't peace enough to die in.' She was wealthy; every day the militia went round collecting something from her. When it was all over the poor thing was very pleased that I'd come with the rent.

The reds didn't bother me much on the farm. They never took any of my wheat or barley; a few vegetables they came for a couple of times. They gave us rations like everyone else. But they tried taking over everything. One day they called a lot of us who had ploughing yokes out to plough the vineyards down on the *vega*. We couldn't say no. We got down there only at two in the afternoon and started to work, taking our time about it. After a while I asked the militiaman in charge if there weren't any raisins about; he sent to a nearby vineyard telling them to send over a box of the best raisins. We stuffed ourselves until, about four o'clock, the militiaman said he was going. 'You can leave when you want.' 'But, *hombre*,' we said, 'we've only just come. . . .'

'I'm off, you do what you want.' So we all came back, no one was going to stay behind.

A rabble they were. When they fled and I saw the first of our lorries coming up the road from Casas Nuevas – that was when I was really happy. Everything returned to order, just as it had been before. Everyone had his own life again.

SALVADOR In 1950 I left here for the first time. I had been called up for military service and was posted to Pamplona in the north. They put us in cattle wagons with a bit of straw for the trip. Four days and three nights it took to get there. We had to urinate where we could, and a friend of mine who was train-sick had to lie in his own vomit. Now and again they'd take us off to feed us; then back in again. We were packed in there like animals; when we arrived our clothes were in such a state you couldn't recognize us.

Up there it was so cold and a lot of people spoke only Basque that it seemed to us we had left Spain. There was a lot of trouble in the camp where I was. They worked us day and night making roads and the food was worse than animals get today. A number of soldiers deserted and got into France. A friend and I took off one night, we were so fed up. We walked and walked like crazy but couldn't find where to cross the river that's the frontier with France. So we turned back. If we'd got across we'd never have been allowed to come back to Spain, never. I don't know what would have happened then. I told my mother once what we'd planned and she got very upset about it.

I wrote my father what was happening. Shortly afterwards I was called in to see the regimental priest. My father had spoken to don Fernando, the priest here, and he had written to the priest in the camp. As a result I was posted to a detachment checking machine-gun nests hidden in the mountains along the frontier to make sure they were in condition in case of war. There were only half a dozen of us and we hardly had anything to do. It was marvellous.

When I came back things were getting a bit better here. It had rained and with water we could plant and live somewhat better. Not well enough to save money but at least to eat.

JUAN GONZALEZ   *Thirty-eight*

Goatherd

The blackmarket was about the only way you could make money. Olive oil was the main thing. The rationed stuff was so thick it was more like tar than oil. My brothers worked in señorita Rosalia Lopez's mill, and when I was eight I got the job of look-out.

From seven in the morning until nightfall I had to stay in a cave overlooking the road in case the inspectors came. My mother had to bring me my food because I couldn't leave. Since no cars came up here then, as soon as I saw the reflection of the sun shining on glass I ran to the mill. Then I went to the square to wait for the car. If the people looked like inspectors – they always went to the town hall first – I ran off again down the mule tracks to warn people coming up with loads of olives. Half of them didn't have official permits. In the mill itself everything was hidden away. At night the blackmarket oil was shifted from here by the lorry-load. A lot of money the señorita made. A lot!

There were all sorts of tricks the people got up to. One man used to fill a skin with water and on top pour a couple of litres of oil so it looked as though the whole skin was full of oil. He'd walk to another village and when he got close to a shop he started to run. 'Here,' he'd say, bursting into the shop, 'take this oil quick, the *guardia* are coming. Give me 2,000 pesetas and I'll be back tomorrow to settle up.' Of course he never went back and sooner or later the shopkeeper would find he'd been cheated. But he couldn't do anything because it was all blackmarket anyway.

Things were so bad in the village that when I was nine my uncle came to take me away to his farmstead in the folds of the sierra to be a goatherd. My father had no land, he was a goatherd himself, and there were eight of us in the family. He couldn't support us all. He asked me if I wanted to go. I never said no to my father, whatever he ordered I always did. You had to have that sort of respect for your father in those times.

For the first couple of months I cried all the time. The work wasn't so hard but it was a life of slavery and I wasn't used to being away from home.

In winter I had up to 150 goats to herd. I'd be out in the

mountains all day, usually with another two or three goatherds from around there. We wore capes made of reeds against the rain. But most days we found shelter in a cave or mine and lit a fire and took shots with our slings. When we came back at night the people on the farmstead used to sniff the air and say how we stank. It was from being huddled over a wood fire all day.

Each goatherd had four castrated males specially trained to lead the herd. Two at the front and two at the back. They answered to a whistle or call and those in front would turn round and start to butt the others until the whole herd turned back. They saved us hours and hours of walking, those goats.

In summer we were gone four or five days at a time. From May to September we came back to the farmsteads only when we needed supplies.

What a lonely life! The only people we ever saw were the outlaws and the Guardia Civil. We were always glad to meet the outlaws because they gave us tobacco. Crying for a smoke I always was, even at that age! The outlaws always had plenty of tobacco; they bought it from the smugglers, I suppose.

Sometimes there were as many as nine together. They carried pistols, shotguns, sub-machine-guns and hand-grenades like those the Guardia had. They were a lot better dressed than we were, with boots and good corduroy trousers and jackets. And they were always clean-shaven. We only managed to get our hair cut every three or four months when we got back to the village. It was we who looked like outlaws and they who looked like farmers.

The only thing they ever took from us was a goat once in a while. The best, the tenderest. We were happy when they did because they left us the meat they didn't want and we could sell the hide. They took the best cuts and carried them off to their hiding places. We never knew where they were, but they must have been the farms of people they trusted. They never went hungry, that's for sure, and they'd often join us for a bite when we were cooking a bit of hog's fat on a wire over the fire – the way you see them cooking in wild west films.

I remember one day when we came across them in a deserted mine. Our eyes nearly fell out of our heads when we saw the bottles of *aguardiente*, *coñac*, wine they had there. And tins of sardines and freshly baked bread. When one of them saw the bit of bread I was eating, hard as a brick and a week old, he took it out of my hand and threw it to my dog. Then he gave me a bit of his. Delicious it was! They were celebrating and one of them started to sing and we stayed there all day, singing, drinking and smoking. A real fiesta, but I never found out what it was for.

They never talked to us about what they were doing in the sierra. One night I came down to my uncle's farmstead and shut the herd up. I went into the house and suddenly I saw two of them there. They were beating my uncle with a rifle-butt. One of them with gold teeth shouted at me to get out and hit me across the head. I ran away and sat under a tree. There was a horse tied up a short way off and I kept thinking of jumping on it and riding to Posadas to alert the Guardia. It was a good job I didn't because when they'd finished with my uncle and came out of the house another one appeared from some bushes right behind me. He'd have shot me if I'd made a move. There were six of them altogether. They called me and told me to ride to Posadas to alert the Guardia; they themselves ordered me to do it.

A whole lot of *guardias* on horseback came and took us all to Posadas where they kept us three days. My uncle had to go to hospital in Málaga; his head was badly injured and he had a broken rib.

Some time before my uncle had been to Posadas and got drunk and started to talk about the outlaws. They had spies everywhere. That's why they came down that day; and they robbed him of a lot of money he'd just made on the sale of some calves.

They only beat up or robbed informers, they never touched anyone else. People who had money were scared, but since not many had any money the majority weren't frightened.

They never stole anything; but they came to the farmsteads a lot to eat. They'd arrive without warning, put their rifles up against the side of the house, like the Guardia Civil, and start to chat. A couple always stayed on guard. When the farmer's wife had got the meal ready she would invite them to eat, as is the custom here. After the meal the outlaws told someone from the farm to alert the Guardia. It was for the people's own protection, because if the Guardia found out that someone had given them food he'd be put in jail and everyone was frightened of that.

They came a lot to my uncle's – before and after they'd beaten him up. My uncle was pretty scared by then; he'd been away for nearly six months after that happened. However, they didn't touch him again.

One summer afternoon I took the herd down to the river to drink. The outlaws were there. It was an open place, but they didn't seem frightened. They never were. They used to ask if we'd seen a *guardia* patrol but it never worried them if we had. As it happened someone from Tajos passed by that afternoon and saw me with them. He told my father. My father didn't know that I often saw the outlaws. He came for me the next day and said I was needed at home. He didn't say anything about the outlaws; but I think he was frightened that now I was fifteen and nearly a man I might go off with them. So I came away.

For a time after that Juan worked a plot his mother had inherited, but the land was too poor. He left the village and got a job in a baker's in Benamalí. 'The first time I nearly went crazy at the sight of so much bread.' It was while he was in Benamalí that the outlaws' leader was killed. 'A strongly built man he was, with a mouth so full of gold you didn't see any white at all. He always liked a joke. They say he visited his wife when she was giving birth in hospital in Málaga disguised as a priest. She lived by smuggling in Benamalí and he came to see her often enough; she had three children by him after he fled to the sierra. He liked the women and that was his downfall. He was visiting one on a farm and a boy saw him go in and alerted the Guardia. They approached and started to shoot. He escaped from a window but was shot through the foot. The woman ran out and threw herself on him, crying that he had been killed. But as the *guardias* came close he shot one of them dead. The other took cover and killed them both, cutting them in half with a hail of machine-gun bullets. . . . It wasn't long before several of the other outlaws were killed or surrendered. Without their leader they couldn't go on.'

MIGUEL MORENO *Forty-Seven*

Fish-vendor

'My father always said to me, "Miguel, we weren't born to be rich. To eat you've got to work hard. We were born to suffer and work." '

For as far back as he can remember his family have been fish-vendors. He started helping his father carry fish up from the coast when he was nine; at thirteen his mother died, leaving five children younger than he and the smallest, a girl, blind. His father couldn't leave the children to go on working. 'I'll take your place and you stay to look after them,' Miguel said. 'At that age I wasn't a man yet but I was always eager to work. And from then on until my brothers were old enough to carry a vendor's basket, I supported the family.'

Miguel stands little more than five feet six inches. His toothless face and body are thin to the point of emaciation, and he looks ten, if not fifteen years older than his age. He speaks proudly of his work, in a way that the day-labourers are never proud. For him it was an individual struggle – a race, not a constant and seldom victorious battle with the *señorito* employers.

I left the house at three or three thirty of a morning to be down on the beach by five. I went barefoot like all of us vendors, and with a sack for my shoulders over an old jacket in winter. Going down the watercourses in the dark I used to be scared; I was still only a child at the start. But I knew I had to go on – what else could I do?

When the boats came in I bought a load of fish. Very often I couldn't pay for it, I'd get it on credit. In the village the demand was only for the cheaper sorts of fish: sardines, *jurel*,* whitebait, sea-bream. You couldn't sell fine fish here.

We foot vendors carried the baskets of fish on our backs with a halter over our foreheads to leave our hands free. Sometimes we'd

---

* A type of spiny mackerel.

put a hand inside the halter to take some of the weight off our heads. And when the basket was on our backs we started to run.

The more you sweated the quicker you sold your fish. If I was carrying no more than forty kilos I could leave the men on donkeys behind. One day my second cousin and I left Casas Nuevas together, he on a donkey and me on foot. When he got to Tajos I'd sold my basket already. Blood nearly came out of my eyes to make it up the last climb which is where I beat him. When one of us vendors said we'd get to Tajos before another, he'd kill himself to do it. My father was the same; he could get to Benamalí faster than a man on a donkey. Running, always running – he died of it in the end; broken down he was from the running. We had to work like that because we were always hungry.

Sometimes I'd get up here and my father would say: 'Miguel, there's no fish being bought in Tajos today.' If there was any, I'd have a coffee and rest a minute or two while he fixed my basket. Then – *pom-pom-pom* – I'd be running to Benamalí. From Casas Nuevas to Tajos is ten kilometres and from here to Benamalí is another fourteen. I could do the twenty-four kilometres in three hours and still have time to spare. Foaming at the nostrils and my mouth spewing fire! I always put everything I had into it.

Five days in a row I ran from Casas Nuevas to Benamalí. Nearly fifty kilometres a day it made. I'd get back here in the afternoon and throw myself down to sleep. After five days I was worn out and had to rest. All that to make a couple of pesetas more.

The brine from the fish – that was before there was ice – brought out pustules on my back. The weight of the basket rubbing broke them open and the blood and pus stuck to my shirt. But nothing stopped me. Neither rain nor sun. I got wet through and got plenty of colds but I never stopped.

If my stomach had been full it wouldn't have been so bad. But I've gone hungry more times than I can say. Just to see someone eating made my eyes pop out of my head. The worst was in the hunger years. We'd kill each other to get a cabbage, lemon rinds, anything. I've eaten lemon rinds and been happy to have them. In my house we always had fish but no oil to fry it in. Grilled fish and barley coffee without sugar – that's what we lived on.

It went on like that for six years or more. All my youth! Very often I didn't sell my fish; I tried to barter it for food. I got home one day and my father said he and the children hadn't eaten all day. The little ones were asleep, that was all they could do. 'We've got no money and even if we had there's nothing to buy in the village,' my father said. I got some fish from the basket. Then I went down into the country and stole two cabbages, some lettuces and half a basket of sweet potatoes. The next morning I went to tell the corporal of the Guardia Civil what I'd done. I said he shouldn't blame someone else if the theft were reported. '*Hombre*,' he said, 'it's not an offence; you did it for the good of your father and brothers. Go back to your house without fear.'

I was always half-starved. One day I got to Benamalí and I saw a woman. 'Señora, I've got to have something to eat. Take whatever fish you want and give me a handful of figs, a bit of bread, anything.' She took me into her house and gave me food. I told her to take the fish but she wouldn't. 'Why not?' 'Because I'm going to buy it from you.'

I used to carry some weight of fish in those days. 107½ kilos was my record, they weighed it when I got to the village. It cost me sixteen pesetas and I sold it for 1·25 pesetas a kilo. That was a day! Three or four kilometres from the village I couldn't carry it, I was so worn out with hunger. I stopped by a woman drawing water from a well and asked for food. She gave me some coffee and a bit of bread with oil and I gave her a kilo of fish. And when I got here I still had 107½ kilos on my back. The will one had in those days!

Some days I could sell all my fish in an hour, standing on a street corner; other days it took four or five hours hawking it through the streets; sometimes I couldn't sell it at all. I often had to beg the women to buy. 'I can't, I haven't the money.' 'All right, take it on credit.' I'd give her half a kilo for forty or fifty centimos and the next day I'd try to collect. As like as not she wouldn't have the money and I'd have to wait until she did. The half dozen people with money enough to be called rich spent nothing buying food. They wouldn't spend even to buy themselves a beer.

Sometimes when the weather was bad no fish was landed on the beach here. I've walked as far as Málaga to buy fish. Seven or eight hours it would take me to get back here with a basket weighing forty or fifty kilos. Hundreds and hundreds of times I've had to do that.

I was always broke. For a day's work I'd make between ten and fourteen pesetas. After the war that was, when the day-wage was nine. I gave everything I had to my father. One morning early – I was twenty-five – I was going down in the dark when a horse passed me. I'd gone about another kilometre when I found a wallet in the road. A merchant's wallet. As I was looking at it I heard the horse coming back. 'Have you seen a wallet?' the rider asked. 'I've lost one.' 'What's in it?' I said. He told me. 'Well, I haven't seen it yet but I'm going to look now.' Everything he said tallied. I didn't get to see the money. 'Boy,' he said – he called me boy – 'here's 120 pesetas. Buy yourself a donkey.' I thanked him. 'And the next time you find a wallet like this lying in the road, don't hang about looking at it. Run.'

Well, with that I bought a donkey for ninety pesetas and had thirty over. So I left off running and started to ride.

Five years ago, after spells of chronic bronchitis, the doctor forced him to retire. In the meantime his sons had become vendors and taken over from him.

SILVESTRE ALARCON   *Forty-six*

Esparto and firewood gatherer

My father and his father before him were firewood gatherers. All of us with the same wealth – nothing; no future of any sort other than hunger and hardship. My parents had fourteen children: seven boys and seven girls. All the boys died except me. A curious thing, I don't know what they died of. Perhaps it was lack of food or there was something wrong with my mother. I don't know.

I started going to the sierra with my father when I was six and a half. No one ever started younger! My father could carry more firewood on his head and shoulders than a pack animal. When he was eighteen they say he brought down eighteen *arrobas* – 207 kilos – in one load; an *arroba* for every year of his life.

By the time I was nine I could carry a load of nearly thirty-five kilos; by the age of ten I was picking and bringing in nearly 120 kilos of esparto in a day. My joy then was the silver *duros* we were paid in. '*Papa*, let me have my money so I can give it to my mother.' What happiness when, after a week away in the sierra and my mother crying at the sight of me so small, I gave her the five or six silver *duros* I'd earned. Twenty-five or thirty pesetas! And for that I'd had to work from dawn until night for a week.

In summer when there was a moon we often left the village at two in the morning to go to the sierra for firewood. It was a six-kilometre climb and it took us an hour and a half to get there. Brushwood we collected mainly: rosemary, thyme, cistus and all the other plants that grow in the mountains. We made bundles of the wood and put a bit of rag or sacking for a pad on our heads and hoisted the bundles up. They covered our heads, shoulders and backs; sometimes all anyone could see of us was our feet.

There were days enough when we couldn't sell the firewood we'd gathered. Two pesetas, 2·50 for a load. We'd pile it up outside the bakers' waiting for them to take it – and as like as not have to exchange it for a bit of bread in the end. When we couldn't sell it we didn't eat. The times I've left my house without anything in my stomach and come back with sixty or seventy kilos on my head and found my mother whitewashing the house. 'And the food, *mama*?' 'If you haven't sold anything what am I going to make a meal from?' she'd answer.

I've picked esparto in every sierra along the coast: Nerja, Mijas, Casares. I know all the mountains like the back of my hand. To work in the sierra you've got to be born to it. It looks easy picking esparto but it isn't. Every year the sierra changes; it's full of crevasses and holes which get covered over with grass; you have to learn how to walk it. The same with the picking, it's an art you've got to practise.

The worst time was in the 1940s when the state took over all the esparto and sold the concessions. It was all we had to live on, and a Málaga businessman put guards on to stop us. When we were caught the esparto was confiscated and we were thrown in jail. One day we told the Guardia Civil sergeant what we felt about the mayor making a living from the esparto confiscated from us: 'This man is alive only because Tajeños are good-natured; otherwise he'd have been dead long ago.' It was a scandal that he should get rich on the blood of the people; today his children can study and prosper while mine have to work.

I had good eyes in those days and I could see the guards a long way off. 'The Monday friends,' I used to call them. I've had them on my heels chasing me and escaped and got back to my house. When I saw them coming through a crack in the door I refused to open. They had to go and get permission to search a house. While they were getting it I hid the esparto in the house next door. Once, after escaping like that, I saw a well-known esparto black marketeer walking through the village. I walked behind him dropping bits of esparto in the street. 'I'll go to jail, but I'll get you thrown out of here,' I thought.

When I reached the square I was ordered to jail. 'For what?' 'For picking esparto. . . .' 'I haven't any esparto, have a look.' They couldn't throw me in jail; instead they ordered me home. 'You'll be a month without leaving the village.' 'A month? Whose orders are those?' I went to the tavern. One of the guards came in. 'Where are you going tomorrow?' he asked. 'For esparto,' I said; and all the others there repeated with one voice what I had said. 'If we don't go we'll come to your place to eat instead.' 'I haven't anything to eat either,' he answered.

They couldn't stop us, there were too many of us. Sometimes these guards tried to shoot at our feet, but we escaped over the mountains like Red Indians and got back to the village. The clothes didn't have time to dry on our backs. You know what it's like when you hear shots fired at you? – you run as hard as you can.

From the age of sixteen when my father died I had to support my mother and sisters. Everything I earned was for them; I've always been very tough about protecting my home. And in matters of love I've been as hard as I've been in work.

I had a woman on a farm in the sierra who gave me all the food I needed. Against her will I left her and went picking esparto in Casares. When I got there there was no work. Three days I went without eating anything except a piece of bread I found in a pig's trough. Thin and humble as a lamb I went back to the woman. She knew what had happened but I said to myself, 'Men have got to be men; the last thing a man can do is to tell a woman his troubles.' So when she asked me how I'd got on I said: 'All right.'

'So much pride still when all you've known is hunger. You who had to hide your shame and ask the mayor and the Guardia Civil of Casares to get you a ride on a lorry so as to come back here. . . .' I looked at her. 'I'm a man and we come first in everything in life, that's why God made man before woman. Goodbye!'

I didn't want a woman with land; she had to marry one of her own class. I married the poorest woman in the village, the very poorest, and I fell in love with her because she was poor and understood me who was in the same state as she. I won her from the arms of another. 'Look, girl,' I said, 'I've got nothing but these,' and I showed her my arms. 'But as long as God preserves them I'll see to it you don't go short of anything.'

She had a *novio*, a fish-vendor, who treated her badly. After I'd taken up with her he wanted her back. 'In the month I've been with her,' I said to him, 'I've put down more roots than you in two years; yours seem to have grown on the top of a rock. Let her decide, and if she decides for you I'll be your best man.' But she didn't; and that's how I came to marry her.

But I'll never tell her I love her, much as I do. She'll die wondering. Women want men to be rich, powerful, strong and then turn them into little dogs. When they've done that they don't love them. As soon as you give a woman what she asks for you're finished. I don't know how it is in other countries, but that's how it is here.

I grew up in the sierra like a deer and I think like a deer. I like to remember those times. We hardly ate, we hardly lived, but we enjoyed ourselves. A friend was a true friend; if you found a cigarette end in the street you'd share it with him. Now some of them have got cars and they toot their horns at you – not so you'll get out of the way but to show that they're in a car and you're on foot.

Well, I'd sooner be poor and remember those times instead of pretending to forget. I came into the world to live; it was my bad luck to lose for I believe I could have made something of myself with better luck, if I'd found a patron. But that's no reason why I should enslave myself now. I'm like an old soldier who hands in his uniform but says, 'I'm not handing in my weapon until God comes for it. . . .'

Concentrated in a solitude from which this has been a rare

outbreak, he sits in silence for a moment. Alone in the sierra while still in his teens, he had the first of a number of epileptic fits. His illness set him apart. He looks up: 'The people think I'm mad, you understand. I see things other people don't see. They say a man goes mad for lack of reason but it's the contrary; he knows too much and all his intelligence is too much for his head. I told a doctor that once: in those moments of fury my thoughts go so far there's no human being who can understand them if he hasn't been through the same thing. That's why I like to be alone; solitude is my companion. Then I'm free.'

Rarely seen in the village, Silvestre still goes to the sierra for esparto which he plaits for the tourist industry. His wife goes out cleaning and he looks after the house, doing the cleaning and cooking. 'Yes, if I'd had the money I believe I could have become somebody. As it is, after a life of misfortune, I'm a nobody. . . .'

And the others, the survivors of the war and the famine years? Miguel, the fish-vendor, has a job as an usher in the village cinema which, with his son's earnings, keeps him alive; Juan Gonzalez, the young goatherd (to whom we shall return), is a master bricklayer on the coast; Manuel Gutierrez's farm has recently been sold by its owner to a foreign property developer and he received 200,000 pesetas for moving out; his son is foreman in a gravel pit for the construction industry; Juana Cuevas remains a *recovera*, but: 'I'm too old, I'm tired and I haven't got the will to make money as I had when my daughters were dependent on me. Moreover, the people eat all the eggs laid here now, you know.'

Finally, Cristóbal Gonzalez, the sharecropper: he is a gardener in a foreigner's house overlooking *El Verdegal*, his old farm. 'Here I am, happy and tranquil. I look down there and bless the day I left.'

RELIGION

Patron Saint and Parish Priest

The Virgin of the Rock, the patron saint of Tajos, is kept in a chapel hewn out of the live rock of the promontory jutting from the mountainside. It is said locally that the statue was discovered in 1586 in the walls of the old castle where it had been hidden to prevent its falling into the hands of the Moors eight centuries earlier.

As in most Spanish villages, considerable veneration is paid to this doll-like figure which is normally brought out only for the festivities in her honour each September – the climax of the village year.

The statue was preserved during the revolution but the throne was partially damaged. In 1959, when he was appointed schoolmaster in Tajos, Eugenio Lopez set about the task of restoring the statue to its former splendour. He recalls how it happened:

One day don Vicente, the parish priest, came to me and said: 'Don Eugenio, the Virgin's throne is in such a poor state that we won't be able to take her in procession through the streets in September; she will be ridiculed by everyone.'

I had just been put in charge of the Brotherhood of the Virgin and I agreed with him. The throne – a beautiful thing of ebony and gold – had been smashed in the time of the reds. With the foreigners who were already beginning to come here, it would have been scandalous to allow our patron saint to appear in public in such poor condition. I set about finding out how much it would cost to make a similar throne. I could hardly believe it when I was told: 40,000 pesetas.

I went and told don Vicente. 'Listen, don Eugenio,' he said, 'this is a chance, let us attempt it. God will provide.' So I asked him to authorize me to go from house to house collecting money.

I went all over the village, even to the poorest streets at the top. 'How can I ask for money from these people when what is needed is that they be given money?' I asked myself. One house was so poor that I passed by; I didn't dare stop there. The man and his wife came out after me. 'Listen, are you passing our house by?' I didn't know what to say. 'No, no, I was just going to this other house first,' I replied.

'No, no, you weren't going to stop at our house. Well, we want you to know that this morning we did without breakfast so that you could have this 1·50 pesetas for the throne.'

I asked the two or three foreigners who were living here then for money too. To overcome my shame I used to fortify myself with a few *copitas* in advance! One of them said to me: 'How can you go round collecting money for a throne when there's so much poverty in the village?' And I said: 'The village people are the first to donate and the Virgin will have her throne.'

From January to the patron saint's fiesta I collected 25,000 pesetas. We were still 15,000 pesetas short. Don Vicente and I went to the bank in Casas Nuevas to see the director who is my brother-in-law and he loaned us the balance. The Virgin came out in procession with her new throne!

During the *feria* I went from table to table collecting money. Before it was over I had 15,000 pesetas. Don't ask me how, I don't know. There were many people from outside the village who came for the festivities and it must have been in part due to their generosity.

In the following years we raised another 25,000 pesetas for the supports for the throne and one or two smaller things.

Then there remained the Virgin's sanctuary to rebuild. I set about it myself after school, working as a labourer while a mason did the building. We uncovered all the live stone inside and left the sanctuary looking as it must have done originally when it was first carved out of the rock. I had to go to the Civil

Governor and the Minister of Information and Tourism because the town hall wouldn't help. That didn't trouble me; I could appeal to higher authorities. The Governor sent us 25,000 pesetas and the Ministry another 10,000. I had become obsessed by the thought of the Virgin and the good name of Tajos. Because my wife is from Casas Nuevas, I could hardly open my mouth at home about what I was doing; she didn't want to hear any more about Tajos. As for my children – they no longer talked about the Virgin of the Rock; they called her 'our father's Virgin!'

VICENTE LOMBARDO   *Forty-three*

Parish priest

My first impression of Tajos is unforgettable. A village of classical Andalusian beauty, a village which breathed the air of the countryside, the scent of wild flowers. . . . It was spring and I'll never forget the poetry and beauty of it, the simplicity of life, its naturalness. It was 1954 and I had recently been ordained. In youth one finds everything more poetic and beautiful!

Then I was sent there as an interim priest. Three years later, when I was appointed parish priest, things seemed different. In fact nothing had changed, it was I who now had different responsibilities, a continuing task to do, and I felt laden with a greater burden. I saw the village more clearly, I talked with more people, I came to understand it properly.

I believe I can safely say that in 1957 the village had changed hardly at all since the beginning of the century. Its economy, its customs and religious practices were the same. Economically speaking, existence was rudimentary, depending principally on esparto; apart from those who had permanent jobs and the small shopkeepers and artisans, almost everyone lived poorly. Of the village population, I'd say more than 60 percent were really poor; but one must bear in mind that the poor lived mainly in the village. Those who owned land or who had a plot to work in the countryside were considerably better off; and one noticed it when they came to the village. Taking the whole municipality I'd say under half were really poor – so overall Tajos was no worse off than many other villages round here.

There was less unemployment, in the pure sense of the word, than under-employment. A man scratching a living from whatever poor bit of land he could find to work can't be said to be fully employed. No more than someone who went to the sierra for a bundle of esparto which brought him too little to eat properly. The proof is that now, with full employment, even some of the best land is no longer cultivated.

One thing that struck me early on was that Tajos was a village largely closed in on itself. Let me explain: there are other villages close by like Benamalí and Arroyo de la Reina which have a tradition of going out into the world. You'll find men from Benamalí all over Spain, many of whom have prospered. But the people of Tajos have been so enamoured of their village that they have hardly emigrated at all, even in times of large internal migrations from Andalusia. In my time there were perhaps eight families working in the coal-mines of Leon and that was all.

I don't believe one can explain this by lack of communications, for the other villages had no better. Rather perhaps by the large extent of the municipality in which the men would always try to find work, even if it meant walking for several hours. And also by the particular disposition – idiosyncrasy, one might say – of its people.

In my opinion this is one of the virtues of Tajos – and also one of its defects. It is a village enamoured of itself, of its customs and traditions. A Tajeño will always say that Tajos is better than anywhere else, that its water is better, its air fresher. There is this village pride and *unión*. I'll never forget, because it made such a deep impression on me, how when someone in the countryside died, 400 or 500 men would come to the funeral. They'd give up their day's work to attend if they had to come a long way. That was the sort of *unión* there was; I haven't seen the like in other villages. Of course, it gave the village an air of fiesta when so many men came to the funeral and afterwards went to the bars. In Andalusia it is the custom that only men attend a funeral while women go to the mass said later for the deceased.

But this enclosed life, this way of exalting everything good that exists in their imagination also impoverishes them. In their isolation they don't see the good that exists elsewhere, they turn away from everything else. And that is a big defect.

In its respect for religion Tajos was in my time a classic Andalusian village. Everything revolved around religious customs, fiestas, folklore and tradition. I could summarize the year by the religious calendar.

A month before Christmas not only the children but men and women went out singing in the streets accompanied by the traditional *zambomba*.* This was both religious preparation and an amusement since there was so little else in those days for the people to do. Immediately after Christmas – and this was strange – they began preparing for Carnival. This was no longer celebrated with masks – they were forbidden in the 1920s because of the danger of crimes – but in villages like Tajos the spirit of Carnival has never been lost. The people danced in rings in the streets and squares and everyone participated in the joy. Lent which followed and culminated in Holy Week was one of the climaxes of the year. People who normally didn't attend church every Sunday now appeared. The Holy Week processions were very simple, crude you could say, but truthful too. A great deal of importance was given to Christ's resurrection; on the Saturday night before Easter Sunday the young stayed up all night taking a procession through the streets and keeping the village awake.

In spring there were the festivities of the Cross of May. This is widely celebrated in Andalusia and is in honour not of the Cross of Holy Week, sad and dripping blood, but the Cross of Salvation and Glory. Young girls in all the houses made crosses which they adorned with flowers; and then – to return to the close connection between religion and popular amusements here – the people organized dances and outings into the countryside. The festivities lasted throughout the month of May, and were the time for the young to find a *novio* or *novia*. The month after there were the very popular fiestas of St. Peter and St. Paul; and in September village and religious life reached its peak with the festivities for the patron saint. A month, two months before, the young men and women were dreaming of the *feria*, of their new clothes, their new shoes – of the very little they could buy then in

* A jar with a skin stretched over the mouth through which a reed is rubbed up and down, producing a hoarse and monotonous sound.

comparison with only a few years later and the advent of tourism.

In November, for All Souls, the whole village went to the cemetery to light a candle for the deceased. The cemetery was open all night; and that too became a fiesta. The bars stayed open, stalls sold sweets. . . . Happiness, sadness, amusement were so much a part of religious faith, which in itself was so strong, that it was impossible to separate these different elements in village life.

As in all these villages, the people of Tajos had a great deal of faith and very little religious education. For this reason, like many another priest in the same situation, I supported the local traditions. In all sincerity, it seemed better to me to try to favour those customs that had some good in them, even if they weren't totally good, rather than try to create new customs to replace them. It's very difficult to create new traditions. For example, the quite undeniable fact, as far as Andalusia is concerned, that men consider the church a 'woman's affair'. The Andalusian man is very special in this respect and he justifies not going to church by saying that women have less to do than he and thus more time for church. In Andalusia traditionally the women haven't worked outside the home – unlike in Galicia, say – and so the woman here has always been a señora. 'Obligations before devotion,' say the men and by and large leave churchgoing to the women who, moreover, have a greater sensibility for religion than they. But the slogan of obligation before devotion is exploited to such an extent that it sometimes seems as though it means getting to the tavern before one's neighbour!

The lack of religious education has gone hand in hand with a general lack of culture. It's no secret that in my time in Tajos over 50 percent of the population was illiterate. There was a bishop of Málaga who said that before preaching about God you had to see that the people were properly fed. That's the truth. And not only that – though it's the most important – you have to see that their minds have been formed, that they have education. What good is there in talking to the starving about philosophy? Or to a man without education about faith and religion which are above culture? This is why, in all that I've been saying about religious life in the village, it will appear that it is of the heart and feelings of the people that I have spoken, not of their convictions.

The lack of education is largely explained, as elsewhere, by the scattered rural population. When I was in Tajos, 80 percent of the country school-age children had no school to go to. One of the finest acts undertaken by Bishop Angel Herrera of Málaga, who later became Cardinal, was to create rural schools throughout the province in collaboration with the state. His basic idea was that the teachers to staff the schools must come from the countryside. He or she must be able to talk to the children in their own language. Moreover, a city-trained teacher would always be looking for ways of leaving the countryside; sooner or later, he or she would succeed on some pretext, and put in a substitute teacher; the school in short would be abandoned. So don Angel created a corps of rural teachers who did a crash course of two or three years. This permitted a number of the rural young to attain a profession, but at the same time their training was not sufficient for them to go to the towns looking for a job.

Six of these rural schools were opened in my time and they've had wonderful results. Half school, half chapel; I used to visit them on horseback periodically to say mass, and it was always one of my joys.

A priest's life in Andalusia is made up of more than his spiritual role. The people think a priest can solve everything, they come to him for all sorts of administrative matters. Someone hasn't been able to collect his old-age pension, another has a relative who has been arrested, the hospital has refused to admit a third. For atavistic reasons, a priest here is thought of as the man who can get everything done. Sometimes I'd say to myself, 'Why was I ordained? To preach the word of God or to spend all my time fixing up papers?' But as St. Paul said, the way to the soul is through the body; the priest's role is as much human and social as religious, perhaps even more so.

This idea, so common among ordinary people in Andalusian villages, must be understood in its historical perspective. In former times the priest was one of the three or four people in a village who were educated, who read the papers. There was a custom then to meet in the pharmacist's backroom – *la rebotica*, as it came to be called. The pharmacist, the priest, the doctor, a few landlords – the village aristocracy – met there to talk and play cards. Anyone who wanted a favour would go there. Since those with education were usually the rich, the priest would be confused with them, though he was poor. The people always thought there was collusion between priest and authorities; there was no getting it out of their heads. 'And who goes?' they'd say when there was an official function. 'The mayor, the priest and all the authorities. . . .' Such is the mentality of the Spanish that the priest, however much on occasion he has had to oppose them, has ever since been associated by the people with the rich and powerful.

This has been a terrible handicap for the church and very prejudicial to religion. The church today is opposed to this power, it wants no longer to be identified with the actions of the state, whatever they are.

Look at what happened before and during our civil war. The people associated the church with the rich, the ruling classes. They attacked and burned churches, killed priests. . . . When the war was over, the defeated associated the church again with the victors. All this has done the church considerable harm. Had the church then adopted the view it takes today of being separate from – though not hostile to – the state, much of what happened might not have come to pass. The church need not have been confused with the state, and consequently blamed for all sorts of social injustices for which it wasn't responsible. Also, had the church not gone on vegetating in its past ways, many social injustices would have been dealt with and the revolutionary outbreak would not have been so sudden, so tremendous. In saying that, I don't want to judge individual ecclesiastics of those times by the standards of ours because, in my view, man's biggest error is to judge another century by the values of the moment. Adopting such a position might mean that the next century will consider us all idiots, or perhaps even heretics and barbarians!

The smaller the village the more difficult a priest's work, in my experience. Not that people are better or worse depending on the size of the village; simply that in a small one it's often more difficult to influence people and get to the bottom of things. The mayor, the judge, all the authorities in a small place are dependent on relatives and friends whom they can't offend or take action against. As priest I would go to one or other of them and he might be willing to correct some injustice; but as it's his brother-in-law who is committing it, well, he's sorry but there's nothing he can do! I mean, if it's the law that a man can't pick esparto somewhere – well, that's the law; but if that man has no other means of livelihood and will starve if he can't pick an armful of esparto, a priest knows that putting him in jail is no solution. I admit I went through some bad moments in Tajos with this sort of thing. Some I could solve, but I confess with all humility that many times I was unable to.

However, one has to admit that those in power in a small village are not open to authentic religious reasoning on the part of a priest. One can't persuade them by moral arguments. No. I had to go to them with stronger arguments, I had to remind them that only a month or so before they had taken no action against X or Y and that this could well become known. I had to threaten them really that some sharp practice of theirs which I knew about would come to light unless. . . . One has to use these rather devious means which, coming from a person of influence like a priest, makes the other say: 'Ah! I'm trapped. . . .'

In Spain a priest is always the subject of criticism, you know. When he does something that's bad he's just a priest; when he does something good then he's don Vicente or whatever his name is. Don X is always good, but not the priest! In a small village, especially, it's not his work that's appreciated; it's whether he's sympathetic, whether he gets on with people that counts. The social mission is as important as the religious one.

It has been a great advantage for me to have been born the son of a small peasant. I come from the village of Junquera in the folds of the Serrania of Ronda. I thank God and with all sincerity to have been born in a poor family, to have known what sacrifice and hard work mean, and moreover to have lived through those difficult post-war years. In the seminary we ate badly and little enough as it was, but during Lent we fasted voluntarily. Until I came down here I had never known what it was to bathe in hot water. In Tajos there was no bathroom in the priest's house. How are those who have all the comforts in their youth going to solve difficulties in their adult lives? No, I give thanks to God for this; he who hasn't suffered knows nothing at all.

Don Vicente was transferred to Casas Nuevas in 1960 after little less than three years in Tajos. Some of the difficulties he encountered with the local authorities, which he refuses to discuss in more than generalities, give an insight into the workings of the village. As the members of the ruling group are equally reluctant to discuss such matters, one incident, amply authenticated, may serve as an example.

Not long before don Vicente left Tajos an order went out from Málaga for the provincial population to be vaccinated against smallpox. The Tajos doctor at the time charged five pesetas per person for the vaccination. In fact these were to be done free as part of the public immunization campaign. When don Vicente heard of the charge, about which several families were protesting, he obliged the doctor to return all the money he had already taken. As the doctor was a powerful man with solid friendships among the ruling group, the latter thereafter did not look with favour on their priest.

Today, it should be added, don Vicente's admonitions about the role of the priest as one of the ruling group have been heeded in Tajos. The present incumbent, recently appointed, plays no part in village politics; indeed his presence, unlike that of his predecessors, is barely visible: sports trousers and open-necked shirt have, under the new Vatican dispositions, replaced the prominent black cassock, biretta and tonsure of a few years ago.

NEW MEN

The Ruling Group

As a result of the civil war a new class came to power in Tajos. Its basis did not rest on landownership as (exemplified by the Tejadas) had been the case up to the war; nor on a mixture of commerce and land as in the case of the self-made Lopezs and Saenzs who, by the 1930s, were threatening the previously dominant landowners' position.

The new class was very much a product of the nationalist victory and the rapid growth of a new bureaucracy. Stimulated by the regime's policy of rewarding the rural petite bourgeoisie for its support during the war, the bureaucracy doubled in numbers nationally in the decade from 1940. Its one and a half million members were then nearly three times as numerous as in 1930.

Enough has been said about the post-war period for it to be unnecessary to stress the reasons for this enormous increase; the bureaucracy's role was one of control. Its growth, however, also served another function: to provide the consumers necessary for economic growth. To fulfil this function it had to be relatively well remunerated. Forming approximately one-quarter of the working population in 1950 it took 40 percent of the national income; the 49 percent of the working population engaged in agriculture received by comparison only 27 percent.

In Tajos as elsewhere state intervention in agriculture, rationing, the corporate trade union, provided this new bureaucracy with its means of ascendancy. Among the new ruling group in the village was a sprinkling of local shop-keepers and professionals, firmly committed to the new regime by background and personal experience. Their allegiance was publicly displayed in a plaque raised on the town hall celebrating the village's liberation from 'the Marxist Hordes' by 'Franco's Imperial Crusade'.

A son of the founder of the Saenz family fortune in Tajos was mayor of the village briefly in the 1940s; it was he who made the victory speech quoted earlier. But from the time of his death in 1942 no landowner of any consequence has again been mayor.

This is not to infer that the remaining landowners are no longer part of the ruling group; but rather to stress that the new bureaucrats and professionals have become the domi-nant members and exercise power on the group's behalf.

In popular idiom the ruling group is identified as *la gente gorda* – the fat people. The villagers endlessly watch, discuss and embroider on their use and abuse of power. However bitter their feelings, they are slow to protest to higher authority; even the private 'appropriation' of water affecting the whole village has, in the past, produced no immediate action.

A certain village *unión* plays its part, no doubt; but the reasons are more complex. The need to keep in with those in power is one. For it is the bureaucrats who are the links with the central authority, it is they who have the 'contacts', who can 'arrange things': the documents and permissions, the pensions and social security arrangements which are too complex for the majority of villagers to handle except through them. In such a situation it seems folly to a villager to run the risk of reprisal by overtly challenging local authority; indeed, until recently, when the system of pay-ment was changed, old-age pensioners 'tipped' the local official fifteen or twenty pesetas each time he paid them their 400 to 500 pesetas monthly pensions. Though such overt 'keeping in well' with officialdom is not common, there are other, more subtle ways. In return those in power often 'bend the rules' to do individual villagers a favour.

The new men – like the revolutionaries before them – were young when they came to power. They continue to form the core of the local ruling group to this day.

FRANCISCO TRUJILLO   *Fifty-five*

Town hall official

A native of Ronda, he and his mother joined his sister in Tajos where she had been appointed as teacher, in September 1936. As soon as he got off the bus he was arrested. 'Simply for not being known. I was held in jail an hour while the communist committee made enquiries and my sister came to vouch for me. The fact of wearing a tie was enough for them to call one a fascist.' He survived without further detentions and served in the nationalist army. Trained as a teacher, he did not want to leave the village for a post elsewhere on his return at the end of the war, and took the examinations to become an official in the town hall. He worked under Jaime Naranjo and later took over his post when the latter retired. At the end of the war he joined the Falange and has remained a convinced falangista ever since.

I became a member because I saw that the Falange's doctrine was the only one that suits Spain. The cause of all the bestiality of the civil war – I'll tell you, it stemmed from ideas imported from other countries. Ideas from the east, ideas of extermination. The communist party was bestial in Spain and it dominated every-thing in the red zone. If we had been left to resolve our own problems there might have been no bloodshed at all.

One man, José Antonio,* had the solution. He was a prophet, just as Karl Marx was the prophet of the communist movement,

* José Antonio Primo de Rivera, son of the dictator and founder before the civil war of the Falange. He was executed after trial in the Republican zone during the war.

and the proof lies in the fact that the Spanish government today is founded on his ideals. But at the time everyone called him a fascist and wouldn't listen to him. He wasn't a fascist, he was one hundred percent Spanish and he died for his ideals.

Spain should be one, great and free – those were his ideals. Being one meant an end to separatism, the separatism of the Catalans and Basques. Great – well, everyone wants their house to be great, don't they? And free – free from any type of foreign interference, for in Spain the English and the French and everyone but the Spanish government ruled the country. No more foreign ideas. We Spaniards have a form of being which cannot assimilate the politics of England or Norway. . . .

'To be a Spaniard is a very serious thing,' José Antonio used to say. 'Spain is a unity of destiny in the universal,' that was the first point in the Falange's programme. Everywhere before the civil war there was disunion, each one went his own way, there were fights. And this man said, no! everyone should be united, everyone should work together in harmony, the employee and the employer, the state should see to the education and employment of the people, create public works.

They compared him to Hitler and Mussolini whose fascist doctrines were in vogue in Europe then. But they were imperialists, they wanted to break out of their frontiers, appropriate other countries. José Antonio wanted none of this, all he wanted was that Spain should be united, strong and free. Great but without imperialist aspirations;* liberty but without libertinism.

For me the Falange is the point of departure, the basis of everything the government has done and is doing today. But I'm not a falangista of the type people like to think, the falangista of the arm outstretched in salute – no, no. Not a fascist, because for me fascism is the salute and being in favour of gas-chambers like the Nazis. I could never be that; people are mistaken if they think the Falange is fascist in the style of Hitler and Mussolini.

I hate violence, all killing repels me. On one side or the other. Of course, the nationalists had to execute people when they captured a place during the civil war. Take this village, for

---

* Point 3 of the above-mentioned programme, now often forgotten, proclaims: 'We have an Imperial determination. We affirm that Spain's historical plenitude resides in Empire.'

example. Here six people were shot by the reds – but fifty people went out to do the killing, all fifty had blood on their hands. When the nationalists came in and caught those fifty they had all to be shot. That's not a black legend, that's the pure truth.

In war it's always possible that innocent people are killed, it's possible there were cases of injustice. But those fifty didn't die just like that, they were tried first by courts martial. What else could be done? Their hands were stained with blood and they had to die. The relatives of those they had shot were demanding it. Perhaps, looking back, it may seem a bad thing, but at the time there was no one who could voice such a thought. I don't believe anyone should have been killed by one side or the other. God creates man, it should be God who kills him, not other men.

War is cruel, all wars are cruel. Ours left a gap for people of my generation; everyone had relatives who died on one side or the other. It's a wound that's healing, it's better forgotten. . . . War is an affair of the big capitalists, of those who produce and sell arms. They don't care whether ten or twenty million people die. The whole of humanity ought to oppose them, rise up and burn down their factories. Instead of using the money to slaughter innocent people, women and children, it ought to be used to bring food to the people of India, to the blacks of Africa. The world would be a much better place then.

Politics is a dirty word for me, I don't believe in it. To me it means demagogy of the sort Spain knew before the war. Politicians would come to a village like this and agree that something must be done, a school built, a road constructed – and once they'd left nothing more was heard of the project. A lot of talk and very few deeds. A good politician, as far as I'm concerned, is one who is entirely dedicated to his country. That's what was lacking before – dedication. A man became a politician because his father had been one. Politics and squabbling were this country's downfall.

Of course, there were tremendous social distinctions then. The aristocrat in his club who couldn't even talk directly to a shoe-shine boy but had to speak to him through the doorman. Such great differences were certainly one of the causes of the civil war. Differences between peasants and middle class, between the middle class and the aristocracy. Such distinctions are always bad, the one who is at the bottom feels humiliated. Why should a man whom society has placed at the top speak with disdain to another as though he were a negro? No, if a person has another's foot on his neck all the time a moment must come when he says: 'This has got to finish now.'

I'm a realist, I believe only in facts. Reality today bears the name of Francisco Franco. In the whole history of Spain, including Ferdinand and Isabella, Philip II, Charles V, there has been no other ruler of this country who has so entirely devoted himself to its people. From the age of seventeen he was struggling to save Spain – and from that you can understand the sort of man he is and why I have such faith in him. He is a Spaniard, he is beyond definition, you can't say he is another El Cid because he is much more than that.

As long as Franco lives we know that we're protected, that nothing will happen, that we don't have to worry about anything. He is like the good father who says to his children, 'Go out and play, eat, don't worry about anything because I have the reins in my hand. . . .' He has lived through all the bad times in Spain, he knows where it hurts when someone steps on one, he knows the virtues and defects of this country.

This is why no one is interested in politics any more. Before, the people were always reading the papers and thinking about politics. Now they don't, now what they look for is sport, football, anything but politics. And that's because they know they're protected by Franco. Of course, he isn't eternal, but I don't believe there's any danger there, because today the Spaniard is better educated; moreover, all the links have been secured, all the cords of the succession firmly tied up.

He leans back with satisfaction in the easy chair, part of a three-piece leather suite which stands in the living-room of his home. Here the traditional whitewashed walls have disappeared under imitation wood panelling and reproduction oil paintings. Carpet replaces the customary floor tiles and 'antiqued' furniture the plain wood chairs and brazier. It is the house of the newly prosperous lower middle class and to date has no rival in the village. He has a car and keeps a flat in Málaga where his daughters are studying; he and his wife spend most weekends and holidays in the city.

Little seen about the village outside office hours (which in summer end at two p.m.), he had one stroke of fortune which may explain the affluence, otherwise inexplicable on a village civil servant's salary, and around which he prefers to draw a discreet veil. In 1949 he staked claims to quarry mica he had discovered in the countryside around the village. He sold part of the rights to a mining company which exploited the mineral and gave work to 400 to 500 people in the village. The quarrying lasted until 1953 when the company collapsed due, according to him, to foreign competition.

MANUEL FERNANDEZ   *Forty-seven*

Vet, ex-mayor, and justice of the peace

Brother-in-law of Francisco Trujillo, who married his sister, don Manuel is the only Tajeño of his generation to have completed a university degree. His father was a baker, his mother the licence-holder of the village tobacco shop. On the village schoolmaster's advice they made the financial sacrifice of sending their only son to boarding-school in Málaga. On his return from the university of Córdoba in 1946, his father wanted him to remain in the village. The post of state-appointed vet in Tajos was held by the vet of Casas Nuevas; in consequence don Manuel set up in private practice. He married a pharmacist from another village and they started what was, until recently, the only chemist shop in the village. The shop and his house are a few doors up from the Trujillos in the square. In 1957, as tourism was just beginning, he was appointed mayor in succession to the man of esparto fame during the famine years.

One day I was working quietly in my house when a man came in. I didn't know him; he introduced himself as the Civil Governor's delegate. 'The Governor wants you to be mayor of the village.' It was a complete surprise, I didn't know anything about it. At first I didn't want to accept. The delegate appealed to my patriotism, to the service I could render my country and village. At last I agreed. Being in my thirties at the time I thought I had the energy to try to achieve something here. Moreover, the delegate filled me with a sense of patriotism.

Mayors are always appointed in this way.* The Civil Governor sends a delegate to a village to ask questions and get suggestions of possible people. It's done pretty much in secret. The delegate talks to the priest, the Guardia Civil sergeant who knows everyone's conduct, the mayors of neighbouring villages and anyone else he wants to. Then he draws up a confidential report on each of the people suggested, their jobs, their personal behaviour and private life, their age, and from this the Governor chooses a mayor.

The village was still poor in those days. The financial situation was the most serious I faced. The village budget was approximately 300,000 pesetas a year but frankly there wasn't anything like that sum coming in, even after the state subsidy which is made up of a percentage of the taxes collected. After the war a tax-farming system was introduced in villages: the tax collection was auctioned to the highest bidder, the town hall assessing the total amount due to be collected. The tax collector's bid was usually something like 20 to 25 percent below the assessed figure. This system, which has been abolished now, had the advantage that the money was paid immediately to the town hall. But all the same, very few of the taxes in force then were being paid. I don't know why but the town hall didn't bother to collect them. So the first thing I did was to enforce payment of all legal taxes in existence – taxes on house drainage, the movement of animals in the village, on lorries and cars using garages, the *plus-valia*.† In the six years I was mayor, the budget rose to six million pesetas annually, in part because taxes were now being collected, but of course largely because of tourism and the number of foreigners' houses being built.

* The system used in municipalities of less than 10,000 inhabitants under the monarchy and reintroduced after the civil war. Under the Republic mayors were elected. The Civil Governor of a province however, has always been a government appointee.
† A form of capital gains tax on the sale of land and buildings.

For a number of years it had rained very little and soon after I became mayor the *mina* from which the village was drawing its water dried up completely. The mayor before me had laid pipes from the *mina* to the village square, a distance of nearly two kilometres; before that people had to depend on springs. That year, 1957, everything dried up. There was only one small spring for the whole village. I got a water engineer to come up: should we dig the *mina* deeper or look for water elsewhere? He said that a few good miners would get water from the *mina* in a month or two. That was fine – but where was the money to come from? The town hall had none. We had a meeting of everyone who irrigated as far as Casas Nuevas with water from the *mina*. They agreed to pay so much for every hour of water they owned, but said the town hall must also contribute. I agreed but without telling them that there was no money available. It was a bit of deception on my part, I'll admit, but with the 30,000 to 40,000 pesetas they paid we were able to start work.

I'll never forget it – the day I came back from Málaga to find the whole village waiting for me – 18 March 1958. The church bell was pealing. An enormous quantity of water had been struck. I went straight out to the *mina* and, although I had a new suit on, I climbed down into the water, I was so happy. There was enormous joy in the village that day.

When the Civil Governor saw that I had managed to solve the water problem with the help of the people, he conceded a credit of half a million pesetas, if I remember rightly, to lay pipes throughout the village.

There's a saying here that a child who doesn't cry doesn't suckle and that's the truth. A mayor's task is always one of crying for money, asking for ten in order to get one. I was always writing to the Civil Governor, going to see him, pleading for money to get things done. That's how at last I got agreement for the road up from Casas Nuevas to be surfaced and widened in parts. I kept saying that as long as it remained unpaved and full of potholes no tourists would come to Tajos.

I had thought for a long time that Tajos could have a tourist future, and the things I set out to do were with that in mind. For a start the people had to be disciplined in the matter of cleanliness. Until then they had been used to leaving their animals in the streets, their pigs in the square; they threw litter in the streets and didn't whitewash their houses often enough. I ordered the houses to be whitewashed and gave various orders about keeping animals. I had to impose a few fines on the more recalcitrant, though I don't like punishing anyone, to set an example so that the people should know I meant what I said. . . .

Yes, I know, the people here like to say that mayors 'eat' money from the town hall. When the delegate came to propose that I should become mayor I had a car on order. In those days it took three or four months to get one. I told the delegate the people would say I had bought it with money from the town hall coffers. 'No, no,' he said, 'they won't say anything.' But of course they did, especially since I was only the second person to have a private car here!

In fact what could be 'eaten' from the town hall when there was so little money anyway? There was only just enough to pay the employees, the street lighting and all the other costs. Being mayor actually cost me money, because in villages of under 10,000 inhabitants it is an honorific, unpaid job. It would be better if it were paid, in my view, because a mayor could then devote himself entirely to his work and not have his life complicated by private business. Suppose, for example, another vet had come here but, because I was mayor, the people had continued to come to me; well, I would have been unfairly in competition with him. And when you've said vet you've said doctor, pharmacist or whatever.

Being mayor cost me money and it cost me friends. We're all human after all, there are always some who don't like what's being done, especially if they see a mayor putting the law into effect. So they turn themselves into the mayor's enemies – well, if not enemies, no longer friends, let's say. That's what happened to me.

It was so demanding a job that in the end I had to go to the Civil Governor and tell him my personal affairs were in disarray because I hadn't the time to attend to them. There was always this or that meeting in Málaga, having to go to Casas Nuevas to greet a visiting government minister, as well as attending to all the different problems in the village itself, being available to see people if they needed something. . . . I had no time for myself, my family or my business.

I went back to running our chemist shop and to my profession.

I've always liked animals and that's why I became a vet. I believe it's quite incorrect to say the Spanish don't love animals. Perhaps the difference is that they don't show it as much as the English, for example. They love their dogs, they love birds – the only animal they have little affection for, I don't know why, is the cat. Every house has one but not because people really care for them but to keep down mice.

I've never known any cases of deliberate ill-treatment of animals. Donkeys are well-cared for as a rule; a donkey is a very useful animal, after all. As a work animal it has the big advantage of not needing a great deal of food and is very economic as a result.

Today my only official position is as justice of the peace. The title sums up my task: to make peace. Most of the cases are settled amicably through reconciliation. They are small affairs as a rule: disagreements about land boundaries, a farmer's complaint about another's goats straying on to his land, things of that sort. If I can't reconcile the two parties in advance I hear the case. Each of the parties is represented by an *hombre bueno* of his choosing; why they're called good men I don't know but their presence means that the disputants don't have to talk or deal directly with one another. After listening to the evidence, the prosecutor – the village postman here – demands the fine he thinks appropriate. I have three days to reflect on the case; the highest fine I can impose is 500 pesetas. If the disputants disagree with the verdict they can appeal to the higher court. It's all kept as simple as possible. But the most important thing is to try to reconcile the parties, to get them to shake hands and leave feeling that the solution is fair to both of them.

REMEDIOS REYES *Forty-eight*

Midwife

Two years before don Manuel became mayor Remedios Reyes came to Tajos as state-appointed midwife. A lively woman, she is a native of Antequera where her grandfather was a large landowner. Her childhood was happy until, at the age of thirteen, the civil war broke out. Antequera fell rapidly into nationalist hands but not before six of her cousins had been shot. Her father, she maintains, was saved because he aged so rapidly under the stress that when 'they' came to search the house her mother pretended that he was her grandparent. Claiming to be older than she was Remedios got a job in a hospital tending the war-wounded. Later she went on to study midwifery. Tajos was her first official post; she has remained there uninterruptedly since her arrival in 1955.

Uy! I don't want to remember the day I came here. I got to Málaga and the village taxi hadn't arrived; it only made the trip every other day. They told me to take the bus to Casas Nuevas and try from there. I saw a taxi driver and went over to him. 'I'm not driving up that road in the terrible state it's in.' I told him I was the midwife and had to reach Tajos. At last he agreed. As we bounced from one pothole to another I kept wondering where the village was. 'You see those few little lights up there,' the driver said, 'that's Tajos.' And I thought to myself, 'Where have I got landed now?'

The village seemed hideous. The people were very poor, living off esparto-gathering and plaiting, there was no life at all. I didn't know anyone, it never stopped raining, and I was so miserable that I shut myself up in my room and cried. All I had was my work.

The first birth I was called to was in a very poor house. The only light in the small room where the woman was lying on a mattress on the floor was a wick dipped in oil. I asked another woman to bring the oil lamp closer so I could examine her. At that moment she had a contraction and her water burst all over the lamp. 'Ay, in God's name light another lamp!' I called. 'I can't, the wick's soaked,' replied the other. All the while the woman was moaning that she was going to die. I put my hand down to feel and there was something hard – the baby's head! Our Lord came to my aid, I know it was He who gave me the inspiration to go on. I felt for the head to see if it had anything round its neck. But there was nothing. I pulled and in a few moments I had a baby crying in my hands. 'What is it?' the mother asked, 'a boy or a girl?' 'Wait, wait until we get a light,' I had to reply. I was so nervous from the tension that when I got home all I could do was cry.

After that my father bought me a torch. I had to use it very often because so few houses had electricity. In many of them I couldn't expect to find alcohol for sterilizing, nor gauze nor anything other than a bit of cotton for tying the baby's cord. No one had a bathroom and not many had toilets. To relieve yourself it was out in the open against the wall of the patio. How many times, during long waits, I've had to hold myself in rather than go out in the dark among the animals in the patio. What a change there has been since then – and it's only sixteen years ago!

Before I came, from what the people say, there were only a few amateur midwives. One of them used to make esparto plaits while she waited. She never washed her hands, she'd lay down the esparto and put her hand in the woman to see how close the birth was. Then she'd use the scissors from the esparto for cutting the baby's cord. There was another who lay in bed beside the woman in labour and kept her finger inside her to be sure to know when the baby's head was approaching. If the woman was too small for the baby's passage it was the custom among these amateur midwives to tie the mother to a chair and – without anaesthetic – to slit her with a silver coin. Why silver I don't know. The incision was never sewn up; many of the older women never healed properly and still bear the marks.

A lot of women used to haemorrhage to death. Thanks to God, it's never happened to me. I've had cases out in the countryside which I've had to attend to alone because it would have taken the doctor two hours to reach the farmstead on a donkey. I'd pray to Saint Ramon Nonato, the midwife's patron saint, and I've always pulled them through. They're rough and tough, these country women; they work like men, they give birth in the morning and like as not they're out washing clothes in the afternoon.

But however tough they are they always give vent to their pain, they cry and scream that they're going to die. Sometimes it's their mothers who are the worst. There's one – God forgive me – whom I have had to throw out of the room. Every time her daughter gives birth she comes in and screams, 'Ay! my daughter, she's dying. Can't you see her face? Look my daughter's dying.'

Most husbands go to the tavern while their wives are giving birth. But there was one woman I remember who insisted that her husband sit by her bed. With every contraction she grabbed him round the waist. He was sick for a week afterwards with the pain.

They say there was a woman once who told her husband he ought to suffer like her. She attached a rope round his private parts and over a beam and each time she had a contraction she pulled. I don't know if it's true but the people swear to it.

When I first came lots of children died young. The people thought a baby's stomach had to be stuffed full to keep it alive. When it got diarrhoea they fed it more. 'This one has got to learn to eat,' they'd say, and they gave it crumbs of bread soaked in anis. Of course that upset their stomachs even more.

They suckled their children until the age of three or four – very often lying with the baby in their arms and their nipple in its mouth all night. 'Look,' I told them, 'you go all night without eating, it's the same with a baby.' But there was no way of getting the older mothers to believe me, and so their babies continued to get sick from over-eating and often enough died. The mothers did it out of pure ignorance. I remember being called to a farmstead and, seeing an old woman, asked where was her daughter who was giving birth. 'Señorita, it's for me.' Her face was so wrinkled I wondered how old she was. Thirty! It came from suckling her children too long and living on too poor a diet herself.

Everyone's diet was insufficient in those times. They hardly ate meat, they said fruit was too dear and the only green vegetables they ate were swiss chard and cabbage. Though you can grow just about everything here – carrots, beetroot, celery, parsley – the people didn't think they were good for them.

Some of the older children had rickets. Mothers fed their babies on barley coffee, thickened with lots of sugar and no milk and with bits of bread in it. When they gave them milk it was condensed, which is bad because it has too much sugar. I used to tell them that this wasn't a proper diet for a baby. 'We grew up on it,' they replied. 'Well, you were lucky then,' I said, 'but that doesn't mean it's right.'

All this has changed now. The people eat properly, they look after their children's diet with great care. When a woman gets pregnant she comes to see me and I tell her what she'll need and send her to the doctor for examination. Many women go to

Málaga to have their babies which costs them nothing thanks to Social Security. There are all sorts of prepared baby foods which they buy: children's health has improved enormously in these past years. Diphtheria, polio, typhoid, tetanus – those are things of the past. The 'summer sickness' which came from alimentary upsets and lack of hygiene in the houses is a thing of the past. Today I doubt whether more than one unweaned baby a year dies.

I believe I've done a lot to help educate them. But the greatest thanks must go to Franco for all these social improvements. What a fine man – he is like God to the people. In all truth, we love him as though he were a father, a father who loves his children greatly and who, from time to time, has to punish them if they do wrong. Isn't that what a father has to do with his children? And now Franco has grown old, not so much with years but with suffering so greatly and taking so much responsibility for us. I would give a year of my life – not only I but the majority of Spaniards – if it would add a year to his.

Look at the Spain Franco took over: ruined, destroyed! And look at it today. Recognized, loved and admired by every country in the world; if it weren't, so many foreign tourists wouldn't come here, would they? It's because they know this is a tranquil country. Yes, I'm a Spaniard and a one hundred percent patriot; for me Spain is the best country in the world.

I've been a falangista since I was a child; in consequence I was happy to be put in charge of the Falange's Woman's Section here. Just as military service is obligatory for men, so every woman has to do her social service. For six months she has to attend classes in cooking, dress-making, running a home, looking after children – a hundred things of the sort. I've got six or seven girls going through now; they start at sixteen. Of course, there are more girls of that age in the village, but they think they don't need to do the course. They forget that the social service diploma is necessary to be able to go to university, to get a passport, to get a state post, even to get a driving licence.

The Falange has done a great job in keeping alive traditional regional dancing. My group has won many prizes for its flamenco dancing and has been to Madrid to appear on TV. I collected the local dances, *fandangos* and *tanguillos* from an old lady here and the verses that went with them. Marvellous they are, I used to wonder how people with so little culture had been able to invent such fine *coplas*. We Spanish all have a bit of the poet in us, you know. Listen:

> Si tu madre no me quiere
> *If your mother doesn't like me*
> Que se haga la puñeta,
> *Let her go to hell,*
> Que en teniendo yo el clavé
> *If I've won the flower*
> Pa' qué quiero la maceta.
> *I don't need the flowerpot as well.*

The people are very witty. They invent nicknames in a flash. Everyone here has one and they're often passed down from generation to generation. Usually people don't know a family by their real name but only by the nickname. There are whole generations of Satans, Little Stars, Bad Feet. I imagine a woman looking at her newborn and saying, 'Ay, what a tiny prick he's got,' because the poor man has been 'tiny prick' for the rest of his life.

There was another custom that used to amuse me when I first came. Every now and again ghosts appeared in the street. The people firmly believed in them. There would be this long white figure with flickering eyes waving its arms to stop anyone passing down the street. A ghost! In reality, some man who wanted to go to see a woman he had no business to be seeing! He'd put one of those round cork beehives over his head, on top a gourd with three holes cut out and a candle inside, and over his body a sheet. Then a 'ghost' would appear and the people were frightened and turned back so that the man could slip unseen into the woman's house.

There were children enough in those days who weren't born legitimately. Those of different fathers and those born a bit early. 'Eating the stew before it's cooked,' the villagers say. Many mothers try to make out that their babies are seven-month pregnancies. I tell them they can try that on other people but I know when a baby is full-term. There was one I remember who had her child two weeks before her wedding. 'It could have waited a couple of weeks, couldn't it?' the girl's mother grumbled. 'What it should have done was wait until nine months after the wedding,' I replied.

ANTONIO MORENO   *Forty-one*

Trade union official

I've been a falangista since the end of the war, since I was a boy.
I joined the youth movement then and at eighteen I became a full
member. My parents were poor, my father made *alpargatas* for a
living. I know what poverty is like; during the war when my three
brothers were serving in the nationalist army we had to try to live
on what my father earned. He couldn't keep us alive by making
alpargatas so he started a small tavern as well. You won't see
anything like that tavern here today; his was just a counter and
three or four bottles. When someone asked for a coffee the bottle
of rum or *aguardiente* was put on the counter and the man
helped himself. As long as a customer was at the counter my
father stayed open. And sometimes that was all night.

I went to the village school; I've had no other education. From
almost as far back as I can recall the Falange's ideals seemed the
only ones for me. I remember the horrors, the bestiality and
destruction of the revolution well enough for that. The Falange
stood for everything that was opposed to such horror: respect
for property which was non-existent before; respect for religion –
whatever religion anyone wishes to profess, though our religion
is catholicism – which Marxism never respected. And then all
the social improvements which didn't exist and which have
raised the country's standard of living.

After I left school I got a job in the town hall, working in the
rations department; for each ration card issued I received twenty-
five centimos instead of a wage. Everything was rationed, including tobacco. The people used to get up to all sorts of tricks. A man
whose wife was called Juana would cross off the final letter of
her name and claim another tobacco card as a man! You had to
be on the look-out all the time. Then there were rumours that the
milk which was being sent as part of American aid was poisoned.
I don't know how the rumours started but the people firmly
believed them. The poor didn't drink the milk – but for another
reason. They sold it to buy bread, and their children were lucky
if they ever tasted milk.

In 1950, when I was twenty, I was appointed to the trade union post I've held ever since. It's the Brotherhood of Farmers and Livestock Breeders which is part of the single trade union, the CNS, in Spain. At that time all union posts were appointed, not elected as they are now.

The ideals of the Falange and of the union are almost identical. Indeed, from the start the Falange spoke of a vertical trade union incorporating workers and employers. That was what was wrong before the war – the employers who thought of a worker only as an element of labour. But no! A man, apart from being a worker, has a soul. As José Antonio used to say, before saving the man one must save his soul which is the bearer of eternal values.

I think it's a good thing that employers and employees are both represented in the *sindicato*. The workers and bosses are more united that way. When there are problems affecting both sides, they meet round a table. 'Come on, all get down to it together,' I tell them. And that's how things get resolved.

Employers and employees have their own section and meet separately except when there are common problems. Each now elects its own delegates every three years and the delegates together elect a president. The workers' section is for the day-labourers; the employers' section includes renters and share-croppers among the landowners. Every worker or person active in agriculture is a *sindicato* member. They don't have to join; we enroll them automatically.

As recently as nine years ago the entire working population was employed in agriculture. There were 920 day-labourers and 1,175 self-employed on the land. By then, thanks to God, there wasn't the unemployment of the 1940s and 1950s; a quarter of the day-labourers were out of work at any one time in those bad years. The *sindicato* had to allocate hundreds of labourers for a week at a time to different landlords during the worst of the winter months so that the workers could earn something.

As things got better one major problem remained: irrigation. What a headache this has been! The hours I've spent trying to get the people to agree. Water there's enough of, but a lot of it is lost. New irrigation channels are needed – but could I get the people to agree how to set about the work! Never! One says the costs ought to be paid by the hour of water owned, another by the metre of channel crossing each farm, another something else. . . .

They can never agree. And what never enters their heads, however much I insist, is the legal and also most sensible solution: by area irrigated. There are always one or two who won't have it.

The government is prepared to give loans for irrigation improvements; but then the landowner with a bit of capital says, 'What do I need a loan for?' without realizing that unless the poorer owners' costs are covered by a loan nothing will get done. There's a certain amount of egoism in all this. And also lack of foresight. The landowner thinks about irrigation only when there's been no rain for a couple of years. Then he clamours, 'Something has got to be done.' But nothing in the end gets done. I've organized innumerable meetings, I've brought up experts, I've tried to persuade the people – but without success.

However, having irrigation committees within the Brotherhood has put an end to all the fights over water that used to occur when people came to blows over their rights. The farmers are a bit more civilized today than they used to be.

There's another important function of the Brotherhood I want to mention and that's the conciliation committee.

Any worker who has a complaint against his employer can appeal to this committee which is composed of a representative of both the workers' and employers' sides and presided over by a delegate. The most usual complaints are over pay and dismissal, though the latter is less common now that there's full employment. The employer is summoned to the hearing and there every endeavour is made to come to an agreement. In my experience it's almost always the worker who is in the right. If he has had to come to the conciliation committee it's because he can't get satisfaction from his employer.

Before the war a landowner could throw a sharecropper or renter off his land whenever he wanted. A man who had perhaps spent years breaking the soil to win a living from it could be thrown out when he got too old to produce enough for the landowner. This government couldn't consent to that and since the war there has been security of tenure.

Through the *sindicato* we've considerably improved the sharecroppers' lot. They demanded it themselves. Before, the landlord provided nothing but half the seed and fertilizer; now he has to pay two-thirds of everything needed to plant the land and in return gets one-half of the crop. The old system was a form of slavery, the sort of thing I meant when I said employers considered people only as work elements.

Today there are only a couple of hundred day-labourers left on the land. Everyone is leaving farming to work in the building business on the coast. Over three-quarters of the work force of Tajos goes down to the coast every day, according to my estimate.

We're constantly exhorting people not to leave their plots or, if they do, not to leave them totally uncultivated. A couple of years ago the 'English' work week was introduced here: that means that people in the building industry can spend Saturday afternoons and Sundays working the land. There are many who do and who save money as a result. You know, there wasn't a bank here until a few years ago and now there are three. That shows there's money around. And the day all this building ends the people will have to return to the land.

I like problems. My happiest work day is when a problem comes up in the morning and by evening I've solved it. Often I have to spend long hours trying to convince someone who wants something that it is not within his rights. One of the problems at the moment is that the 'English' work week doesn't apply to people working the land or in shops. These people complain a lot about that – and that's one thing I can't solve for them.

But there's one problem I – or rather the *sindicato* – doesn't have to worry about: wages. In the past, of course, we took up any case where an employer was trying to get away with paying less than the government-established minimum day-wage – though that hardly ever happened. Now the minimum day-wage isn't even directly relevant here. The last collective agreement negotiated in the *sindicato* between employers and workers set the agricultural day-wage at 180 pesetas. That already was fifty pesetas more than the national minimum. But you can't find anyone who will work on the land for less than 300 pesetas a day. A building labourer gets that, and a mason who can't read a plan makes 500 pesetas. The land isn't rich enough to pay wages like that.

The workers are becoming increasingly aware of the *sindicato*'s importance. In the past there were some workers who thought the *sindicato* was the tool of the employers but that's no longer the case. The elections we've just been holding for delegates proves what I'm saying. 52 percent of agricultural workers voted and only 40 percent of the 800 employers, small-holders, renters and sharecroppers. Amongst the building workers in companies employing more than six people we had a 98 percent turnout and 80 percent in the other companies. And all this on an ordinary working day!

Up to the last elections I was the National Movement's local secretary. The Falange no longer exists as a separate entity, you see; it is now an integral part of the Movement.* An integral and integrating part of the Movement, I'd say. It is more than a political party because it covers everything and everyone, whatever their ideals.

The Movement's role in a village, as I see it, is mainly concerned with the youth's education, intellectual and physical, with keeping alive traditional types of dancing, giving classes to the girls on looking after a home. . . . Above all, keeping the village united.

The youth is becoming more educated; up to now they've been a bit apathetic, more concerned with sport than political matters. The Movement's vice-secretary said so himself recently, it was in the papers. The youth's formation has been neglected; it's a question of giving them a political education, of orienting them. But there's still time to remedy it; we can't afford to lose our youth. They have lived their own lives without caring about any-anything else, without realizing that if there are no ideals there's nothing to live for. We – I say we because I'm of the Falange – want the youth to understand what we're made of and what our ideals are.

My generation was certainly more political than today's. But wrongly so. They went for the fire rather than the oven. That's to say, their ideas weren't sufficiently formed. The country was more political – but in the sense of the ballot box. And so out of that came all those bad practices, things like buying votes and all the rest. And that ended in the destruction and bestiality of the revolution. . . .

For me Franco is the finest and greatest person in the world. He has done wonders in every sense of the word. That is why he is our lifelong leader. May God preserve him many years because while he is preserved so too are we!

* The only legal political party in Spain.

ENTREPRENEURS

Endemic poverty, isolation and illiteracy have not in Tajos – if they have anywhere – fostered an entrepreneurial spirit. In a village where, for the majority, the optimum was to have sufficient to eat; where the landowners lived as rentiers, neither working their land directly nor investing in improvements; where the size of holdings and lack of communications made market production for the small-holder virtually impossible, it is hardly surprising that so few have become self-made men. To 'get on in the world' would in most cases have meant leaving the village; the very enclosed village life, which don Vicente Lombardo has remarked on, seems to have reinforced a lack of vision of the world in which the possibility of 'getting on' was nullified for most before the thought could become decision.

With the coming of the foreigner the world began to break in from outside. It was a slow fracturing, however; from 1952, when the first foreigner bought a farm, to 1956 only two more purchased land; from 1956 to 1960 perhaps a dozen. Not many Tajeños* were foresighted enough to see what lay over the horizon of the mid-1960s. The majority, if they had land, waited with the lottery player's mixture of hope and fatality for the foreigner to select them as the recipient of fortune

---

* Nor Malagueños generally. The Costa del Sol was largely the creation of northern Spanish and foreign capital. Málaga landowners and bourgeoisie failed to prospect the goldmine which lay on their doorstep.

and relieve them of land at prices that – amazingly – bore little relation to agricultural values. With the proceeds in those early stages some bought more land; others salted the money away; others simply squandered it. The landless, the few who were lucky enough to find employment, were glad of the opportunity of becoming wage-earners off the land.

Some, however, if no more clairvoyant than the rest, were prepared by previous experience to profit from the new situation. They became the first wave of the newly wealthy, whose ranks were swelled later as more and more small-holders and landowners sold out.

Despite their new wealth these self-made men did not accede to the ruling group. In varying degrees, the latter had made money from their privileged positions either in the bureaucracy or through the monopoly of their profession. Wealth and position were too closely enmeshed to permit wealth alone to become the criterion of power.

ISIDRO GARCIA   *Forty-three*

Taxidriver

One of six children, Isidro Garcia was taken in by the owner of the local taxi at the age of seven when his mother died and his father, a fish-vendor, fell ill. It was during the civil war. Isidro got board, lodging and clothes in return for helping to run the taxi, a 1928 Packhard which had been converted to run on charcoal. All the tips he earned from running errands in Málaga he handed to his father who could no longer work. . . .

Every morning I got up at five to fill the boiler with charcoal and light it. It took an hour to get a good clear blue flame which showed that the gas was all right; then I started the taxi. Not that it had a starter, nothing like that. It had to be left on a slope every night and run down to get it going. I drove it to the square and loaded up the *recoveras*' eggs, chickens, kids and all the other things and went to call my chief.

By six we were on our way. With a bit of luck we'd make the thirty kilometres to Málaga by nine-thirty or ten.

The taxi was in no real shape for the road. When you stepped on the brakes a couple of times they heated up and no longer worked; the gearshift was always jumping out of position and we'd shout at a passenger in the front seat – there were usually three or four – to grab hold of it. We couldn't buy sparking plugs and we used a bit of wire and a mother-of-pearl button to keep them going. But the worst were the tyres. We had no spares, only a few inner tubes and the rubber on them was practically worn through. There wasn't a trip when we didn't have five or six punctures. One day I remember we got to within three kilometres of Málaga when we had no more spare tubes. My chief told me to go and pick grass from alongside the road. We stuffed the tyre full of it and that's how we arrived – with the smell of burning grass filling the car.

Rain or shine I rode outside, hanging on to the back of the taxi, so I could jump off and put a rock behind the wheels if we had to stop on a hill. One rainy day my chief gave me his jacket to put over my shoulders. That day, by chance, the Guardia Civil stopped us on the road. I bent down behind the spare wheel at the back and put the jacket over me because I wasn't supposed to ride outside. I was so small the *guardia* never saw me; not only that, he actually wrote out his *denuncia* on my shoulder without realizing I was there!

My chief liked the bottle a lot so by the time I was twelve he let me drive the taxi with him sitting beside me. Not that usually he was in a fit state to help if anything went wrong. To reach the pedals I had to have a five-litre petrol can between my back and the seat, and a jacket or bit of blanket under my backside. Even then I could only just see out. They were heavy, those old cars, without syncromesh or hydraulic brakes. But I loved the life, I loved cars.

We never got back to the village much before ten at night. The return journey took longer because we couldn't make the climb up to the village in one go; we'd have to let the engine cool for an hour or so. There was a small reserve tank of petrol which we switched on for the climb – on charcoal alone the taxi would never have made it. As soon as we arrived I had to be preparing the charcoal for the next day, cleaning the filters and boiler until midnight. So I slept only five hours. In Málaga the next day, after getting everything ready for the return trip, I'd get another three or four hours in the back of the taxi. Two shifts of sleep, that's how it was.

One day when I was fourteen my chief got a trip to a village about forty kilometres the other side of Málaga for a wedding. We made our daily trip to Málaga but by the time of setting off again my chief had had a few too many and he told me to go on my own. I was the other side of Málaga when a pair of *guardias* waved me to stop. It was four in the morning by now. I brought the car to a halt about seventy metres beyond them because the brakes wouldn't stop it quicker. They came up and looked at me; then one asked how old I was. 'Fourteen? And you're driving this car?' A story flashed into my mind. I told them my chief's mother had fallen seriously ill and I had to fetch her. 'And you know how to drive?' The younger of the two *guardias* started to write out a *denuncia*. Then the older one said, 'Come on boy, we'll go in here, you must be cold,' and he took me into a tavern and bought me a *copita* of *coñac*. Perhaps he felt sorry for me; anyway, he told the other *guardia* to tear up the *denuncia*.

So I set off again. To get to the village I had to climb a road like the Tajos one, and half way up I had a puncture. At that time there were outlaws in all these sierras and I was scared. I tried jacking the car up but I couldn't manage because it was on a slope. I started to cry. Then I heard the sound of hooves and I got really frightened. It wasn't dawn yet. But they weren't outlaws, they were black-marketeers bringing down wheat. When they saw me crying they stopped and helped me put the jack in and change the tyre.

I got to the village at last. Mine was the first car ever to drive into it. The only street was so narrow I had to drive over the front doorsteps to get to the square. All the kids were around cheering and waving me on. I arrived in time to take the *novia* to her wedding in another village and drove back to Tajos to find my chief. . . .

At the start we'd be lucky if we had half a dozen passengers. My chief charged eighteen pesetas the round journey to Málaga and that was a lot of money for those days. But as things got a little better we were often carrying as many as twenty or twenty-five. They'd be squashed inside, they'd be riding on the roof and hanging on to the running boards. We used to put a tarpaulin over those on the roof in case they went to sleep and fell off. We were stopped once by the *guardia*. 'What's this?' the lieutenant said. 'The Tajos taxi,' I answered. 'It doesn't look like a taxi – it looks like a boat,' was what he said. My record is forty-two passengers one night going down to Casas Nuevas. You couldn't see the car for people hanging on back, front and roof.

After military service I worked in a transport company in Málaga and by 1953 I'd saved a bit of money. I had a friend in Benamalí who sold me a 1928 seven-seater Buick for 19,500 pesetas. Of course, I hadn't the money but he said I could pay by the month.

It had eight cylinders and drank up the petrol. Even though I sometimes took as many as thirty passengers, about all I could clear a day was twenty-five pesetas to give my wife. My friend warned me about the instalments. Just then I had a stroke of luck. A man came up to me in Málaga and offered to buy it for 45,000 pesetas.

I went to Madrid looking for another big old car, but I couldn't find one cheap enough. Then I found a 1929 Nash in Granada for 26,000 pesetas. It was a good car and I made some money with it in the next year and a half. Outside of going to Málaga I might get a trip to Casas Nuevas once a week – things were getting better here, you see! I sold the Nash well, too, for 40,000 pesetas – but there my luck ended. On the 1935 Buick I bought next I lost 30,000 pesetas when I came to sell it.

When I started on my own there was one other taxi in the village. One day coming back from Málaga I was stopped by the police. 'Where's this taxi going? To Tajos? Don't you know only one taxi in Tajos has got permission to bring passengers every day to Málaga?' And the policeman gave me twenty-four hours to give up my taxi.

I knew this couldn't be the law. That night I went to a farmer I knew and asked him if any of his goats had had kids. 'Give me a couple of tender ones by tomorrow.' The next day I found out where this policeman lived and I took a couple of lads along to carry the kids. When I knocked on the door his wife opened and asked what I wanted. 'I've brought you a present.' 'Come in, come in,' she said. While we waited for her husband we skinned and cleaned the kids and she put one on to cook. When her husband arrived, she said, 'There's a señor here who's brought us a present.' He looked at me. 'What are you doing this for?' 'Because I wanted to talk to you and I couldn't come with empty hands, could I?' I had him then because I had the two lads as witnesses and his wife had the kid on the stove.

'I've come to see you because I've got to go on working. I've got a wife and a young daughter to provide for and the taxi to pay off yet. I've got as much right as that other person in Tajos to run a taxi. I know why all this is happening – it's because the other owner has been putting pressure on you.' 'No, no,' he said. 'Yes, yes,' I said. He went on denying it but in the end he agreed I could run my taxi and that he wouldn't trouble me any more. And that was that!

After I sold the Buick I worked for a couple of years on the coast as a bus-driver. Then a relative stood guarantor with the bank for a loan of 50,000 pesetas and I bought a 1947 Seat. The tourist boom was beginning then and between one thing and another I was able to build up my business until by 1964 I was running all three taxis here.

Not so long ago I sold one of my taxi licences which cost me 900 pesetas many years ago from the town hall for 415,000 pesetas. The first one I sold longer ago and got 63,000 pesetas. I'm asking 600,000 pesetas for my last licence. If I get it I'll buy a licence in Málaga which costs 1,200,000 pesetas and set up in business there. I've just bought a house in Málaga so that my daughters can go to school there. I want them to study for the *bachillerato*; to get anywhere today one's children have got to leave the village to study.

I started with nothing and only went to school a couple of years, and I didn't learn much. Ever since I was a child I've been struggling to make a living. I want my children to have a better future than I had at their age.

JESUS PEINADO   *Forty-six*

Farmer and president of the Brotherhood of Farmers and Livestock Breeders

In 1940 his father bought the farm he had been renting from Antonio Tejada's daughter for 50,000 pesetas payable in three annual instalments. It included five hectares of irrigated land and an established lemon grove. '50,000 pesetas was a lot of money then – it would be worth ten times that today,' says Jesús. 'The cost of living was beginning to rise but landlords weren't allowed to raise rents. It was more profitable for them to sell if they could find someone to buy. My father was one of half a dozen renters at most who had the money. But then we were a small family. . . .' Jesús, the only son, and a sister. Later, when agricultural prices went up, his father had enough capital to buy another plot for 15,000 pesetas. 'He didn't like to have money sitting around. He knew that to make money you've got to spend it. He could read and write and kept accounts, which was very rare among smallholders. He was more advanced in his ideas than most. I suppose that's where I get it from. . . .' In the late 1950s Jesús took over the running of the farms.

One day, in 1961 or 1962, I heard a new factory had been set up near Benamalí for processing onions, leeks and the like. I went there and they told me the office was in Málaga. There I found the head of the company, a German he was, who explained the business. They paid a guaranteed price of 2·50 pesetas a kilo for onions and provided the seed; they had to be white onions, not the sweet, pink sort, and they would take as many as I could grow. They told me how far apart to plant them, the quantity of fertilizer to use and later they sent an inspector to see they had been properly planted.

Well, I said to myself, this is a new factory they've put up, it'll be a few years before it can crash, so I'll go ahead. It was a risk but if you don't get on the boat you'll never get seasick, will you?

I've always liked planting in quantity, not a bit here and another bit there like most people. It's not worth transporting a little by donkey – you want to have a lorry-load at a time to make it profitable. Even so, when my father saw that I'd planted nearly a hectare with onions for the factory he thought I'd gone too far. He feared it would fail. . . . But it didn't. I employed boys to plant – they're more nimble-fingered than men anyway – and their wages were half that of a grown man: about thirty pesetas a day. I had a few adult day-labourers too to weed and hoe the crop, but even so at sixty pesetas a day, which was the basic minimum then, that wasn't too dear. It was a time when wages were still low enough to be able to make something out of the land.

Moreover, I had another advantage. The company gave me a commission on all onions grown here especially for the factory. I got some other small-holders together and told them about the scheme and they planted too – not in as great a quantity as me, but enough so that when the crop was sold the commission covered all my own planting costs.

I don't remember how much I had to spend but I do remember I got 70,000 pesetas for my first onion crop. That was a lot. Most of the small-holders weren't making that much in a year, if they were making even that.

To make that sort of profit from the land you've got to be prepared to spend money. I would go for manure by the lorry-load to villages some distance away where it was cheaper; and I spread it by lorry. I'd already decided that donkey transport came out too dear so I cut a dirt road into the farm. I was the first to do that here. The old farmers thought I was crazy, but I reckoned the cost would be covered in two or three years simply by saving on transport, by being able to get the lorries right down on the terraces. I used the first bulldozer that came to the village. . . . Of course, I had learned from my father just about everything there is to know about cultivating the land. It's not that easy, you've got to know the times to plant, the moons when you can sow. There are plenty of crops you can't plant when the moon is waxing, and others when it's waning. The May moon is bad, for example; if you plant beans then they make a mass of stalk and no fruit. You have to plant seedbeds of onions, lettuce, melon and pumpkins with the waning moon as you do vetch and alfalfa. If the latter is planted at any other time the livestock swell up and die when they eat it. That's the truth. I don't know why it is, but everyone here knows it.

I went on planting for the factory for three or four years. The onions and leeks were ground to a powder and sent in plastic sacks to Germany, for soups and things I suppose. But little by little the company began to go downhill. What with tourism and building, wages began rising and not enough crops were being grown here. They tried bringing onions from the north where wages were lower, but even then they said they could get them cheaper from Egypt. I don't know whether wages were lower there or yields higher along the Nile; but I expect it was wages. Everything depends on that.

When the company folded, I went on planting for market. Tomatoes especially, the winter crop. They grow very well. Instead of trying to sell them locally, I'd ring round the different markets, even as far away as Seville. Wherever the price was highest that's where the lorry went.

There were others here who didn't do as well as me out of the factory. They didn't cultivate the onions properly, they'd sow seedbeds and let them get overgrown with weeds; they didn't fertilize enough and the onions would be too small. There aren't many who know how to cultivate the land properly, even though they've been born to it. They go on planting as their fathers and grandfathers did a century ago. I think in part it has to do with the fact that our grandparents were used to vine-growing and weren't as developed in other forms of agriculture. The people of Posadas and Benamalí have been far more industrious than us here.

It's also a fact that the landowners here – and not only here but in Andalusia generally – haven't wanted to invest in their land. All the money they made was put on deposit in the banks which invested the money in new industries in Catalonia and the Basque country. Nothing went into making the land more productive. That has been the ruin of Andalusia in the past.

For the last six or seven years I've been president of the Brotherhood of Farmers. Not that I've got time for it but I was voted in and they said I had to take it on, so what could I do?

I preside over the commissions which look after the cleaning of irrigation channels, keeping the paths in condition, trying to organize the building of lorry tracks in the countryside. There's usually a fight over the latter because small-holders, especially when they're old, always imagine that thirty square metres of land or a fig tree is worth more than a road. They don't realize that the value of their farm will be much higher once a road reaches it. They can transport their produce more easily and, with an eye on tourism, sell off any plots that aren't good for cultivation to the foreigners.

I'm also involved in the conciliation process. A lot of the time we succeed in settling disputes between workers and their employers; it's good if we can. But we don't always succeed. It's not easy having to defend both employer and worker. Many people end up going to Málaga after all.

In other villages the *sindicato* has organized cooperatives to buy agricultural machinery which it rents by the hour to its members. We've never had anything like that here. There could have been, I suppose, but this isn't agricultural land any longer. There's hardly anyone working the land; everyone is in the building business. The land is pretty well abandoned, to tell the truth.

Jesús himself has given up the land; for the past four to five years his farm has remained uncultivated. The cost of labour is too high. 'No one wants to sharecrop and even if someone wanted to rent it, which no one does, I wouldn't be interested. I may sell it to a foreigner one day and if I have a tenant I'll have to pay him to leave.' Nowadays he helps his wife run one of the two state-concession tobacconists, which she inherited from her father, and does up houses in the countryside to rent or sell.

JUAN ALARCON *Forty*

Shopkeeper

I was standing in my shop here one afternoon a few weeks before Christmas when I heard a lottery seller calling out numbers in the street. *Hombre!* I suddenly remembered I hadn't bought a ticket for the Christmas draw which I usually bought in Málaga. I called the seller into the shop – he wasn't from here but from Velez-Málaga – and bought a tenth of a ticket for 500 pesetas. 550 pesetas to be exact because I had to give the vendor a fifty peseta tip.

I sold my mother fifteen pesetas worth. I intended selling each of my four brothers and sisters twenty-five pesetas of the ticket, but my brothers insisted on having twice that amount. So I sold them what they wanted; but since my sisters didn't insist they got only twenty-five pesetas worth. I gave each of them a receipt.

I put the ticket away and didn't think about it any more. I had my shop to attend to. It was a general store then which had belonged to an uncle of mine. When he died in 1955, my father's four brothers and he divided up everything and I took over my father's share. He had a three-hectare small-holding to look after and a couple of ploughing yokes: one to rest while the other worked. The only one who never rested was my father!

I sold just about everything in the shop when I started. *Alpargatas* and sombreros, berets and cotton thread, farm implements and food; the shop counter served as a bar and men came in after work to have a *copita* on their way home. One of the things I sold most of was paint. You couldn't buy factory-made paint here then, so I mixed my own. The only colouring available was a bordeaux red which came as powdered earth from Málaga, and I bought it by the hundred-kilo barrel. I mixed it with linseed oil, varnish and a drying oil. The people used a lot of it because it was so bad that windows and doors had to be repainted every year!

The shop wasn't much more than the front room of the house. The beams were tree-trunks and the branches of trees and at some time my uncle had put up a tarpaulin to hide them. The mice used to scamper round on the tarpaulin and a lot of the women got scared when they came to buy. 'What's that noise?' they used to cry out.

There were only two other shops the size of mine in the village then. I sold about 300 or 400 pesetas worth of goods a day. That was good business in those days! It was the time when things were just beginning to improve a bit economically.

Well, Christmas came round and as usual here everyone listened to the draw on the radio. Nowadays people spend a lot more than they used to on the lottery and there are authorized vendors in the village. Then – it was 1964 – there weren't any. But everyone listened to the radio just as they do now.

When I heard the number of the first prize sung out, I thought: 'What's that? The radio's all right, isn't it?' I ran to look at my ticket. I had it in a drawer here in the shop. I read the number: 20,426. I went back to the radio again. 'The first prize has gone to number 20,426. Part of the ticket was sold in Vélez-Málaga!...'

'That's it,' I said. 'I've won part of the first prize.' My mother came downstairs and said, 'The people are shouting that Martinez has won part of the first prize.' 'I know,' I said, '*chiquilla*, I've won part of it too.'

3,700,000 pesetas my tenth of a ticket was worth. It was like a miracle from heaven! The village went wild that afternoon – in all something like 12,000,000 pesetas were won here on that one number. It's the only time anyone can remember the first prize in any draw falling in this village. Our joy was troubled only by the grief that my father hadn't lived to see this day.

After paying my mother, brothers and sisters, I had something over 2,000,000 pesetas left. I hired a local taxi and took my mother – may she rest in peace – my wife and child on a tour of Spain. We went all the way up the coast to Barcelona and from there to Madrid and back down again through Granada, Córdoba and Seville. What a trip! 1,000 pesetas a day I paid the taxi and it was well worth it. When I saw Barcelona all lit up at night and the people and traffic I stood there gaping. I'd never seen anything like it in my life.

When I got back I bought the house and did over the shop completely. I put in the first display window ever seen in Tajos! I expanded the shop and took out the old-fashioned double doors to the street and I modernized it throughout. I gave up selling food and wine and went in entirely for clothes, shoes, toilet articles and the like. I could see that with tourism here to stay there was going to be more money about and that people were beginning to buy off-the-peg clothes instead of making their own.

I've got about half a million pesetas worth of stock, I'd guess; I don't keep accounts. I know what I sell, and re-order the lines that go best. Classic things – men's trousers, neither too tight nor too wide, women's dresses that aren't over-done, a lot of children's wear. But I have to stock some novelty stuff for the youth because that's what they want. Mini-skirts, striped sweaters, bell-bottomed trousers. All that sort of strange stuff. I've even got a dozen mini-shorts in stock. I don't think local girls over the age of twelve will buy them but some foreigners might. It's a small village, you know, and people are always ready to criticize; the girls' mothers won't like it. I don't blame them. I think it's a ridiculous fashion myself.

Mini-skirts caught on here though. All the girls bought them and a lot are still wearing them, though a bit longer this year. It took a bit of time but everyone liked them. After all, a young girl with nice legs who shows them off can't be reproached, can she?

Nowadays everyone wears brighter colours than before. Not so long ago when a woman reached thirty she'd say, 'I can't wear those colours, I'm too old. I've got to wear grey.' Not any more. Men's cotton trousers are a thing of the past, too. Today everyone wants man-made fibre.

The youth today spend what they earn straight away. They watch the fashions and as soon as there's something new they want it. If they've just been paid the young girls don't think anything of spending 300 to 600 pesetas on a dress. Not that all the youth pay on the spot. There are some who say they haven't the money on them and they'll pay later. It's mostly the young men, who go off and spend their money in a bar. I've got plenty of debts of that sort.

However, the custom of bargaining for everything is going out. The people are beginning to know that a fixed price means what it says. Sometimes I'll knock a very little off, the price of a cup of coffee, but not much more. My average mark-up is 20 percent and on that I can't afford to give away much. I sell between 2,000 and 3,000 pesetas worth of clothes and other articles on average a day. That's a change from what I used to make when I started. But even so, the money then was worth more than it is today.

Now that Juan has achieved one ambition – to own and drive his own car – his main concern, as with most fathers in Tajos today, is to ensure that his children get a good education. He has a daughter and two sons, all under eight, and he will send them to boarding-school in Málaga if necessary to get 'the education they can't get in the village'. For this he is prepared to pay and doesn't count on scholarships. Not all his lottery winnings have gone into his business; some have been invested in fixed-interest utility bonds.

PEDRO TORRES *Thirty*

Contractor

I was seventeen when, after a lot of persuading, I managed to get my father to agree to let me go out to look for a building job on the coast. He couldn't understand anyone leaving the land, it simply didn't enter his head. Even at the time of the mica mining he never left the farmstead he rented. The land – that was all there was for him.

I knew I had to find work. I'd go of a Sunday to church in the village and I hadn't the money to go to the cinema or have a drink. I never dared ask my father for money. He was a very stern man and when he told me off I used to tremble; it was worse than if he had hit me. Not that he ever laid a hand to me, but just to hear him shout was enough to make me want to die. My sisters and I respected him more, I believe, than most children their fathers.

I and two friends went to Casas Nuevas looking for work. They were bigger than me and were taken on immediately. I had to go nearly to Málaga before I found a job on a new hotel. I didn't know anything about building, I couldn't mix mortar or plaster, but I could carry materials. It was such easy work after the land! On the farm we hadn't even a donkey and I had to haul all the firewood, manure, wheat on my back. I started when I was six or seven; I very well remember one of my milk teeth coming out when I was weeding wheat alongside my father.

I had only sisters and so I had to work harder than most boys of my age. And also because my father wanted everything done his way; he cultivated the land as though it were a garden. Even if he could afford to he never hired a labourer because the man wouldn't work the land the way he wanted him to. Other renters spent less time on their land so as to go out for a day's wage; they earned more than my father that way.

Working on the hotel was like being on holiday. My companions kept shouting at me, 'What are you running for? Where are you going?' I was always worried that the foreman would say I wasn't working hard enough. I always wanted to do more.

I came back after a month and found my father furious. I handed over the 1,600 pesetas I'd made and he gave me back twenty-five pesetas. I'd only made that much by working extra hours in the evenings, sleeping on cement sacks at night and cooking my own food. But for my father the money I'd earned wasn't important; what mattered was that the land should be properly cultivated. He wanted me there to help him and I decided to stay.

The next year I got a job for a month digging trenches in Casas Nuevas. I left home every morning at six to walk down and got back at nine at night. Walking back was the worst, after ten hours of digging. But there wasn't any work here; if you could get a job somewhere as a building labourer for six months you thought yourself a *capitán-general*! It was only too easy for a boss to say, 'I don't like the look of your face, I'm going to find someone else for the job.'

When, in about 1960, a foreigner bought some land close to my father's farm I was desperate to get a job building the house. I persuaded my father that, as it was summer, I could work the land for an hour in the morning and a couple of hours in the evening before and after work. It was one of the first houses Sr Avery built up here; he must have taken a liking to me because after a while he asked if I wanted to be his gardener. Since I had been put to work on the concrete-mixer and wasn't learning anything about building, I agreed.

I was with Sr Avery for a couple of years and during that time I used to watch the men when they built an extension or did repairs to his house. The more I saw the more I liked building. In the end I told Sr Avery I wanted to become a bricklayer and he agreed to give me a job in his company as an assistant at thirteen pesetas an hour. That was a lot better than four pesetas an hour as a gardener for a start.

The building boom had got under way then. Lots of people 'wielded the trowel' for the first time and became bricklayers overnight. The old masons didn't like it much; they said we didn't know how to work and in some cases it was true. But at least I was always trying to learn. . . .

I only had the job eight or nine months before Sr Avery wound up his company. Like everyone else I was laid off. Sr Avery wanted me back as his gardener but I was determined to stay in the building business. For a time I did odd jobs; then one day a foreigner asked me to build him a swimming-pool. Uy! The idea scared me, I'd never done anything like that before. I had to give him an estimate: 29,000 pesetas, an enormous sum; I'd never seen that much money in my life. And all the time I was thinking, 'What if it comes out at 30,000 pesetas, where am I going to get the 1,000 pesetas from?'

I was lucky. I got credit for the materials and, with three young men I recruited, dug the hole and finished the pool in record time. I had 12,000 pesetas over, more than I'd ever had in my hands before, and with it I opened a savings account.

All the time I was working I paid myself a day-wage and handed it over to my mother. I didn't tell my parents about the profit I'd made but all the same they had nothing to complain about. My father still wanted me to work the land in the evenings and on Sundays.

Then the same foreigner wanted another storey added to his house. He had plans drawn up. I had no idea what a plan was, I couldn't read it; but I said I'd do the job. Every night after work I'd spend three or four hours trying to figure out the sheets of paper they'd given me.

One day I had another bit of luck. My brother-in-law was reading a wild west novel when a postcard from something called the American Institute fell out. On it they offered all sorts of courses and there was one for builders. I sent away for the course and the books came by return. I studied them and it didn't take long to learn to read drawings and understand about the loads different types of beams could bear and that sort of thing. Once I'd got what I wanted I didn't bother to go on studying.

I never went to school. My father can read and write but I couldn't learn from him because he'd tell me off and I'd burst into tears. My sister taught me a bit. Later I went to night-school for a month. I told the master I wanted to learn only arithmetic; in that month I learned to multiply and divide. Numbers come easily to me.

Sometimes I paid a man to go to work on my father's land on a Sunday to save me going. It was my only free day and I was using it to build a small house on a plot I'd got from my brother-in-law who hadn't been able to pay for some work I'd done. But my father got furious when I didn't go, he didn't like the way the man worked. Although he never said anything to me, he complained to my mother a lot that he'd worked all his life to raise his children and as soon as they were old enough to work they'd left the farm.

With the help of friends I got my house finished. Meanwhile I had been recommended by the foreigner to friends of his and had got more work building three villas in Casas Nuevas. I'd become a builder without knowing it – and without any papers or insurances for the three or four men I employed! I had to go to Málaga and take out papers as a contractor, pay taxes and get insurance for the workers.

One day I went to my father and told him he should tell the landlord he was leaving. 'That I'm leaving?' he said. He was frightened. 'But where am I going to go?' 'To the village.' 'But what am I going to do there? What am I going to live on? I can't work there.' 'I'll provide for you, I think I'll make enough for us all to eat.'

He was sixty-seven then; it was five years ago. He had 30,000 pesetas in the bank which the owner of a bit of land he also worked had paid him to leave when he sold it to a foreigner. That's the only money he's ever been able to save.

'My 30,000 pesetas will only last a year. What will happen then?' 'You won't have to touch your money,' I said. And nor has he ever had to. But I didn't say that I'd been planning this move a long while, all the time while he had thought I had deserted him.

I think he's proud of my success. Nowadays he doesn't bite my head off or get angry. Every tool I have, every scrap of left-over building material is sacred to him. But he doesn't and never will understand how I work or how I became successful. I never tell him or my mother when I've made money or lost it. If they thought I'd lost 50,000 pesetas on a house it would seem like a disaster to them – much worse, in fact, than it would seem to me.

I know I've made and lost money but I don't know how much. I've kept accounts very badly, to tell the truth, because I wasn't used to book-keeping. A friend of mine is going to help me with it now. But I know I pay out 85,000 pesetas in wages and another

35,000 pesetas in social security a week. I've got thirty-eight men working for me now. To my father all this seems like something from another world. 'A house for a million pesetas,' he says, 'ozu!'

I haven't got any capital, other than about 75,000 pesetas worth of equipment. I live from one job to the next. All the same there are plenty of people who are jealous of my success. 'Look at him, he used to dig the land and now he's got a car.' I don't pay any attention, that's the way people talk in a small village, and there are plenty of others who admire the way I've got on.

There's one thing, though, I don't understand: why none of the men who knew a lot more than I when I started ever tried to become contractors. One or two, when they saw me no longer working with my hands, did attempt it; but when they found out it wasn't a matter of just driving round in a car they gave up. Everyone here wants to make a lot of money, but they won't venture into something new. They'd rather stick to the old things, they don't want to get on in the world.

I suppose they don't want the worries. When I was working in the fields my muscles and bones ached at night. But I never had the worries I have now. The thousand and one preoccupations of running your own business. . . . Still, that's part of going out on your own and trying something new, isn't it?

Tourism has brought all the prosperity that has come to this village. Everything has changed for the better. When I go inland, to Córdoba for example, and see the women working in the fields – the sort of thing I remember here after the war – I realize how much we have the foreigners to thank for.

CRISTOBAL MORENO   *Thirty-eight*

Handicraftsman

Unlike Pedro Torres – lean, pale and smartly attired – Cristóbal retains a robust, rural appearance. Tall and broad-shouldered, he comes from Los Peñones, a derelict hamlet on the track to Benamalí, where his father worked a half-hectare plot of the poorest land in Tajos. The eldest of eight children which included two sets of twins, Cristóbal started work as a goatherd at the age of seven during the worst of the famine years. 'We could think of nothing but food. Day after day with empty stomachs. All year we waited for Easter Sunday to eat the only egg in the year my mother had saved for each of us. For nothing! Our stomachs were so weak that as soon as we'd eaten we had to go behind the house to vomit. We were worn out by hunger, we couldn't imagine it would ever end. . . .'

His father had a donkey and sent his son out to sell lime in the neighbouring villages because the land didn't bring in enough to keep the family alive. The lime was bought on credit, sold on credit. 'Once I got rid of 2,500 pesetas' worth of lime in the villages and at the end hadn't a peseta to buy myself a cigarette. Everyone was going to pay when they could. I knew what it was like – it took me six years to be able to pay off a debt of 850 pesetas.' He took to lime-burning and managed to save a little money. In 1959, when he married, he used his savings to start a small store in Los Peñones. . . .

The people came and bought all right, as they always do when a new shop opens. On credit! By the time I realized what was happening I was 20,000 pesetas in debt. 'We're going to have to leave this,' I said to my wife, and I went off to the sierra for six months to burn lime.

That's another risky business! You spend two or three months cutting brushwood and breaking and carrying the stone to burn say 50,000 kilos of lime – without knowing whether you're going to make anything at the end of it all. All the brushwood has to be carried on one's head because a man can manage more than a donkey in that sort of terrain. Once the kiln is charged and the fire alight you've got to work day and night to keep it going. And then if it rains you lose the lot. That's how I lost that 850 pesetas I couldn't repay for so long.

I and two other men lived in a hut and worked day and night. It was winter at the start and it was so cold we had to keep a fire burning all the time. We made several kilns, and then a lorry which came for the lime ran over my foot and broke four toes; I had to go to hospital. I went back to work before they were healed and went on cutting wood. When it was finished and we added up what we had made I found I had 30,000 pesetas. There was a lot of demand for lime then because the foreigners were beginning to build. I came home and the people couldn't get over it. 'Cristóbal has made 165 pesetas a day for the time he's been gone.' At that time a day-wage was thirty-five to forty pesetas. Well, I paid off my debt, bought a plot of land, a horse and some pigs to raise. Then my wife fell ill and all my money went on doctors and medicines for her.

But it was the shop that changed my life in a strange way. In payment for some of the food people bought I had to take esparto plaits. That was all they had. A cousin of mine who also had a shop in Los Peñones worked plaits into donkey panniers and baskets; when I wanted to sell him my plaits he offered me less than I had taken them for. He wanted my shop to fail.

'What am I going to do?' I thought. Then I had an idea: I'd make panniers myself. Easier said than done. The first ones I tried came out all the wrong shapes. I kept looking at panniers on donkeys, wondering how they were made. My cousin heard what I was up to and almost immediately two *guardias* came to my shop. Was I working esparto? 'Well, you know something about panniers,' I said. 'This looks more like a boat than a pannier to me. What do you say?' 'Ah,' they replied, 'you need a permit to work esparto.' 'Good, and where do I get the permit?' 'That we don't know. . . .' 'You ought to. If you've come to stop me working, you ought to know where I can get the permit to go on working.' 'No, we don't know.' 'Well then, I'm going to go on making them.' And so on. Finally they left, but by then I was angry.

It was anger that taught me to make the panniers. I set about it and it wasn't long before I had the trick. Once I'd learnt, I took my panniers to all the places my cousin went. If he went to Benamalí of a Sunday, that's where I went. If he went to Posadas or Arroyo, I went too. I sold mine cheap – and he had to sell his cheap too. But in any case things were getting bad in this business because every day fewer and fewer donkeys and mules were being used.

With my wife's illness after the birth of our only child, which over the past twelve years has cost us 100,000 pesetas or more, we couldn't go on. I had to find something else. I've never liked working the land, I've never liked the idea of going from the house to the fields and back again day after day, knowing exactly what's going to happen and how much I'm going to earn; knowing, too, that as a labourer, one has to work harder than one should simply to keep the job. That was nothing but loss as far as I was concerned.

I thought that if I could find something closer to Tajos one day I might perhaps be lucky ... I came and talked to the sharecropper who had taken over *El Verdegal* from Cristóbal Gonzalez and who came from Los Peñones. He told me of a farm close by whose owner was looking for a sharecropper. I went and saw him; the next day we moved to the farmstead and the day after I had the seed and fertilizer bought and the cows were ploughing the land.

I sowed the whole farm, I bought two calves and a couple of pigs – and then I discovered that there wasn't water enough to irrigate the whole farm. It wouldn't produce enough to support the three of us – let alone divide the crop with the landlord. I went back to making panniers and taking them round the villages.

Then I had a stroke of luck which, when I think of it today, makes me wonder whether I'm still not dreaming. A foreigner had started a shop in the village. One day he called me in and asked if I could make donkey heads and sombreros. Yes, I said, though I'd never made anything of the sort. The first donkey heads – you should have seen them, they looked more like elephants than donkeys. But there was no one else in Tajos ready to try his hand at the thing. The foreigner offered me fifty pesetas a head. When I went up with the first load he gave me fifty-five pesetas each. Ozu! Some days I could turn out a dozen heads. The sombreros I made he paid me seventy-five pesetas each and sold them for 180 in his shop. I began to think, 'If he can do it why can't I?' But I hadn't any capital.

'*Chiquillo*,' my wife said, 'have you thought it over well?' 'Yes,' I said, 'I'm going to the village to see if I can find a room to rent.' I had 1,900 pesetas – and they weren't mine, I owed them to the chemist. It was 1966 and the people were asking 2,500 pesetas a month for a place to live and work. At last I found a man who rented me the doorway of his house and a small room next to it for 800 pesetas a month. The room was so small my son had to live with my mother-in-law; we couldn't get our own furniture into it. I sold my horse for 12,000 pesetas and the next day, coming back to the village from Vélez-Málaga I found a foreign company making a film here. They hired me to sit in the square sewing esparto. Another bit of luck! A whole week I sat there at 1,200 pesetas a day, and the stuff I made I could sell. Between the film and the horse I had about 20,000 pesetas.

I sat in the doorway sewing esparto, with the things I'd made hung from the lintel; soon the tourists who came up from the coast for the afternoon were beginning to buy. Whatever I made I sold. I didn't keep accounts but I reckon that first year I made 250,000 to 300,000 pesetas. I worked day and night and never shut the shop. Sunday was my busiest day.

I went on for four years like that. During that time I managed to build a house, thanks to the mayor who gave me a plot. It took me four years to build because my brother and I did it in our spare time. But when it was finished I found it was too far from my shop. Another stroke of luck – I found someone who was willing to exchange it for a flat close to the shop. Underneath the flat there was a shop-space which no one wanted because it was hidden from the street. They were asking 100,000 pesetas down payment; I hadn't that sort of money to invest in premises. A commercial traveller who is a friend of mine heard about it and asked if I wanted a loan. . . . I went to bed thinking, and I got up thinking, and I went to bed thinking. At last I accepted his offer.

I've had the new shop only five months and I've already sold 650,000 pesetas' worth of goods. I don't know, it's as though God were helping me. Things I can't sell in my old shop I put in the new one and they go. Last Friday – and it's not summer yet – a group came in and in twenty minutes they'd spent 15,000 pesetas. I know the tourists now, I have all the prices marked in dollars as well as pesetas so they don't have to waste time asking the price.

Most of the esparto articles come from Jaen nowadays. I hardly make anything any more because it's more profitable to be selling than making. On average I mark up most articles by 80 percent to 90 percent, though on glassware and ornaments which are fragile I put on as much as 125 percent. Ponchos, rugs, bags and that sort of thing I mark up much less.

I reckon this year, if the summer is good, to make a million pesetas profit. My business has the advantage of buying on three to four months' credit and selling for cash. Sometimes I've sold all I've bought on credit in a couple of weeks. Using other people's money to make money for oneself – that's the secret. The other day, for example, a salesman from Jaen came in and left me 50,000 pesetas' worth of fans to be paid for only when they're sold. I can't lose on that sort of deal.

I'm not the sort of man, and I never have been, who sits still because he's made 10,000 pesetas. Most people here, when they've made fifty pesetas, are only thinking of spending the money tomorrow. But I'm always thinking of how best to use the money to make more. I'm not interested in money for money's sake. I'm only interested in it if it works for me.

He looks out the tavern window to see if anyone has stopped by his doorway shop. Most of the day he can be found casually pacing the narrow street between his two shops and the tavern, his eyes on the alert. He never goes out, never shuts up shop on a Sunday or a fiesta (though the law obliges closure from Saturday noon to Monday morning), and has travelled no further than Jaen. He doesn't own a car, though he has completely refurnished his flat and has a washing machine and television. 'I've only one real desire – to have enough put by when I get to be sixty-five or seventy to be able to spend my old age in some sort of comfort. That and to see my son gets an education. For that he'll have to go to boarding-school in Málaga because all he does here is play truant. He doesn't know as much as he should – although he already knows ten times as much as me. I only went to school for a year and so I can't correct him, you see. He'll have to go to Málaga.'

And the tourist boom? Will it continue at its ever-increasing rate? 'As long as neither we nor the government do wrong by the tourists, as long as three-quarters of them go home happy and tell their friends what a good time they've had, I think they'll continue to come. More and more, I hope. I've put all my faith in tourism – it was thanks to the foreigners that I got out of my hardships, wasn't it, after all?'

MEN AND WOMEN

Engagement, Marriage and Parenthood

JUAN BLANCO   *Thirty-eight*

Tavern-owner

I think Spanish women are extraordinary. Well, all women are
divine, the best thing God put on earth for man, but Spanish
women are enchanting in a way no other woman is for me. They
have a sweetness, a softness that is quite special. I don't know why,
perhaps it's because they're more difficult to conquer. I've had
English and American and Scandinavian women – the Swedes
are a marvel! – and it's enough to know them a couple of days
and you're in bed with them; they have grown up in a different
environment to ours. But Spanish women, especially Tajeñas, are
difficult – so difficult that I like them all the better for it.

Spanish men aren't like the English or Americans who believe
that men and women should be equals and have the same rights.
Spaniards are jealous, they want to assert themselves, be more
than a woman, more than another man. The man says, 'I am here,'
and that is enough: he commands, imposes his will on the household. In other countries man and wife both work, but in Spain
the woman doesn't leave her house. The husband earns the wage
and he thinks that gives him the right to dominate his wife, to
consider her a slave. 'I've got my work, I earn the money, you've
got your house and if you complain I'll put my foot on your
throat.' That's how 70 percent of men here think. I don't know
whether it's lack of education or intelligence, or because since
childhood they've seen nothing else but that women are inferior
to them. . . .

I don't believe this attitude is right. I think more like a foreigner in this respect – a woman should have equal rights with a man and each should respect the other. The foreigners' way of living is much easier, much better than we know here – at least we Tajeños – because for the foreigners a man and a woman are equal. If they get on and understand each other, neither has to worry about his partner; each respects the other and they can live together happily. And if not, well they can go their own ways. Why make life more difficult than it already is? I've always thought like that even before the foreigners came.

There's a bricklayer here I'll tell you about: Paco Alarcon. Everyone knew that his wife was being unfaithful to him but no one wanted to tell him. At last a friend said something that made him suspicious. He pretended one morning to go to work as usual and came home a bit later to find his wife in bed with a man. He threw him out but without hurting him. Then he went out for bricks, sand and cement. When he got back he started to build a brick partition through the centre of the house, with his wife on one side and he on the other. With every brick he laid he called out to her, 'And this brick is for you, whore.' And that's how they've gone on ever since, he on one side and she on the other!

He had a lot of calm to do that. I don't know whether I would have had it. Not so many years ago a *novio* killed a *novia* who left him; he called her out at night and slashed her twenty or thirty times with a knife. I know a man whose *novia* left him seven years ago and every time he sees her his hair stands on end and he wants to kill her. As she comes down the street his friends say, 'Look, here comes your *novia*, here she comes . . .' and he suffers because of his pride. He says to himself, 'Here I am – and she has left me,' and that's what wounds his self-esteem. He's always thinking about what his friends will say.

I don't think there are many men who think as I do here. Certainly not among the youth. They're semi-men in my opinion, they don't want to be men in the way we grew up to be. I've seen a girl go up to a young lad and ask him to dance, and he answer quite calmly, 'I haven't got time at the moment.' Imagine that! What sort of behaviour is that for a man? When a woman asks a man to dance he gets up to dance with her whether he feels like it or not, whether he's drunk or sober, whether he's got shoes or not if he calls himself a man. But the young are a bit effeminate, they're not like the men before the war.

What is a man then? A man is tough, *macho*, a real male. The most male of all males. An extraordinary being whom God has put on earth to be as he should be. Agreed, he shouldn't assert himself over women, but he ought always to know a little more than a woman. He it is who takes the initiative while the woman does what he orders – as long as what he orders is correct, as long as he doesn't consider her his slave. The man should always have the sure certainty that he is a man and the woman should keep him company – with the same rights as he, while respecting his manliness.

A bachelor, Juan nearly twenty years ago became the *novio* of Isabel Gamez; their *noviazgo* lasted ten years. Though he prefers not to discuss the reasons for their break-up, he refers to Isabel still as his '*novia*' and, at heart, seems set on marrying her one of these days – if she is willing.

ISABEL GAMEZ   *Thirty-seven*

Cook

A plump, attractive-faced woman, who for the past twelve years has worked for a foreign family living near the village, Isabel has no hesitation about discussing what happened with Juan. Her life has been marked by the post-war years. When she was thirteen her father's provisions store failed and the family became nearly destitute. Her father had taken up with a woman and failed to pay the rent to their landlord – one of don Salvador Jimenez's relatives. The family was thrown out of the house; Isabel was taken out of school to look after her young sister. Because the family couldn't make ends meet, Isabel was taken in at the age of sixteen by an aunt in Málaga to look after her children. She stayed in the city four years.

I left Málaga and my aunt's house when I was twenty because my aunt wanted me to marry a widower. He was wealthy and was looking for a woman from our village to marry because his first wife came from here. She had been a servant in Málaga and he had fallen in love and married her. My aunt kept telling me I ought to marry him because I had no other future, because my family was poor and needed help.

'Why should I if I don't love him?' I said. He never came and spoke to me, it was through my aunt that everything passed. And she got very bitter when I refused. I had worked very hard for her all those years for my keep and the twenty-five pesetas a month she paid me; I was grateful to her for having kept me from going hungry, but I wasn't prepared to agree to this. One day, when she was going on about it again, I said to her: 'You'd better wait for your daughter to grow up so she can marry him,' and that night I left and came back to the village.

For three years before that Juan had been my *novio*. He worked with my father – despite everything my father has always been a good worker and he had been made foreman in the mica mine. Juan often came to our house to talk to my father; but one night he came to see me. I wasn't expecting him. 'There's a boy here who wants to talk to you,' my mother shouted. He asked her permission to sit down and took a chair by my side. Normally, he would have asked my father's permission first, but my father didn't want any part of it so that, if later we fell out, he wouldn't be involved. . . .

We became *novios* and every Tuesday, Wednesday and Friday nights he came to my house. That was the custom then – and on Sundays the cinema, after which the *novio* wasn't allowed in. Whenever I wanted to go out with him I had to ask my father. Or rather I had to ask my mother to ask him. That's the custom, the children ask their mother to ask their father because it's easier; the mother can more often get round the father than the child. In the family the father is the boss. Not that my father ever hit us or told us off as our mother did, but we knew he was the boss.

The man here is the boss in everything. As soon as you've got a *novio* he tries to dominate you. After three months he's a lot worse than one's father. When he comes visiting of an evening all he can say is: 'Don't wear that dress, don't have the sleeves short, don't put on make-up, don't get your hair cut. . . .' One thing after another. My *novio* was like all the rest: he wouldn't even let me go to mass. It wasn't that I'm all that religious but afternoon mass in those times was a way of getting out of the house. I used to have to go down side streets so he wouldn't see me. . . .

I don't know why he should have wanted to deprive me of the little amusement there was then; what else was there to do? Go for a walk along the road of an evening, the *paseo* in the square, wait for the taxi to come back from Málaga. We used to watch for it coming up the road from Casas Nuevas and when it arrived we'd all be in the square. If there was a stranger in it – ay! that was an event. But hardly any strangers ever came. The smallest distraction became something big. Ay! How long time seemed when I was young!

Once my *novio* and I went into a bar with four or five other pairs of *novios*; it was a fiesta and we were having a good time. It wasn't long before three of our mothers, including mine, arrived. My mother slapped me across the face twice for being in the bar. Wherever we went our mothers had to come too.

At that time no woman here would wear trousers; that was unheard of. Nor could she wear short sleeves; it wasn't decent to show any part of the arm or shoulder. No woman would cut her hair, the husbands and *novios* wouldn't allow it. All the girls were very frightened of their fathers and *novios* about this. When a new fashion came in the 1960s and, with some others, I cut my hair just a little and got a perm, my father wouldn't talk to me for several days. My *novio* and he were always at me too for using lipstick. I wouldn't stop though I had to promise to use less. As for dresses, I had only three; one from the last *feria* for Sundays, one for working in, and a dress for the next *feria*. It wasn't until the 1960s that all this began little by little to change. . . .

Juan and I were *novios* ten years. In all that time I don't think we ever talked about anything important, about life. Nor did the other *novios* to my knowledge. Perhaps it was because of the little education we had, I don't know. Many an evening the *novio* spent his time smoking while the girl looked at the wall without saying anything, especially if they'd had a quarrel.

It's a bad system, this *noviazgo*, at least the way I knew it. Talking for a couple of hours a few evenings a week you don't get to know each other. A mother doesn't allow it, she's always there. I remember once, I must have been twenty-four or twenty-five, my mother left us alone for a moment to go across the street. My *novio* gave me a kiss and she saw. When he'd gone she got angry and said I had no shame. 'You were only waiting for me to leave to give him a kiss.' 'But *mama*, what's wrong with that between *novios*?' She wouldn't have it, she was angry with me for several days.

It was always 'Don't do this, don't do that'. *Novias* allow themselves to be dominated because they're frightened the *novio* will leave them and they won't get married. That for the women of my time was the main thing. The only thing – to get married and have a house of her own. Whether the couple would get on well afterwards or not they couldn't know because they never got to know each other before. That's why so many of the marriages I've known have been failures.

I've seen it among my friends. The husband is never at home except to sleep. That's not living together, that's not being happy together. It's the custom for the men to go to the bar in the evening; but it shouldn't be the custom to fight and eat each other alive about it. No woman likes her husband to be out every night. No woman wants to be left at home all the time and never go to the cinema or for a walk. That's what happens.

My *noviazgo* ended ten years ago. It happened like this. A foreign woman came here and she used to go to Juan's bar a lot. I didn't think anything of it because Juan has always had foreigners in his place. The people probably knew but they wouldn't tell me. Then one day a woman said, 'Look, Isabelita, Juan goes to that woman's house every night and leaves in the morning. . . .' When I told him he said it was a lie. But the gardener in the house where I work told me one day he'd seen Juan in Málaga with the woman. That night I said to him: 'There are two roads here, the high road or the low road. I don't want you coming to my house and then going off with that woman. . . .'

It cost me a lot to say this after so many years together, but there was nothing else to do. We quarrelled and he went off. We didn't go out together again. A couple of months later his mother died. A woman came to call me, persuaded me to go to their house. I shouldn't have gone – but after so many years of being *novios*, what was a quarrel of a couple of months in these circumstances? I was wrong. As a result a woman cousin of Juan's began to talk behind my back, saying that Juan's mother had told her I had slapped Juan during our quarrel. It was a lie, I never slapped him. That is a very bad thing for a woman to do to a man; and yet if I had I would have had the courage also to say so myself. But the people believed the gossip and that made everything worse.

So with all this there was no going back. Since then two men have wanted me as their *novia*. Each time Juan has managed to turn them away. This happens often if a former *novio* doesn't want his *novia* to get married; he'll call the new suitor and have a talk with him. Juan told them I'd been his *novia* from the age of seventeen. 'Yes,' answered one of them, 'but I've known her these past five years and I haven't known you as her *novio*. You don't come to her house. . . .' 'No, but she has been my *novia*. . . .' The man came to me later and said things would be difficult. A suitor can't stand the insinuations and criticism of a former *novio*. To speak frankly, a suitor believes that after a *noviazgo* has lasted so long, something must have gone on between the two; the *novia* must be 'rotten' as they say here. And in all those ten years nothing happened – nothing but a kiss. A woman can't sleep with her *novio* and if she does she must get married immediately. But a suitor always imagines the worst.

From time to time in the past couple of years I have talked to Juan again. His conversation seems more interesting to me now. Perhaps it's because he talks to more intelligent people than before, more foreigners. He seems to understand more of the world. But there's one thing he's still frightened of – leaving the village. At thirty-eight! He's come again to ask me to marry him and I've told him that as long as he has his bar where, as his wife, I'd have to work for nothing as part of the family, I'm not having it. Years ago I'd have done it, but not now.

I don't care where I live, as long as I live well. Although in many ways I like the old customs, there's one thing about village life I hate: the gossip. In a city – in a place like London where I've been two years – everyone lives their own life. But not here.

Nor is there freedom enough. Not by a long way for women. The young girls want their freedom but they don't get it. The boys have it but not the girls. That's something that hasn't changed.

One of the two or three village women who have been abroad in recent years, Isabel did not find London, where her employers took her, particularly impressive. 'I didn't like the customs there much, especially those of the youth. They say they sleep with each other and I don't like that.' But she believes divorce should be allowed as in England. 'I've seen so many unhappy marriages here that it seems wrong a couple should have to stay together; or that the man can leave but the woman has to remain with a dead life in front of her.'

Isabel's younger brother married the sister of Juana Gonzalez; the latter is married to Juan Gonzalez, the young goatherd, now master bricklayer, we met earlier. They are second cousins though they hardly knew each other until they became *novios*. Juana is the daughter of Cristóbal Gonzalez, the former sharecropper of *El Verdegal*, and grew up on the farm; today she and Juan and their children live in a house opposite Isabel Gamez while the latter's brother and wife, Juana's sister, live next door.

JUANA GONZALEZ   *Thirty-one*

Housewife

I always said to myself, 'I don't want a *novio* from the countryside, never. Let it be a man from the village so I can live there instead. . . .'

It's not that I don't like the land. But I saw how hard my father had to work and for what? Nothing. From the age of thirteen I worked alongside him. Any country girl without brothers at home had to work the land; and my only brother was away a lot, working on the coast. Sometimes I went out day-labouring, picking beans, carobs, olives to earn forty or fifty pesetas for twelve hours in the fields. My mother let me keep the money for the things I'd have to buy to get married one day.

Our house was small; we had no electricity, no bathroom, no toilet – we had to go out into the cowpen – no kitchen, no water. Two bedrooms, one just big enough for a single bed for my brother and the other with two beds, one for my parents and the other for my sister and me. We cooked in the hearth and heated water to wash ourselves over the fire.

The only time I went to the village was on a Sunday, except for the three years I was at school. My father took me away at the age of thirteen because he needed me on the land. After that I came up so rarely I used to go mad waiting for Sunday to come. I had to go with my parents or with the parents of two girl-friends who lived further down in the country. The only place we young girls could go together alone was to the cinema. What a pleasure that was!

When I was seventeen a foreigner started to build a house on a bit of land close by *El Verdegal*. Juan was a labourer on the house and I used to see him on the path when I went to the spring for water. One day I got a letter from him saying he was going to come to my house to talk to me. I told my mother. 'He'll come for nothing,' I said, because I didn't trust him. He'd had a *novia* for twelve or thirteen years and had just broken with her.

'Don't write him or answer,' my mother said. I didn't. Then one night he pushed his way in and sat down next to me in the cinema. He said he was coming to my house the next Wednesday. 'Don't come to my house,' I said, 'I don't want you. . . .' 'Yes, on Wednesday I'm coming, you wait for me.'

My mother didn't want him at all. She nearly hit me one day because of him. She was angry that he had left his former *novia*. 'The same will happen to you, daughter. He'll go back to her in a couple of months.' I thought the same but I liked him too much already.

He came to my house the night he said he would. I didn't turn him away. He came again on the Friday and that meant we were *novios*. The fact of coming to one's house makes a man one's *novio*. As soon as a man says he's coming to one's house one knows what it's for. A few weeks before another suitor had come to my house but I had told him not to come back.

We were *novios* a year and a half. That wasn't long. The reason most people take so long is that they can't get the money together. Not that I had anything saved. Before getting married I had to buy the linen, towels, kitchen utensils which are what the *novia* has to provide. The *novio* buys the furniture.

Each time I got 200 or 300 pesetas together I'd go to Málaga. To help me my father gave me a pig to fatten. I had to hide it because otherwise the landowner would have claimed her half share of it since my father was a sharecropper. One day the señorita came down and my father shouted, 'Juana, the pig!' I hurried to take it to the next-door farm where I tied it up. Almost immediately afterwards, while the señorita Rosalia was talking to my father, the pig arrived at the door. 'Where does that pig come from?' my father exclaimed. 'Oh, that belongs to Maria de la Cruz,' I answered. 'Imagine that pig coming all the way over here,' said the señorita. How we laughed among ourselves when she had gone!

I sold the pig and made 700 pesetas. Off I went to Málaga again. All in all I suppose I went three or four times. The last trip I remember I had 1,000 pesetas – ay! what a lot of money that seemed ten years ago!

We got married in 1960. Because we were cousins we had to get a dispensation from the bishop of Málaga. It meant filling out forms with the names of the family as far back as our great-grandfathers. No one in the family could remember them. We had to get an old lady in the village, who remembers everything like that, to give us their names.

Everyone knows everyone in the village. But ask for a person by his proper name and no one knows him. Ask for me as Juana *del Verdegal* and everyone knows me. When they ask my daughter who she is she says, 'My mother is Juana *del Verdegal*.' All our family on my father's side is known from the name of the farm. On my mother's side all my relatives are known by the nickname of *Petrolero* because my grandfather used to sell paraffin. . . .

My first child was still-born. I was very unhappy and I made a vow to the patron saint that if she gave me a girl the next time I would name my daughter after her. I have a lot of faith in the Virgin – all of us do – and my faith was rewarded. I went and prayed to her and she gave me a daughter! I had told Juan what I had done. When he came back from the hospital my mother-in-law asked what the child was going to be called. 'Maria of the Rock,' he answered. That was the start of all the trouble with my mother-in-law.

She wanted the child named after her, as by custom would have been right.* But I had made my vow and couldn't change it. When I explained it to her on my return, and said the next

* First children traditionally receive their paternal grandparents' Christian names, succeeding children their maternal grandparents' names.

daughter would be named after her, she said it made no difference. But behind my back she went round saying to the neighbours that I hadn't called my daughter after her because I found her name ugly. One day when I had gone out to watch a Holy Week procession she came upstairs and had a fight with my mother about it. Ever since she hasn't looked on me with a good eye.

The day I have grand-daughters I won't care whether they're called after me. I can understand that if one's mother-in-law has an ugly name like Catalina or something one wouldn't want to call one's daughter after her. But Teresa, Juana – those aren't ugly names. This business of names seems very antiquated to me; but my sister will have the same trouble with her mother-in-law, Isabel Gamez's mother, if her first baby is a girl, that's for sure.

When my daughter was born I put ear-rings on her straight away. Two or three days after the birth of a girl the mother is always running round looking for someone to pierce her ears. It's a custom here, like dressing a baby girl in pink and a boy in blue. That way, when the people see the ear-rings they know it's a girl and don't have to ask.

My second child, a boy, we named after Juan's father, and our third after my father, Cristóbal. I don't really want more children. Nowadays most women want smaller families than in the past, three children or four at the most. They know they can't enjoy life with a big family. My grandmother had eight – and her only amusement, she used to tell me, was going to mass. She had to work as hard as a man on the farm and, because there was so little food, she breast-fed her children until they were three. My father remembers getting hungry out in the fields with the men and running home to ask his mother for the breast. Imagine how strong she had to be with eight children!

When I worked in the fields, I never felt ashamed, though it's not woman's work. I've said this to my husband — 'Why aren't men the same?' But no, my husband won't do any housework, he won't wash a dish, won't sweep up – nothing. Not only he, almost all the men are like that. They say it's woman's work and it's shameful for a man to do it.

It's the same in the home, the woman can't be boss of anything. If a woman tries the people talk about it all over the village. 'So-and-so is the boss, ay! why has her husband so many pairs of trousers?' That happens when a woman tells her husband he's not to go out one night. Usually it's the husband who says, 'I'm going out,' and the woman who has to shut up. I've never said anything because it seems ugly to me to do so – and anyway what does it matter to me? A man is a man and it's he who's the boss. But there are a lot of women who try to keep their husbands under their thumb.

Only on Sundays does the husband take his wife and children out in the village; the other days the wife stays at home. I don't mind, it's not worth fighting about. Since I got married I think I've been to a bullfight in Málaga with Juan only once. He's been more often; he'll say, 'I'm going to the bulls tomorrow. . . .' Once, when I knew my mother would look after my daughter, I said, 'You'll take me with you, won't you?' 'No,' he replied, because a whole group of men were going. I got fed up then, but on the other hand I thought, 'What would I have done alone amongst so many men?'

Life today for the young is beautiful. *Novios* can hold hands in the street, the man put his arm round his *novia*'s shoulder. Only ten years ago, if my mother had seen me do that she would have hit me. When I went to a dance before I had a *novio* I couldn't dance with a boy; it had to be another girl. Now you never see two girls dancing together. When I was Juan's *novio* I could dance only with him – and since he doesn't know how, I could only dance with a girl. The youth today is much better off. There's more freedom – too much, I sometimes think.

Parents can't control their children at all. Plenty of mothers with young daughters say, 'When this one grows up I'll kill her.' But they won't be able to. I tell them, 'No, we'll all have to put up with it.'

My daughter who is eight knows a lot more than I do. I keep telling her to study hard to make up for the little I and her father know. Next year, perhaps, she'll be able to start learning English. As long as she has an education she'll be all right; she won't need a profession because here in Tajos what position would there be for her? What I want is that she gets a good job in a shop or something like that and stays in the village.

No, no! I wouldn't want her to leave the village. If she got a scholarship and could study for a profession – well, I suppose we'd have to let her go. . . . But she says she doesn't want to leave the village to study. She never wants to leave my side. When she travels she gets sick in the bus; we went to Casas Nuevas and the poor thing vomited straight away. To leave me and spend the night away – oh no! Perhaps when she gets older she'll change. But in truth I would like her to stay in Tajos.

Such sentiments as Juana's are not rare; the reluctance of parents to see their children leave the village is very marked. Fear of the outside world, of travel, of the sickness which is invariably said to accompany it, are induced early.

Juana's daughter Maria often accompanies Isabel Gamez to the house where she works to play with the foreigners' children. Once it was suggested that she spend the night there. She seemed happy at the idea but it was greeted by cries of 'Ay! she'll be frightened', from her mother and tales of ghosts and monsters on her father's part. Maria, however, overcame her fears, aided in part perhaps by Isabel's presence overnight in the house.

Juan Gonzalez, a good-looking man, does not overtly subscribe to the wish to see his sons or daughter remain for ever in the village if they are to have a career; his doubts are more concerned about the possibility of their achieving a profession. From goatherd by way of being a building labourer, he has become a self-taught bricklayer earning 500 pesetas a day down on the coast. For himself he has no further ambition than to finish building a house of his own. . . .

JUAN GONZALEZ   *Thirty-eight*

Bricklayer, former goatherd

Finding somewhere of our own to live has been my biggest problem since I got married. At that time my parents had just bought a house and they let me have the attic. A stroke of luck, I thought at the time. I put the little money I had saved into making a flat out of it. When I'd done that I found that my parents wouldn't let me put it in my name. Nor would they let me open a separate doorway into the street, so we always have to go through my parents' part.

I think one or more of my brothers or sisters has put them up to it because they were frightened that I was somehow going to get half the house for myself. They wouldn't get their share of the inheritance, they thought, if that happened. How they think I could have managed to do it I don't know, because the whole house is in my parents' name. But what was certain was that when they died I was going to lose the flat because the house would be divided among the six of us children. When that happens my brothers and sisters will see the trouble I can make! Between the six of us each one will get about two metres of house and the portions will be drawn for by lot. If I draw a lot in the middle, then they'll see because they won't be able to do anything without my consent.

The trouble is there's no public housing in Tajos as there is in many other villages round here. There's a terrible shortage of houses and land on which to build. And nowadays a building site fetches the same price for one of us as it does for a foreigner.

My mother had a bit of land which a foreigner, who died soon afterwards, had bought. As he hadn't paid for it in full it reverted to my mother. Things got so bad over the years with my wife and mother quarrelling, as always happens, that at last I told my mother, 'Either you give me a bit of that land or I'll break down the wall to make a door to the street.'

She said she'd have to give a bit to each of my brothers and sisters if she did that. 'Don't think of it,' I said. 'The further away I am from them the better.' At last I persuaded her, but even then she wouldn't give me the deeds. She keeps them in an old chest no one can open – I know, I've tried often enough! Finally one of my sisters, who understands a bit more of these things than the others, explained to her that there was no way in which I could make off with all her land. That's what all this time she had feared.

I'd put about 35,000 pesetas into my flat. For that money I could have built a house ten years ago! But not now – prices have tripled and quadrupled since then. For my bit of land I've had to give my mother back the flat and pay her 10,000 pesetas on top. So the land has cost me 45,000 pesetas.

For the last two years in my spare time I've been building the house. My uncle, who is a mason, and my father-in-law have helped me too, and so have those whom I've helped in the past on their houses. For the sake of one's looks no one will help, but to repay work I've done to help them they will. And my brothers and sisters have helped too. They're happy to see me building my own house because they know that the day our parents die there'd be trouble if I was still in the flat. I wouldn't have money enough to buy the whole house and I wouldn't have let anyone throw me out of my part. Not if all the *guardias* in the world had tried!

There are plenty of other problems when you're married and have got children. Take schooling. I and many other fathers have been to talk to the school director about it; it's not properly organized. One of the girls' schools is held in the slaughter-house. I know it has never been used as a slaughter-house but all the same it's not properly equipped for a school; there aren't proper lavatories, it's open and draughty and the kids are always catching colds. The director says until there's a new school complex built here he can't do anything about it.

Then there's the problem of a state-run nursery school. They say they're going to provide one but they haven't yet. I've had my five-year-old boy in a sort of school run by a policeman's daughter. It was frightening the number of kids she had in an old house without any ventilation. Eighty or ninety there must have been in there; I was sure one day they'd suffocate. I don't know how some of the rich allowed their children to go there.

They've stopped that now and some of the children go by special bus to Arroyo de la Reina. 3,500 pesetas a month that costs! How can I find that sort of money when it's more than a week's wage for me?

I'm quite satisfied with the education my Maria is getting, though. She has learned to read and write well, something I've never been able to do because I only went to school a few months. But I won't be able to afford to give her a profession. As it is now, even if she gets a scholarship to go to Ronda for secondary studies I'll have to bring her back. That's what has happened to a number of parents; they can't afford the costs that aren't included in the scholarship, the books, clothes, linen and a whole series of things.

Unless this new law the school director has told us about comes in. It's going to mean that there will be full scholarships for all kids who are bright. Later, when they're earning, the students will have to pay the state back so much a year. But if a *señorito*'s son isn't clever he won't get a scholarship. The new system sounds excellent. Why should a worker's child have to suffer because his father can't afford to give him a profession? Up to now, if you were the son of a labourer you had to die a labourer. Or a bricklayer. What other profession could you learn in the village?

Another big problem is medical care. When a child is always ill, you want the doctor here to give you a slip to see a specialist in Málaga on the social security. But the local doctor wants to cure everyone himself. There's only the one doctor here now and there's a population of 10,000 between village and countryside. He can't attend to everyone and he's always protesting about the number of social security patients he has to attend to. He forgets that social security costs us 300 pesetas a month – and he gets paid something for each patient. On top of that he likes a tip when we go to him! Well, one has to keep in with a village doctor, otherwise. . . .

The other day we had to take my youngest son down to a doctor in Casas Nuevas because this one hadn't cured him of a cold he's had for several months. We were worried it might become chronic. The local doctor had seen him four times and prescribed more than forty injections in different series. The poor kid is so frightened of injections now that he has to be held down when the *practicante** comes.

Well, the doctor in Casas charged me 300 pesetas and the medicine he prescribed cost me another 434 pesetas. None of that was on social security, of course. And even when it is, it still costs money. I had a bad chest cold this winter and the local doctor prescribed a course of five daily injections, a box of twelve suppositories and another of powdered vitamin. Each medicine was a separate prescription and the lot cost me ninety-four pesetas. And that was the second course of treatment; I'd already had a week's medication before which cost even more though I can't remember the exact sum.

Parents always want the best for their children, don't they? Last year when both my older children needed tonsil operations I went to a private doctor who said he'd charge me 6,000 pesetas for the

* Medical assistant whose principal job is to give injections.

two unless I could get a certificate showing I was on the poor list. I went to the mayor and explained my case and he made me out the paper immediately. The two operations cost me 105 pesetas. The same surgeon and everything! I didn't want my children operated on by a social security doctor. I don't trust them, it might have been one who was still studying or something.

How things have changed since I was young! I was minding goats when I was my daughter's age. I had a respect which amounted to fear of my father – we all did in those times. Not that he ever hit me, never in his life. But he only had to say 'that' and we obeyed. No one answered their father back, no one smoked in front of him, no one went into the same bar as he, everyone called their father *Usted*, and not *tu*. Even at twenty and older I, and all those I knew, went in mortal fear of our fathers. There was no escaping it. Nowadays all that's gone and it's not a bad thing. I don't want my children to be frightened of me. They have a certain respect, but they don't mind answering back; I think that's much better than what I knew.

When my children grow up life is going to be even more different, I believe. My sort of childhood and youth in which one couldn't breathe has already gone. I remember the mother of the *novia* I broke off with after twelve years coming out of her house shouting and wanting to hit me every time I passed. She had it in for me – until her daughter got a new *novio*. Then the people came to me saying I ought to tell him that she had been my *novia*, to warn him off. But I said no, she didn't interest me any more; I knew Juana was the woman for me. Otherwise I'd have scared the man off.

Prosperity which has come with the foreigners has changed so many things. Not all for the good. There's more envy than there used to be. The women especially are always going on about a neighbour who has just done up her house, got new furniture or something or other. They lay bets as to whose sons will be better dressed. They're jealous, very jealous, women here. They won't say anything directly to their husband but they'll tell a woman friend and her husband tells him what his own wife has been saying. The trouble with women – Spanish women at any rate – is that they're always trying to dominate a man. It's one of those things that makes marriage difficult here. When a man wants to go to a bar in the evening, when he wants to go to Málaga for the

day, they don't want him to. They're always after the one thing –
to be boss of the man.

Perhaps that will change too, but I doubt it. All the same when
my children grow up, if things go on at the rate they're going, it'll
be like living in a foreign country. Three kids from here, the
youngest can't be more than fifteen, just ran away to the
Canaries because their parents wouldn't let them be, wouldn't let
them grow their hair and all that sort of thing. So what's it going
to be like in eight or nine years when my sons are that age?

Well, I won't really mind as long as they've learnt enough to
get on in life and keep out of trouble. If my daughter can make a
career as a schoolteacher or something like that she'll have to
leave the village. And so will my sons because there are no professional posts for them here. I hope they are clever enough to
learn a profession; a father always has more hopes for his sons
than his daughters because a man has more problems about
getting work than a woman. Anyway, as long as they know how
to look after themselves, here or abroad, what more could a father
ask of them?

A FOREIGN COUNTRY

'My name is Juan. I'm your guide. Juan, don't forget. Now we are going to Tajos – twelve miles and we climbing all the time. . . .' The air-conditioned bus lurches off the coast road with its cargo of pre-packaged tourists. A couple of years ago one of the tour companies on the coast put Tajos on the map; and now, three times a week, its streamlined buses disgorge their cargo of day-trippers in the square.

'The road is very bad, it will take forty minutes. 1,500 feet we climb. The weather is a little wet. It is only the second time it rained. Here on Costa del Sol sun shines 300 days a year.' The day-trippers stare at the damp land and the sea sprawled limply along its rim; inexcusably, the hot 'sun-and-sea' tourist scenery has disappeared for the day.

Juan is undaunted, as befits his profession. On the outskirts of Arroyo de la Reina his voice takes on a new urgency: 'Here everyone building. Costa del Sol is only twelve years old, you see, so everyone building very hard. Here you see the beautiful private houses. . . .'

Through firmly-fastened wrought-iron gates and over the high walls there is a glimpse of gravelled drives, spacious gardens and swimming-pools. The bus crawls past them; a hundred yards up the road the empty portals of an *urbanicíon* stand beckoning to the vacant land beyond. 'Plots to Sell', proclaims the enormous billboard in five languages. 'Water, light. . . .' Under the scrub which now covers the land the faint traces of terraces can still be discerned.

Looking for more natural enhancements to the landscape, Juan starts pointing out olive trees, almonds, figs. His eye catches something and he exclaims: 'Look – look at that woman doing her washing down there!' The figure in black looks up briefly from the irrigation channel, then returns to her clothes. The day-trippers – a small cross-section of the twenty-seven million tourists who visited Spain in 1971 – crane forward in silence; it is not for such sights that they have come.

On the coast Tajos is advertised as the classic, whitewashed Andalusian village; more importantly, as the place where the handicrafts sold in tourist shops on the coast are actually made and can be bought cheaply. '15 percent cheaper than Torremolinos or Marbella,' says Juan as the trippers get off the bus and stand bemused in the square until he hurries them off. Cristóbal Moreno's shop is the first port of call.

When these bus-tours first began, Tajeños stood in the square and stared at the day-trippers in their exotic garb. Girls in mini-skirts if not in bikinis on hot summer days aroused considerable comment. 'They have no shame,' said a middle-aged woman. 'Of course not,' replied another, 'here they aren't known. In their own *pueblo* it would be different. . . .' The men were equally disapproving; but their comments were cruder and betrayed the ambivalence that the sight of 'undressed' women aroused.

Today no one stares; the day-trippers are part of the scenery, bringing an influx of cash to shops and bars. Both have increased in numbers, the bars especially, for tourism is not confined to the thrice-weekly buses; more and more tourist cars find their way to Tajos now.

It is not this type of tourism which has brought affluence to the village, however. That – or rather the full employment which is its cause – comes from the coast. The village alone cannot provide jobs for more than 30 percent of its working population: each day the local buses transport the remaining 70 percent to the coast; bricklayers and building labourers among the men mainly; shopgirls and hotel maids among the women.

For the first time this century – indeed perhaps in history – every able-bodied Tajeño has work; for the past three or four years full employment has meant jobs not only for men but for their sons and daughters as well.

In the past dozen years money wages have increased almost tenfold; by north European standards they are still low. A bricklayer or mason earns about £16 a week, a labourer about £11 and a maid about £6. Inflation, worsened by tourist prices, has pushed up the cost of living astronomically. Despite this, it remains that where several sons and daughters are working *family* incomes have increased very considerably.

Some of the changes in the village over the past years can be quantified. In 1957 there were two lorries, two taxis (of the vintages described by Isidro Garcia), one motor-scooter and no private cars. There was no public transport and the mail arrived by donkey from Casas Nuevas each night. Television was unknown, only the better-off owned radios and about a dozen newspapers were sold every day.

Today, fourteen years later, there are more than twenty lorries, five modern taxis, close on ninety private cars and a swarm of small, noisy motor-cycles. Buses go to Casas Nuevas every hour and to Málaga twice a day. The tiled roofs have sprouted television aerials in every direction and 125 newspapers are bought daily.

Most of the houses have been 'done up'. Bathrooms, gas cookers, refrigerators and washing machines are commonplace. This progress, whose effects on health and hygiene the midwife has described, is taken by most as a matter of course. To the old, however, it often seems like a miracle. 'Compared to my youth – ozu! The difference is like day to night.' An old goatherd remarks how happy he is to see the tourists in the streets. 'Every time I can help one I do it gladly. Isn't it thanks to them that this village is prosperous now?'

Dress, so important in Andalusia, has lost its significance as a distinguishing mark of social status. Everyone dresses more or less alike; everyone goes to more or less the same bars. In consequence it is widely put forward by the ruling group and by many workers as well that social distinctions are non-existent today. At the day-to-day level of human concourse this may be true; but at other moments the differences are clearly felt. 'Look who goes,' say the workers as members of the ruling group prepare for some official function. 'Whose sons can get an education? – only those of the rich'; 'If I had money all the authorities would be my friends.' Even burials incite the ironic comment: 'You can tell when a rich man dies, they toll the bell for a couple of hours. For the poor just a few tolls, that's all.'

Resentment is sporadic, localized, individual; in the larger political perspective it is usually unformed. Consumerism is steam-rollering over the past as progress has concreted over the streets and the square. Gone are the old cobbles through which the live rock once penetrated, gone the beaten earth surface of the square. On its periphery the two bars have been modernized; but here something of the past remains. The old men gather to play dominoes, cards and watch television; workers come in for a *copita* before going to work; in the evenings men crowd round the counters before going home to eat. No concessions are made to tourists: it is as though the villagers had determined that the outside world should not enter here. The square has become a redoubt; some fear it may become a ghetto yet.

'These baskets made of cactus plant – very strong. Before we make shoes of that stuff,' Juan says, pointing at the wares outside Cristóbal's shop which is in a side street off the square. Inside a young English girl is trying on a Cordovan hat. 'I don't suppose anyone wears them,' she says. 'Yes dear,' her mother answers, 'I'm sure Spaniards do.' Re-

assured, the girl joins the other day-trippers milling around
Cristóbal who is fully occupied at the till.

'They sure trust you the way they leave these mantillas
around,' says an American woman by the door. Her husband
grimaces. 'They're watching you, honey, they're watching,'
he replies. Juan begins to round up his flock. The twenty
minutes allotted for shopping are just about up.

'Well, it wasn't bad,' says the middle-aged English woman
on the return trip. 'No, not bad at all,' says her husband. 'I
quite enjoyed myself.'

At the back of the bus American voices rise over the sound
of the diesel in first gear for the descent. 'It made me feel good
all over to be in a place like that. . . .' 'Yes, happy. . . . The
trees and the mountains. . . .'

Under darkening clouds the sea below has turned purple.
Orange trees stand out against the lighter green of a terrace
of sugar-cane. Here and there small pockets of maize, barley
and tomatoes are growing. Everywhere there are more signs
of the bulldozer than the plough.

The bus flattens out for the run across the *vega* to Casas
Nuevas and its festival of lights. Lightning flashes across the
horizon. Juan breaks a long silence as the bus takes a curve.
'And from here you see the lights of Tajos – heh, that's where
we were. Tajos, you know.'

FOREIGNERS

The Coming of Tourism

The villagers distinguish between day-trippers and residents; the former are 'tourists', the latter 'foreigners'. There are now about 300 foreigners living in the Tajos countryside, most of these at some distance from the village itself. The majority of the new villas have been built in the last few years as rising prices on the coast forced foreigners to look for cheaper land elsewhere.

ANTHONY FERRER   *Fifty-six*

A former British diplomat, Anthony Ferrer was the first foreigner to buy land in Tajos. Of Anglo-Spanish parentage, he was serving in Madrid when, in 1951, he came to the coast looking for a house. One afternoon out of curiosity he drove up to Tajos.

When I got to the village after a terrible drive up the dirt road it seemed as though the whole population had turned out. People crowded round the car to watch me get out and when I walked through the streets I was followed by a crowd of young boys who gawped at me as though I'd come from another planet.

The village struck me immediately as very beautiful but also very poor and isolated. The streets were full of mule and goat

186

droppings and the houses weren't very white. In the poorer streets at the top there were a great many thatched hovels, and even in the lower streets a lot of the houses were dilapidated.

I didn't stay long – in fact I didn't think any more about Tajos until one day I got a letter from Lazaro Lopez whom I'd met offering me a twenty-five-acre farm with a thousand trees and a house with a spring a couple of kilometres outside the village. The asking price was 200,000 pesetas.

I thought about it. It struck me that I'd rather have a farm up here than a plot on the coast, so I wrote back saying I was interested. I came and saw the farm and liked it very much. The house was a classic Andalusian two-storied farmhouse with tall windows and a large front door. After the usual bargaining, I bought it a year later. I paid 160,000 pesetas which was about £1,500 in those days.

By the standards of the times the farm was certainly not one of the poorest. And yet, you know, there were swallows nesting in the rooms where people were living, and in what's now my kitchen they kept their goats. The man who was living here I kept on as a gardener at a monthly salary of fifty pesetas. Not that he had much to do because there wasn't sufficient water to irrigate a great deal.

It was a mystery to me on what people lived. The value of agricultural products was so small I couldn't see how they made both ends meet. Quite a few, obviously, didn't have enough to eat – though the majority did. They lived very simple lives, really; their outlook on life was so limited, it seemed to me, that they didn't realize what existed outside the confines of the village. As you might expect, they were very superstitious; their religion was largely an idolatrous catholicism. I was brought up a catholic in Spain, so I'm comparing urban with rural practices; no doubt the same differences are true of Italy, for example.

Men here have often related to me the visions they've had in the mountains, and when I laughed have said, very seriously, that this was no laughing matter. My gardener, who is forty, firmly believes that menstruating women, simply by looking at plants or trees, have the power of making them wither and die. Goatherds think that a sleeping place in the mountains near a nest of *lagartos** is safe because if snakes approach the lizard will manoeuvre its

* A large lizard with the appearance of an iguana.

tail into the man's ear and wake him up. Any woman called Maria is protected from snakes because on the flight to Egypt the Virgin Mary warded off a snake. . . . And so on.

At the material level they knew so little of the outside world that the smallest thing was precious to them. I used to have to go to Gibraltar quite frequently and my gardener would ask me to bring him back a bicycle lamp, for example. That for him would be a prized and treasured possession. Now he'd sneeze at a bicycle, he's got a motorbike and it's a car he's really hankering after. The change in expectations has been enormous.

When I came here I knew hardly anything about village life in Spain, and for the first few years I only came on holiday. All the same I was surprised, I remember, by the way the village saw itself as a family. When I went – indeed, when I go – to Málaga villagers whom I know purely by sight will stop and greet me affectionately simply because I too come from Tajos. When a villager meets another outside the village they're of the same family!

It operates within the village, too. People who commit misdemeanours aren't as a rule denounced to the Guardia Civil or police. Actually, there weren't any municipal police here until 1956 or 1957 when don Manuel became mayor. No, they're usually admonished by the mayor. For example, a policeman who was involved in some money business was simply removed from the police and given a minor job in the town hall. A man who makes a living as a middle-man buying and selling land 'sold' some of the municipality's land on one occasion. He was told off and warned not to do it again but no further action was taken. There are many such incidents I could relate. Conciliation is a very important feature of village life.

The village 'family' functions in such a way as never, if possible, to throw anyone out. Up to a point the corollary of what I've just been saying is that the authorities aren't denounced by the people either – at least not until the situation has become quite flagrant. There is always plenty of open criticism but little immediate action. There's the well-known case of the man who for a time was mayor and feathered his nest very nicely during the famine years by selling half the village rations and pocketing the proceeds. Later, during a long spell of drought, he used his position to dig a *mina* and sold the water. The fact that tampering with water is a serious offence and that he was reducing the village supply didn't trouble him at all. The people were very voluble in their criticism but not to the point of actually doing anything. It took two successive mayors and a considerable fight which involved the Civil Governor in the end before he could be restrained.

The point I want to make is that the *pueblo*, the people, are very patient. But in the long run they will always revolt against improper use of authority.

The Spanish character is one of an intense feeling of equality. Everyone feels himself as good as the next person, the lowest as good as the highest. It has – or had – nothing to do with financial status; it's a matter of innate feeling. But today I'm no longer sure. The enormous changes brought about by tourism, all of them packed virtually into the last five or six years, are having their effect. The people have become more grasping, more demanding, more arrogant even. If you as much as remind them of how they lived in the past they get on their high horse and tell you that is not how people live today. I think this change has brought with it a feeling of unrest and consequently of unhappiness too. From television they've learned about a world they had never even dreamed of before; in effect this means that they're now aware of all the things they can't have.

Status has entered into it. Before, no one was much better or worse off than his neighbour. Now one may be quite a lot better off because he has sold a plot of land or something of the sort. So he has a car. 'Why can't we have a car too and go on picnics on Sundays?' the neighbours say.

I've always liked the local craft-work, especially the esparto donkey trappings and that sort of thing. I used to buy these from a man in the village. He was so poor he was on the point of emigrating. He was always asking me to come in with him, and eventually I did; I set up a small shop and employed him on a good salary and commission. The business went fairly well and he became quite famous; his work was displayed at national and international exhibitions, he was on TV and in the papers. He was able to buy his own house, furnish it completely, buy a TV and eventually to set up on his own. When he left he said I had to give him a golden handshake.

Under our contract I wasn't obliged to. However, I said I'd give him a month's wage for every year he had worked which would have made about 25,000 pesetas. He demanded 125,000 pesetas. 'Nothing doing,' I said. He came back and said he had been to the *sindicato* and that I owed him 400,000 pesetas. I consulted my lawyer who agreed that legally I wasn't obliged to pay him anything; but he suggested that this man could give me so much trouble by making me defend the case before the *sindicato* in Málaga that it was better to settle with him. In the end I did – for 50,000 pesetas.

I cite this only as an example of the change of mentality in recent years. New values are replacing the old because of the sudden prosperity brought by tourism. Here was a man who was virtually impoverished if not on the verge of starvation, who became famous and comfortably off largely through my efforts; yet when the moment came he bit the hand which had fed him.

Over the years Anthony Ferrer has restored and converted his farmhouse into a permanent home. He spends his time nowadays developing the rest of his twenty-five acres on which he has built a number of houses for sale to foreigners. Excluding these, he estimates that the land which he bought for £1,500 twenty years ago would be worth something between £90,000 and £120,000 at current building prices.

AVERY MARK   *Forty-two*

Architect

Four years after Ferrer's purchase, Avery Mark, a South African architect, visited the village for the first time. Twenty-seven years old at the time, he had been staying on the coast and heard about the *feria* in Tajos. Told it was impossible to get there by car, he took a chance and reached the village.

I was bowled over by the village immediately. I remember walking up the street to the pine trees on the mountainside and looking down over the tiled roofs, the church and the land to the sea. The view was so dramatic I wondered whether it wouldn't be too overpowering to live with! And then the people – I had the immediate feeling they were sympathetic. The *feria* was marvellous, all the people in from the countryside to join the villagers in the great social and festive occasion of the year.

I decided I wanted to live there. I asked around and Lazaro Lopez found me some land outside the village. When he pointed it out I thought he was crazy. There I had been looking at plots down on the coast and here he was offering me three acres of farm. But the price of £600 was about right. I borrowed £200 from a friend who thought I was crazy and signed the contract. The owner put his thumb-print on it and that was that. All done on trust, without my being able to speak a word of Spanish really.

I designed and built my own house. It was then that I discovered how right my feelings about the people had been that first day. It's hard to describe their generosity and honesty. While I was building a guy who came to stay – a foreigner – conned me out of practically everything I had. I had no money to pay the wages or anything. I wanted to stop building but the men wouldn't stop. No one would take money from me in the village, they went on for at least a month building before I could pay them. When my wife and I went to South Africa for a while, all the workers' wives brought us presents – at least twenty chickens and dozens of eggs! Our welcome back was even greater – far warmer than anything when we got to South Africa.

Generosity and honesty is a basic part of the people's character. In all my time in Tajos I never had anything stolen, never locked my house. . . . Living among Tajenos I learned a normality that I'd never known. I discovered that the forms of human concourse, which had been worked out over centuries through thick and thin, were beautifully simple and fulfilling. This was when I started to learn to design, working together with the craftsmen.

Mediterranean peoples have a feeling for form; their building materials are simple and, left to themselves, they don't mess them up. Coming from South Africa where there's no tradition at all, where everything is designed to be seen – as opulent status symbols – I was very influenced by village architecture. Here everything is hidden. You go off a little street into a door in a wall – and it's not until you're inside the house that you see what it is. They're proud but they're not boastful, and that makes all the difference.

The craftsmen impressed me by their particular skills at stone work, tile laying and plastering. The traditional materials have been stone, lime and earth from which they made mortar. The size of the houses and the pitch of the roofs was limited to the timber they had: olive, originally, and later poplar. The lime in Tajos is very good and the constant whitewashing is like painting on a coat of cement. That's why, when a house is unlived in for a time and not whitewashed, it just falls to bits.

Where the craftsmen come to grief is when foreigners without much idea of building try to give them new ideas. They're so polite, so reluctant to offend that they never refuse; but of course it usually comes out badly.

This politeness can go to extraordinary lengths. There was a time when the whole village started talking a terrible Spanish. They were too polite to correct me and instead talked the way I did!

It has its drawbacks too, this reluctance to offend, because they'll tell you only what they think you want to hear. But when you start to think the way they do, things work out very nicely. I don't like Germanic efficiency and I'd be unhappy to see that here. On a building site everything gets muddled up but no one ever says, 'That's not my department'; everyone is always willing to pitch in and help.

One day a foreigner came across my land. It was John Black who, in his marvellous way, had taken the wrong path down to Casas. He and his wife Ruth came in and we had a couple of glasses of wine and the next thing I knew I was building a house for him. Then, for something to do, he put an ad in an English paper saying: *Have you ever thought of owning your own castle in Spain?* He did it more for the pleasure of answering letters than doing business; but as his answers were so amusing people actually began to want to come here. Suddenly I found I had a building company.

There weren't such things as quantity surveyors in those days to work out prices, but I had a feeling for what things would cost. It was in 1960 and the first people to come with money were wanting to build houses, to retire to mainly.

From nothing in a couple of years the company expanded until it had its own carpentry and iron-work shops and was employing 150 men. It was the biggest enterprise in Tajos since the *mica* mining company; all in all we built about thirty houses in the countryside around here.

I wasn't really interested in the company to make money; I was interested in designing houses for people who wanted them. I didn't have contracts and variation orders and all the things needed to protect one in this sort of business and soon I found that clients weren't paying for all ·the extras and modifications they wanted. Quite frankly, I was a very bad businessman and didn't know about capital. I expanded too fast, and the company was always under-capitalized.

At that time work wasn't easy to get, there wasn't full employment by any means. Nor was there the terrific poverty there had been when I first came, with people walking down to Casas and back just to look for a job. Talking about that, I was always impressed by their ability to absorb poverty, probably because of their incredible family sense. There wasn't the unhappiness and sadness which I always associated with poverty. They managed to manage.

The way they worked, too, when they had a job! Seeing it made me realize for the first time how lazy we are. On my house they wanted to put in twelve hours a day. It was too much; a guy can't work that many hours. It was the same in the company. Instead we gave them piece-work. We'd estimate a day's work and pay them for it and they could leave as soon as they'd finished. They worked even harder, a damn sight harder then. They'd finish a couple of hours early – and then work those two hours as well. There was no such thing as overtime. Finally we reduced the work day to ten hours for which they got the equivalent of twelve or thirteen hours' pay.

We paid above the government-fixed minimum wage so there was never any problem with the *sindicato*. The union would be used by a man only if I sacked him. Unless I had a cast-iron case I would be certain to lose. I liked that because it defended a man against my exploiting him. At the same time it could be a drag because you couldn't get rid of a man.

Having the company made my relations with the village easier. It was like a big family. I became more involved in their problems

– family ones as a rule. I never felt they were envious of me; they knew I had limited means myself and that my work was giving them work. Six days a week guaranteed work meant more to them then than the wage. Moreover, we were building houses for foreigners with a completely different style of life, and the local people didn't really want to change their ways. They were curious, not envious. And also, the new houses were going up in the countryside and a Spaniard doesn't want to live in the country, he wants to live in the village.

In the end, because of the under-capitalization, the company folded. We cut back and laid off men but it didn't solve the problem. If I hadn't bought land and made a profit I would have been wiped out. My own land I bought in 1956 for eight pesetas a square metre; by 1962 I was paying a hundred pesetas a square metre for large parcels which, sold as small building sites, fetched double the price.

You'd never believe it: as I was forced to lay off men they and their families all came to see me and bring me presents. Some even offered money. These were men who had been fired! Where else would a thing like that happen?

After the company's failure, he moved down to the coast where, after a time, he began building again. 'In fifteen years I've had some very up-and-down times. For all that I've had a far more fulfilling life here than I believe I could have had elsewhere. It's mainly due to the people's basic honesty and friendliness. Perhaps a commercial, capitalist spirit is missing; we who came from outside saw the opportunities and grasped them. It's precisely this lack of graspingness, I think, that makes Spain such a popular tourist country.'

JOHN AND RUTH BLACK

As Avery Mark related, John and Ruth Black came to live in Tajos by chance. John is a writer now in his fifties; tired of urban life he and Ruth came from Melbourne in 1959 looking for somewhere to live. A New Zealand friend liked walking up hills. 'One day when we were in Casas Nuevas, he said, "There's a village up there." So we walked up. We found the place more sophisticated than we'd imagined. By that I mean it wasn't as grossly of the seventeenth century as some other villages we'd recently visited. There was no begging, no sense of importuning. One reads of other villages where stones are thrown at strangers but nothing of the sort ever happened to us or anyone I know here. Indeed, the people were intensely hospitable. . . .'

RUTH: But poor. You could see that from what they ate. A bit of chicken, some chick peas and a piece of lard was a special Sunday treat in those days. I'd say the children weren't getting an adequate diet. They were eating enough but not properly. Even if their parents had money there were so many things you couldn't buy then. Butter, fresh milk other than goat's, a lot of ordinary vegetables, tinned foods. . . .

JOHN: Yes, the men lacked stamina because they lived on so little, because of their poor diet. There was an air hanging over the village of nothing happening, of nothing going to happen. A lot of men had probably lost the desire to work because of the chronic unemployment. The poorer they got the less drive they had. I remember giving a boy ten pesetas for bringing down a crate of beer to our house. I offered him the same for returning an empty crate. 'No,' he said, 'I exist on ten pesetas a day and since I've got it, that's it. Tomorrow if you want. . . .' Well, that's not the dynamic that's going to breed a Henry Ford. By which I don't mean they're lazy, far from it. I've seen them working like the backside of hell, to use an Australian expression, in the blazing heat smashing away with picks.

RUTH: There was no market here. When you went shopping you had to peer into all the little doorways. In the front room of someone's house there'd be a few packing-cases of tomatoes, oranges, potatoes, a couple of bars of soap. There were dozens of these front-room shops eking out some sort of living. Stuff like sugar, flour, chick peas, rice they kept in drawers and scooped out. You had to pick through everything because there was usually something foreign in it.

As a matter of fact until a few months ago there was still one of these old shops in the village. The people are stubborn about changing their ways, as I suppose any small enclosed community is. They can't be told anything; they distrust foreign ways even while delighting in helping a foreigner. You can tell them so and so is done in Australia or America and they simply reply, 'It's not the custom here.' For years we tried to get our maids to use a mop on the tile floors. But they preferred to get down on their hands and knees and scrub them as their mothers and grandmothers did. It's only in the last couple of years that they've changed.

JOHN: Most of the important changes in village life have been technological. The introduction, for example, of butane gas about ten years ago has revolutionized their domestic lives. They can cook and heat with the portable gas cylinders and no longer have to go to the sierra for firewood. They eat better for it. Television has been another major factor of change. It has opened a world to them. People who can't read, or if they can don't, now *see* what is going on around them. At a lower level, the introduction of piped water into the houses since we've been here; sewage, dust-carts in the last year. . . . All this progress made possible by the influx of money, by tourism.

RUTH: Yes, that's true. Look at plastic — another innovation. Before, you carried a basket and everything was tipped into it. Now almost everything you buy is given you in a plastic bag. Supplies come pre-packaged in plastic from Málaga. People certainly live and eat a lot better now. What was a special treat before is now an ordinary meal. The market, which was built about six years ago, has made a big difference; there's a much wider range of fruit and vegetables. You can get things when they're out of season like Canary cucumbers, for example.

But the market hasn't had any effect on bringing down prices. Tajos is considerably more expensive than Málaga, and the quality there is usually better. Last week I saw green peppers in a shop here at seventy-six pesetas a kilo. A couple of days later I found much better and bigger ones in Málaga market at thirty-six. Cucumbers were forty pesetas a kilo here and twenty-four in Málaga. The same differences are true of fish. Pork and beef are perhaps two exceptions, being a bit cheaper here; but then it's difficult to get beef in the village and the quality in Málaga is always better.

It's true even of vegetables grown in Tajos. Potatoes are always dearer here than in Málaga – and if they've just been dug you get a quarter of a kilo of dirt with every two kilos of potatoes. In Málaga they look as if they've been washed. I don't know how you explain the difference unless it's middlemen and transport. If you remark on it to the shopkeepers locally they just look at you and laugh. The locals know it, of course, but they don't know why either.

JOHN: It's not because of tourism. As far as I can remember food has always been cheaper in Málaga than here. But what I wanted to say was that all this progress hasn't really changed their social attitudes very much. The strength of the family which impressed us so much when we first came hasn't lessened, I believe. They're a very family people. A man's brother-in-law or his cousin is more important than a non-relative any day.

And then there's this business of losing face, I think one could call it. This hasn't changed. A Spaniard finds it very hard to say 'no' to your face. He says, 'Come back tomorrow week' and when you do he's probably out because he doesn't want to hurt you by admitting that he can't do something for you. Nor put himself in the position of losing face. I remember once a mason agreeing to repair our roof. That was four years ago and he hasn't shown up yet. When we see him we're mutually pleasant and buy each other drinks – but he wouldn't say then and there he couldn't do the job. One thing one must never do is to press a Spaniard to the extent of his losing face. He becomes crestfallen and perhaps unpleasant; one has to work out some face-saving formula.

The impact of tourism has been enormous. It's a great money-spinner. In fact I fear that in a decade or so, if the foreigners start buying up houses in the village, Tajos could strangle itself, become a foreign ghetto like Torremolinos and some of the other places along the coast. There are signs that it's starting.

In the tourist areas the Spanish aren't quite as nice as they used to be. In the old days I remember I didn't think twice about going away for the weekend and leaving the front door unlocked. I wouldn't do it today. Though in all fairness, a lot of the petty-thieving that has started is the work of foreigners on the coast!

JOHN BERTORELLI　　　　　*Thirty-four*

Silversmith

Another foreigner who, like so many, came to Tajos by chance, John Bertorelli was on his way from New York to Italy in 1966 when he got off the boat in Málaga to visit the village which a friend in New York had told him about. He has stayed ever since, and is one of the few foreigners actually working in the village itself. A commercial artist with a practical bent for mechanics, he turned to metal casting and silversmithing and has built up a flourishing business, supplying shops as far afield as Torremolinos and Marbella.

After the stink and noise of New York, Tajos seemed like a paradise. Mountains, sea, fresh air, olive trees – I was overwhelmed by it and still am; it's the most beautiful countryside I've ever seen. But the village, no. I don't like it and I want to get out.

I suppose I wouldn't like a small town anywhere. I'm sure they're all the same. I don't like the gossip and one-party lines and talk about people behind their backs. I'd rather live in a big city where I don't know anyone.

I didn't feel like this at the start. After two or three months I really came to like the people. They seemed natural, free people, all exposed. Naked in the sense of not having any artifice, really basic. That's how I felt them then. I don't any more.

I'm of Italian origin and I've spent quite a long time working in Italy. The Spaniards are polar opposites of the Italians. The Spaniards are tragic, black – an earthiness that has something to do with the tragedy of life: I see it in the black-shawled women overwhelming their kids, and there's a side of my personality that identifies with this.

So I tried to get to know the people better. It's easy at a superficial level. You can talk about the land or about money; how much something cost, how much it went for which is what they love to talk about. But after that there's a barrier. Even with the young people, among whom I've made several friends, I have never been able to get to know them as I would an Italian. I never felt a barrier in Italy; I moved right into the people, felt very close to them. It was easy there and here it's the opposite.

I've been trying to figure out what this barrier is; I don't think it's my fault, I believe it's theirs. They're very warm, genuine, sympathetic but there's always an area where a shield comes up; there's an inner rapport which I've never been able to make, even with friends. Something's missing in the way they relate. I've been willing to expose myself for the sake of making a rapport but I've never met communication at the same level.

It gets me down that after five years here the people still stare at me with a sort of animosity when I walk through the village. I felt that at the beginning and I feel it now. I don't know whether it's paranoia but I know a lot of other foreigners who feel that way too.

The animosity comes, I think, because they resent the intrusion of the foreigner, the outsider. The village is a very tight, incestuous family. They need the foreigner but they resent him. He's an intruder – especially in summer time when tourists come up – and because I'm here all the year round I feel it in a way that the tourist doesn't. No foreigner is ever going to get into this village, be accepted as part of the village. I know Spaniards from outside who've lived here for years and they're still considered strangers. They're not accepted. I've had one say to me that he feels like a foreigner here. The changes that have taken place are only superficial really, and this village tightness isn't going to be broken. Not for a very long time, if ever.

Don't get me wrong. The people have been very helpful and kind in their way, especially when I was scraping along at the start. The mayor has done everything he could to help; he even got me the site for my workshop rent-free for five years. But I know now that I'll never be a member of the village. It gets me down and I'd like to move – out into the countryside where I'd feel freer.

Part of this closed-in way they live their lives, I suppose, is their unwillingness to try anything new. I've had a man working with me four years filing buckles after they've been cast. It's dull, repetitive work. He's a self-taught electrician by trade and very good with his hands. I wanted to teach him to weld – it would have helped him and me too. 'Oh no,' he said, 'I don't know how.' 'But don't you want to try?' 'No, no.'

I tried three or four other people whom I thought had good hands, always with the same response. It upset me. I just cut off; I don't push it.

I offered this guy a seat so he shouldn't have to stand all day. He refused. I put in a coffee-machine and said, 'Make yourself at home,' but he just answered, 'Oh no', and went on filing. He's a very good worker and he's thought bright in the village and I think so too. But if I ask him to take on more responsibility he just falls apart. I pay him well, and I'd like to pay him double to widen his range of skills – but no. He seems happy to do this boring job.

I know what he would really like. He'd like me to shave off my beard, cut my hair, put on a tie and a suit and stand with him and the mayor and other dignitaries in the square on a Sunday and watch the people. He's inferred that this is the way of being a good Tajeño. To put on a clean shirt after work and stand in the square to see and be seen. If I did that, he'd respect me.

But even then, even if I did, this invisible barrier would still be there, this shield would come down, and I wouldn't be part of the village. No foreigner ever will be as far as I can see.

YOUTH

'The Good life'

When I tell them what hardships I went through at their age they stand and gawp at me. They don't believe it. Once one of them said: 'You must have been stupid to put up with it.' And I answered: 'Stupid we were. Don't you ever be as stupid as that.'
An old day-labourer

With their long hair, bright clothes and mini-skirts, the Tajos youth of today is indistinguishable from the young tourists, except that the Tajeño is, if anything, better dressed. Pop music, sport, fashion and the opposite sex are their major concerns; drugs, seriously watched for and heavily repressed, have made no inroads among them.

One elemental experience separates the young from the old; anyone under twenty-five today has never known what it is to go hungry. In childhood they may have eaten badly but they never went, as did their elders so frequently, without any food.

Many have known the hardships of the land; but few since they entered their 'teens have been unaware of another culture and standard of living developing around them as foreigners began building in the Tajos countryside.

As the impact of tourism generally brought change to the village, so the young found themselves increasingly in a world of two cultures: the indigenous and the foreign, the old and the new. Changes which previously had worked themselves

201

through in the course of a generation or two were now compressed into half a decade.

The point at which these have made themselves most critically felt is in the traditional form of relationship between the two sexes. Seemingly impervious to much else that is new, except perhaps the superficial 'style' of life, the youth confront here an apparent breakdown in the traditional culture. There is no young man or woman under twenty-five who does not reflect in some way on this problem.

What, apart from the concerns already mentioned, interests or moves them? What do they know about their history or the contemporary world? (They, as anyone under the age of thirty-five, have lived all their lives under the Franco regime.) In an attempt to make a rudimentary assessment, I asked each of the seven young men and women who appear subsequently a few standard questions.

What, in their opinion, were the causes of the Spanish civil war; what did the Falange mean to them; what was happening in Vietnam; did they consider themselves religious; would they consider leaving the village for good; had they any particular work aspirations?

All said they were religious and went to church, the women more frequently than the men; none, however, had confessed or communed within the past two years. Only one had a clear idea of where Vietnam was, who was fighting there and why; only one – the same young man – had any idea of the Falange's ideology. Taking the following answer as sufficient, two were able to advance landlords' oppression of the workers as the cause of the civil war. None could imagine leaving the village for ever; and none had work aspirations which significantly transcended their present situations – unless becoming a housewife is considered as such.

So small a sample is not statistically meaningful. Such, however, is the homogeneity of village culture that I doubt whether an accurate sampling would reveal very different results.

JUAN AND ENCARNACION MARTÍN

Restaurateurs

Few people have more contact with village youth than Juan and Encarnación Martín. They come from a small town in Galicia and run a restaurant in the village. Juan, who is twenty-eight, did his military service in Málaga and came to love the south. 'The way of life – this living from day to day without thought of the future – awakened something in me that had been missing all my youth in the north.' After military service he returned to Galicia and became a merchant seaman, sailing all over the world; for a spell he also worked in a factory in England. When he and Encarnación married, they came south for their honeymoon and spent some time in Tajos. They liked it so much that, after Juan had spent another year at sea, they decided in 1968 to return. Eventually they invested their savings in restoring an old village house and turning it into a bar where the youth could meet.

JUAN: When we first arrived we noticed that nothing was organized for the youth here. It surprised me because in my home town no one thinks anything of a girl going to a bar and having a glass of wine and a cigarette. But not here! I talked to a lot of young people and they all complained of the same thing: the taverns were full of old men and they, alone or as *novios*, had nowhere to meet.

So I set up my bar as a place for the youth. It failed very soon. I blame the men entirely for this. As soon as a young girl set foot in the bar the men talked about her. 'Ah, she's one of those who goes to *El Portón*,' they'd say, as though that were something bad. The very ones who had complained of having nowhere to go didn't have imagination enough to bring their *novias* with them for a drink. No, no. For them a *novia* has to stay at home, do what her *novio* tells her, wear what he wants her to wear, not go to a bar alone or even with girl-friends, not smoke. . . . I found myself up against customs ten centuries old and there was no changing them.

So I turned the bar into a restaurant mainly for foreigners, and it has become very successful. Upstairs I've kept a room specially for the young. But the girls who come are totally 'lost' as far as the men of Tajos are concerned. Their only hope of marriage is with someone from outside the village. 'When you go to Galicia bring back a waiter,' they say hopefully.

I could hardly believe that men could have such an 'Arab' idea of women as they have here. You have to hear the way they talk about girls. I'm thinking of one seventeen-year-old in particular whose *novio* left her after a couple of months. 'You don't want to go with that one,' the men say to each other. 'She was with so-and-so and you can't tell what they got up to, can you?' They insinuate the worst sort of sins, not only to prevent any man from taking up with the girl, but to blacken her reputation as well.

For the men it's quite a different matter. They can go off with other women. In fact it's become a thing here now for the men to stay with their *novias* in winter and, in summer, look for some excuse for quarrelling so that they can go down to the coast and chase foreign girls. A local girl made up a rhyme about it: *Tajos, ciudad de invierno, en el verano cuernos.** When their *novio* returns in winter, the girl takes him back! Why? I don't know, unless it's because she's scared of never getting married or because of this 'Arab' style of things in which a woman expects a man to have relations with other women.

ENCARNACIÓN: The desire to get married is carried by girls here to an extreme I've never come across before. In Galicia, young girls, however poor their background, try to become something before thinking of marrying. But not here – here they've no other future than marriage; they can't study, the only work they can get is as a maid in a foreigner's house or a shop-girl on the coast. So once they've got a *novio* they'll stick to him despite everything. If you point out their *novios'* defects they don't understand, they simply bow their necks to whatever he wants.

They're frightened, not just about remaining single but because of the ridicule. 'Little old spinster' is what the men call a girl of eighteen or twenty who hasn't got a *novio*, and they laugh and make jokes about them. A spinster is an object of ridicule. The

* 'Tajos, city to winter in, and in summer be cuckolded in' – a take-off of the tourist slogan of Málaga as 'the city to winter in'.

terrible thing is that the girls think the same. 'Even if they have to stick a red hot nail through me, I'll get married in the end,' they say. 'I'd rather marry a drunkard, a good-for-nothing, than become an old spinster.' I can't understand it. I can't imagine living on bread and onions and misery just for the sake of getting married.

The girls who come here often ask my advice. It's almost always, 'Do you think so-and-so would think it bad if. . . .' I always tell them, 'Why do you worry about what he thinks? Why do you let yourself be subjected to what he wants?' Many of them have had *novios* and they can't understand why they left them. 'I only used to go out when he wanted; when he wasn't in the village I never went out; I didn't wear what he didn't want. . . .' Sometimes I say that their *novios* left them perhaps because the girl hung round his neck too much. She shouldn't show so much interest in the man. But all the girls are so anxious to get a *novio* they can't see it.

Many of them would make excellent wives. Very often they run foreigners' houses single-handed. After all, that's all a man considers a woman to be here – a house-cleaner, a person to look after the children. He never thinks he has any obligations in the home. He won't pick up a broom or help his wife wash up. Never! The trouble we had getting our waiter to sweep the floor. He was scared out of his life someone would see him with a broom in his hand and laugh· at him for being a woman. Each time someone passed he'd hide the broom!

JUAN: Imagine a society in which any man who didn't get married was considered a queer. That's the position these girls are in. They know they're discriminated against, but in a way it's so rooted in custom that they see it as natural. They lack the education to understand the real situation. Instead they deal with it individually, accepting or rejecting the particular man.

They talk about it quite openly. They've got a hundred times more problems than the men. Psychological problems too. They get depressions. Whether it's caused by their situation, by their lack of sexual expression, by menstrual problems, I don't know. It doesn't seem to be chronic; it goes by stages. Depression today and as like as not tomorrow they'll be singing. Everyone lives by the day here.

I've been very surprised by how openly they do talk, even in front of me. About sexual matters particularly. They seem to have no shame at all. There are things that happen during a *noviazgo* here that I don't believe happen anywhere else in Spain. The *novio* demands a lot of the *novia*. For example, that she masturbate him. This is considered as normal and ordinary as giving a kiss, and the girls talk quite freely about it. They don't mince their words either, a spade is a spade.

ENCARNACIÓN: This practice, I believe, is why *noviazgos* are still so long drawn-out here. There isn't the excuse any more of not having money enough. In the north *noviazgos* don't last anything like as long; but then there a man's physical necessities aren't satisfied like this. Any girl who has been a boy's *novia* for a year is expected to do it. She won't sleep with her *novio*, though. If he left her after that she would be more than 'lost', and if he didn't he could do what he wanted with her for the rest of her life. Her only hope would be to become pregnant so that he had to marry her.

Another demand the *novio* makes on his *novia* is that she send him money regularly while he's doing his military service. I've never heard of anything like that where I come from. There the man has to fend for himself. But not here. If the girl doesn't comply it's cause for breaking off the relationship. It's not a lot of money, no doubt; 200 or 300 pesetas, depending on what the girl earns. If she can't manage that every week, then 1,000 pesetas a month when she can, that sort of thing.

JUAN: Due to tourism, the young men have been taken from a totally prohibitive world into one of perhaps exaggerated freedom which they haven't been able to assimilate. They think only of sex. Any foreign woman, in their minds, will sleep with them. But this sudden change hasn't produced conflict in them: the old and the new don't clash. If they ever went hungry, which most of them didn't, they've forgotten it; not only that, they've forgotten the lives their parents had to live. In the bar they often laugh about their parents' past. Their capacity for forgetting is so great that it has made them quite capable of adapting to this new way of life without assimilating it properly.

Their only talk is about women, football and bullfighting. Sometimes I try to stir up a conversation about things in the village: why aren't there enough schools, why is the road in such poor state? It's only the few with a bit more education, like Lazaro the electrician's son, who are willing even to think about such things. Even then it's only with reference to the village. If you try to talk about the news they take it as a joke. In the three years I've been here I don't think I've had what one could call a real conversation with anyone about what's going on in the world.

Anyway, the young don't know what's going on anywhere. They don't read anything except the sports pages. Actually, 95 percent of the youth over fifteen is illiterate, if you consider illiterate someone who knows only how to read and write a little and add two and two. But there's something else. Spain, let alone the world, doesn't exist for them; only Andalusia exists. Because I speak Castilian I'm a 'foreigner' to them. I've had them say it to me: 'Ah, you're just another foreigner come here to get rich.'

Well, if Andalusia is the world to them, then Tajos is the capital of the world! This self-centred love of their village is, actually, one of the things I like best. When they go to Casas Nuevas or Málaga they look at people and say, 'Ah, look at those fools. . . .' They consider themselves superior to everyone else. In Galicia we have the same pride in our *patria chica*, but we don't think ourselves everyone's superior for that reason.

ENCARNACIÓN: It makes me laugh. If you're going down to Casas Nuevas they say, 'Are you going on a trip?' as though you were packing your suitcases and going a long distance. Their mentality of space is very restricted. I can understand it among the old – after all there are old and illiterate people in the north who've never seen a map – but not among the young who not so long ago left school. They don't know whether Madrid is to the north or south of Pontevedra – for them Madrid is simply the north. 'You're from the north, you must know so-and-so who lives in Madrid.' Catalans, Basques, Asturians, Galicians – for them the different regions are indistinguishable. Just 'the north'.

The young women talk mainly about men, fashions and new pop groups. Very rarely one of them tries to start a serious conversation. Then the others make her sweat blood. They say she's trying to show she's better than they, set herself apart; and of course she gives up straight away.

Fundamentally they're bored and a lot of the time I wonder if they even realize it. They never try to do anything about it, never say, 'All right, I'm going to break with this and try something else.' And if they do, it's because it might offer the chance of marrying rather than because it's something they want to do. 'I might meet someone or someone might meet me.' A couple of days later they hear a *fandango* and forget it. I don't believe it's a psychological problem for them; rather a number of problematical moments when they come face to face with reality and say they're going to break with the situation. It lasts a day or two and that's it.

Not only are most of them illiterate, as Juan says; they're so used to village idiom that they don't understand a lot of ordinary Castilian words. They often stop me when I'm talking to ask the meaning of something. Once I was talking about some crime that had been in the papers and used the word rape (*violar*). None of them had ever heard it. 'What's this about *virolear*?' they asked. Such a word doesn't exist. Juan was listening, and for weeks after as a joke he used to say to the girls, 'I'm going to rape you.' 'You're going to virolear me?' they'd answer. 'All right, virolear me then.' It got to be such a thing that we had to stop it. When I told them what it meant they were quite taken aback.

With such a poor understanding of words it's no wonder it *cosís* them a lot of trouble to read a book. Photo-novels is about all they can manage. Romances with little writing and a lot of pictures so they can follow the story more easily.

JUAN: Most of the young men are so bored that some of them are even bored with being bored. But they take it as natural. Even those who have cars and the afternoons free come in saying, 'Oh, I'm bored!' They're so used to it – perhaps because for so long the village was isolated – that they don't even try to think of ways of amusing themselves. On a rainy day the young building workers come in and they too complain of their boredom.

However bored, however few prospects they have here, they won't leave the village. Even those who've got into trouble, whom it would pay to leave. 'Yes, yes, we're leaving' – but they never decide to do it. To leave would be like dying for them.

In Galicia we're always thinking of tomorrow. Here there's no thought of the future. I've been surprised how many intelligent young men are quite happy remaining building labourers as long as they get paid. Out of pride I'd try to become a bricklayer at least, so that no one could boss me about. But not they. I believe they're frightened of responsibility, don't want to have the pattern of their lives disturbed.

ENCARNACIÓN: They've got no ambition, that's true; or they're prevented from having any. A couple of girls I know who are serious about wanting to leave the village can't do so because of their parents. Anyone who leaves is frowned on, even by their own families. Their parents insist they've got to find work in the village or on the coast and return home every night. There's one girl who works in Málaga and when she comes back for a day or two to see her parents you can hear the men talking: 'Look at so-and-so's daughter; what do you think she gets up to in the city on her own?' The fathers who are listening, or even making the comments, don't want to expose themselves to the same criticisms.

They're always thinking, *qué diran*? What will the people say? This attitude is stronger here than in Galicia. It's a very superficial one. 'I don't do this, not because I feel it's wrong, but lest someone see and criticize me.' There's no inner morality in that. Once the doors are closed and no one can see, *amigo mio*! There are girls held up here as models of correctness whom I know for a fact do what the others do only in secret. Even married women. It's all a matter of what the people see. . . .

JUAN: Or say. The young men have very little idea of their rights. Not so long ago one of them came in saying the Guardia Civil sergeant had told him to get his hair cut. 'He's got no right to tell me that,' he said. I agreed. A couple of days later the sergeant repeated the order and told him to report to the barracks that evening with his hair cut. I told him he shouldn't do one or the other. But young men in the bar disagreed. Finally he went and got his hair cut and reported. 'I didn't want any problems,' he said when I reproached him. The fact is that they believe – and they've said this to me – that a *guardia* can do and undo as he pleases. That shocked me coming from the north where a *guardia* is considered as someone who keeps order, not as one who meddles in people's private affairs.

In this sense things haven't changed here since the beginning of the century. 'The authorities' – the sergeant, the mayor and the doctor – these are the real powers. 'Command and we have to obey.' That's what they say.

Seen from outside there don't seem to be any social distinctions between the young today. The parents of most of them are earning more or less the same money; if the father of one is a policeman, the other's a mason or lorrydriver. They dress and talk alike; there's no distinction of speech and not much of education. They'll meet and talk and drink together. But from inside they make distinctions. The young men who work in the banks or in the town hall tend to stick together. They perhaps feel a cut above the rest, though it doesn't stop them mixing. On the other hand it's very rare for the youth from the centre of the village to mix with those of the *barrio*. That old distinction still exists.

ENCARNACIÓN: Among the girls it's much the same. There are exceptions like the doctor's daughters but even there the young talk more about the parents' pretensions than about the girls themselves. 'My daughters – do you think they're going to continue mixing with the sort of people they know here? My daughters have a different future in front of them. I'm going to present them in society.' That sort of thing. But then they are from outside the village anyway.

No, the major distinctions among the young girls are between those who feel themselves more 'puritan' than the others; one of them goes to a bar, smokes, goes dancing – and the other doesn't. She feels herself superior to the former. There is certainly an antipathy between girls following these two styles of life.

JUAN: Where we come from there are hundreds of possibilities for a worker's son with a bit of intelligence to get on. Scholarships, Labour Institutes, even the parents scraping to pay for his education. These don't seem to exist in Andalusia and even less in a small village. Or people don't try to make them exist because they're not thinking ahead. Even the rich, almost without exception, live from day to day.

This is why tourism hasn't been the shock it would have been in my part of the country. There the people would have been much less sociable, would have seen tourism as much more of a problem. Here it's not a problem – here it's solving a problem by providing jobs and money. The people know they're living off that money, and living comparatively well. They don't think about more than that, unless something goes badly wrong. Then I've heard young men say: 'It's thanks to us that that foreigner is living like a king here,' and talk about the fact that the pound sterling is worth 166 pesetas.

Underneath their show of 'modernness', which has rubbed off from the foreigners, they remain peasants. It's understandable because they've no real perspectives on the world which has formed them. In the end they'll be like their parents, with the same ideas, the same number of children, marrying a girl from here or a neighbouring village.

MARIA CUEVAS   *Twenty-four*

Maid

'Today we can laugh at the world. Yes, really; life here has changed that much. My father, my three brothers, I and even my youngest sister of fourteen are all working. Between us we earn plenty of money. My mother can stay at home now like a real señora.' As though to make the point she chuckles; she can remember the time when her father sharecropped a plot of land belonging to her mother's sister-in-law; when her mother had to go out to work whitewashing because the land didn't feed the family. She herself had to leave school, which she had attended infrequently, at the age of eleven to care for the three youngest children, to cook, wash and look after the two-roomed house while her mother went out. Until nineteen Maria stayed at home working; then, with her father employed as a building labourer on the coast, she found work as a maid in a foreigner's house.

I earn 3,000 pesetas a month cooking and cleaning. It's a big house, four bedrooms, three bathrooms, three shower-rooms, a bar, a sauna, a swimming-pool. . . . The owner has built it to rent, so we get different people throughout the year. I could earn more in other houses, but sometimes in winter there are no tenants and I still get paid. It's a permanent job, no one bosses me about and I'm happy there.

I've only ever worked for foreigners. From what my friends tell me I wouldn't want to work for a *señorito* from here. I had a friend who was earning 500 pesetas a month cleaning house and looking after the children of a town hall official. She left last month – after eight years. She had to work every day, including Sundays. One day she offered a friend who had come in a cup of coffee while the children were having their tea. The children told their mother and she told this girl she wasn't ever to give anyone coffee in her house. Now she's left them and their children won't even greet her in the street. After eight years! The Spanish have little charity for their maids.

The foreigners are much more considerate. They give their maids the same food as they eat themselves; they treat one as a human and not as a pack animal. Of course, the *señoritos* are having to change because no one will work for them any more. We don't have to be frightened nowadays of losing a job; there's plenty of work to be found.

Of course, there are some foreigners who aren't polite and considerate. Anyone who owns a house here is a *señorito* for us because he has money — but they don't all behave like one. Apart from money, a *señorito* must dress and behave properly, like don Manuel, the vet. He's a *señorito* all right. 'Don't compare yourself with that person, he's a *señorito*,' the people say. But most of the local *señoritos* aren't like him, they're stuck up. If they see me in Málaga they won't even greet me, though I'm from the same village, because I'm poor. Not that I care, I know what they're worth.

Sometimes I look at the house where I work and think, 'How hard it is, these people have all the money and we don't have enough for a house like this.' And all the time, as a maid, one has to put a good face on everything and be nice. Just the other day, when something went wrong, I was thinking: 'one doesn't have the right even to feel sad in a job like this.' But then I think of the past, think of a friend's house and the poor state it's in and that she hasn't even got a bathroom, and I'm more sorry for her than I am for myself.

My father has managed to do up our house; we've got a bath-room, my sister and I have a bedroom to ourselves, my brothers the same, there's a kitchen. I've bought my mother a washing machine and my brother bought her a TV set. This summer we're hoping to buy a refrigerator and my father wants to build on some more. . . . No, I can't complain. We eat and we sleep well – what more can one want?

How things have changed! Just in these past two or three years. I had a *novio* when I was nineteen. He was killed in a building accident two years ago. I went into mourning for a year and a half. During all that time I wore black and didn't go out of an evening at all. Nowadays everyone can choose how long they stay in mourning. When I was young the custom was seven years for a parent, four years for a brother or sister. Seven years and longer for a husband. But the custom is disappearing – the church has always been against it, saying it had no meaning. Pray but not wear mourning, the priests always say.

Anyway, eight months ago I became the *novia* of a young man from Posadas. When I think of the differences in my two *noviazgos*! My first *novio* came to my house three evenings a week and we were never really alone. He was a good man but he often annoyed me. He was always telling me what I shouldn't be doing. I couldn't go out even with my girl-friends when he wasn't with me; during the twenty-one months he was doing military service I didn't go out at all. I put up with it out of love; anyway, what was the point of going out? He never let me dance with anyone else; he said one could never know what the other's intentions might be.

With Salvador, my new *novio*, things are quite different. As soon as we're out of the house he puts his arm around me and gives me a kiss. We go out alone whenever we want. Just in these two years life has become freer and it's much better this way. If I want to go out with my girl-friends, all he does is laugh and say, 'Ay, what a tourist you're becoming!' I have a picture of my first *novio* in my bedroom and Salvador doesn't mind. If it had been the other way round my first *novio* wouldn't have allowed it. He used to complain that my mother kept a picture of her first *novio* who died when he was twenty-two. My mother!

I wouldn't put up with that sort of thing any longer. That's one of the things I love about Salvador – he lets one be free. The youth today doesn't care any more what the people say; we have imposed our ideas on our parents. I used to be frightened when Salvador first used to take my arm in the street. 'The people . . .' I'd say. 'Ah, you're stupid,' he answered; and in these past eight months I've seen that he's right.

We go to his home in Posadas sometimes. Things are still old-fashioned there. His mother doesn't want me to sleep upstairs with his sister because Salvador's bedroom is next door. But in my house, where he stays very often because he works on the coast, he sleeps in my brothers' room next to mine. Here quite often we're alone in the house, but his mother won't let us go out alone; we have to take Salvador's sister with us. Not that I would sleep with my *novio* – no, we don't take things to those limits.

I have to ask my mother to ask my father if I can go to Posadas. He doesn't like my leaving home; he says that to my mother though never directly to me. But he says even less about my sister. She's just fourteen. What a difference! She doesn't do anything round the house, not even make her bed; I do it. My mother looks after her clothes – and she's got more clothes than I could have dreamed of at her age. She won't cook, and if she tries washing up she only chips the plates. To think, when I was her age I was cooking for the whole family and carrying her through the streets to where my mother was working so that she could give her the breast!

And she's always the last home at night. My brothers and I have to be home by midnight – but not she. My father doesn't say anything to her. Nor my mother. That's the really big change – with girls of her age, not mine. . . .

Maria will marry when her *novio* has built a house which, she expects, will take another two or three years. 'I'm in no hurry,' she says tranquilly. She has already spent between 60,000 and 70,000 pesetas on linen (seven pairs of sheets, thirty towels, eight tablecloths, five bedspreads) – many of these articles hand-embroidered – kitchen equipment, glass-ware and crockery for her home. Meanwhile she is content to go on working as a maid.

'Some of the girls who work in shops on the coast think they're better than us who work as maids. They'll talk to me here but not if I meet them in Casas Nuevas or Posadas. "Señoritas without money," I call them. I'd far rather work in a house doing different things than be stuck in a shop putting up with the whims of the owner and tourists. And having to work Sundays as well.'

LAZARO RODRIGUEZ *Twenty-seven*

Bank clerk

Son of the local electrician, he was eleven when a group of young priests came to the village to talk about the seminary. 'They said you played a lot of football, that it was a happy life and you learnt a lot. They didn't talk about religion or celibacy. I liked football and I wanted to learn, so I spoke to the local priest. My parents hadn't the means, so the priest wrote to my godmother, the wife of the electricity company owner in Málaga and she agreed to pay for me. The priest took me to the city to sit the exams. There was one long division sum I couldn't get to come out and he helped me a bit. . . .' Along with ninety other boys, including two from Tajos, Lazaro was accepted as a seminarist; it was 1959.

At that time I suppose I thought I'd become a priest. At the age of eleven what does one know? My parents were happy; it's a good thing for the son of poor people to be able to study, isn't it? And I was happy enough for the first few years. I enjoyed studying. Religion, Latin, maths and Spanish were the main subjects; history, geography and music were secondary courses.

Of the ninety who started only forty remained at the end of the first year. The majority of us were from poor families; only a few had foam-rubber mattresses instead of our wool ones. One of the two boys from Tajos left after a fortnight. He was fourteen and already thinking about women and that sort of thing; his family gave him a wrist-watch and the priest tried to persuade him to stay – but he refused. It was only because I was younger that I put up with things.

To begin with I found the atmosphere very happy. But little by little I began to feel a police-like vigilance. When I came back here on holiday – only in summer for the first three years – I remember I was always looking round to see if anyone was watching me! We had a superior, an older seminarist, who lined us up and sent us to the refectory on our own because he had confidence in us, as men, not to break the rules and talk. That's what he said, and then he'd hide to see what we did. That was an ugly thing to do and I came to hate him.

In fact, looking back, one's brain had been washed after a couple of months. From time to time they showed films – comedies mainly – and if there was something they considered obscene the projectionist put his hand over the lens or stopped the film. It was funny; a film lasted twice as long that way. Sometimes they made a mistake and left in the scene they meant to cut and blocked another. No one ever said anything, everyone just sat there in silence. After the showing the older seminarists discussed the film and told us what was good and what bad. It didn't take me long to believe everything they said.

They discouraged all special friendships; they wouldn't allow us to talk to seminarists who were in a different year's course. They wouldn't say why. '*Noli me tangere*,' they said, and forbade us to touch one another. When we went to bed we had to undress under the sheets. Showers were always alone.

After four or five years I began to understand what it was all about. That was something I disliked – they would never talk openly about sex. I didn't know anything and once I asked. All I got was that it was necessary to reproduce the species and so on.

Little by little, as I saw clearer, I began to feel I hadn't a vocation. Earlier, especially during the spiritual exercises which lasted a week, when one priest after another talked to us of death and that we were destined for heaven, most of us, including me, would go to confession crying. The Jesuits were the best of all at this. It was a bit like being in the army and being trained to the point where one is capable of killing. But a week or two later I'd forgotten it and during meditation periods I thought about other things, about girls. . . .

Tourism was starting; there were more people about. I began to envy enormously all the local boys when I came home. I didn't go to the cinema, didn't go to a bar, didn't go dancing. My sister's friends used to touch me, give me a kiss and I'd tell them to keep quiet; but inside me I had terrible desires. It was no longer the innocence of before, although I still felt great humiliation from the teachings they had inculcated in me. And still do, psychologically. Little by little all the seminarists who came from along the coast began to leave.

With two friends I used to go to the visiting room where we could see other seminarists' sisters. The superior got to hear about it and called us up. He asked me what I wanted. 'Freedom,' I said. 'What do you understand by freedom?' I didn't dare answer. 'To walk out with a girl, go to the cinema, that sort of thing?' he said. 'Well, *hombre*, that's natural; it's nature.' 'Yes, but I like all that a lot,' I said at last. 'Ah, those are just things that happen at your age.' He persuaded me to stay on; it's difficult to persuade them you haven't got a vocation. But my two friends left.

I lasted another year. Then the strain became too great; I couldn't go on. I knew definitely I could never become a priest. In the middle of the year I left.

It has marked me. The other night I saw a foreign woman drunk in a bar and the world seemed to crash around me. Prostitutes in Málaga – they're like a mystery, mysterious things. There's a lot I haven't got over. But the education was good, that's for certain.

After a while I got a job in a bank here. I was earning 6,000 pesetas a month and I only worked mornings. I liked that. I was able to save and buy a Seat 600 on hire purchase; I live at home and it doesn't cost me much. Also I had time for other things. The mayor asked me to become chief of the Falangista Youth, and not to say no I took a course in Málaga. Politics in a small village is a bit like that. The course wasn't anything much; they talked a lot about politics.

When I was nine I had been to a Falange holiday camp on the coast. Most of the time we spent on sports, nature excursions, ceramic classes. I remember the only pair of boots my parents were able to borrow for me were so large I spent all my time trying to keep them on! One evening I missed the Falange ceremony by mistake and I got a whack across the ear for that – I remember it all right because it left me deaf for two days. But what they said about the Falange's ideas I can't remember.

Although I was elected local councillor of the Movement at the last elections – the youngest in Tajos – I hadn't really known what the Falange was until recently when I read the novel *Los Cipreses creen en Dios*. Of course, today the Falange doesn't exist as such, everything is the Movement. According to the book, José Antonio wanted a fascism like Mussolini's but with the main ideals being catholicism, patriotism and unity. The idea was good, I like it. But like all ideas it got deformed in practice. The same with communism – a magnificent ideal, almost the same as Christianity, but unrealizable. Here the older people talk about fascists and communists, but I don't believe there's anyone who knows what communism in Russia or Cuba really means: police repression and all that.

We Spanish are always critical of any regime, however good it is. So there are people who criticize the Falange for occupying a privileged position, falangistas for getting preference in jobs and making money and that sort of thing. But when foreigners talk about it we don't like it.

We're too rebellious, too individualistic to have democracy here; that's what they say. I think that was truer before because now people are learning that it is only those who deserve it who get on in life. We were always jealous before of the more advanced countries, but that's changing with tourism.

The tourists have brought more freedom. How shall I put it? Spain has always been very religious and for that reason hasn't advanced. Well, the new ideas brought in by tourism have opened people's minds. A person can no longer think like someone who believes in religion. At the same time there are drawbacks. Morality is on the decline; the people see foreigners who are divorced, who have children in one place or the other. We want to understand all this but we can't.

The biggest threat is that if tourism continues at this rate we're going to become pariahs. Shortly we'll all be entirely at the service of the foreigner. I don't like it. Nor do the people. 'We're in Spain and these foreigners have become the bosses of everything.' They think they're superior to us, too, and the people resent it; the foreigner wants everything his way. As soon as he buys a bit of land he fences it off and if anyone comes too close to his house he'll throw him off.

It's the people's fault, naturally, because all they want to do is sell their land to the foreigners. At the start it was all right, the people liked the foreigners – but now they're so many, things are changing.

Tourism has rid us of a lot of hypocrisy; if it hadn't been for tourism it would have been 1980 or 1990 before we reached where we are today. But the Spanish are curious. They'll put up with a lot and keep quiet – but when they blow up they really explode, as they did in 1936. Well, now we're putting up with it because we're relatively well-paid, and that's something we've never been before.

TERESA GAMEZ *Twenty-one*

Shopgirl

Isabel Gamez's sister, Teresa, has been working for the past three years in a tourist shop in Casas Nuevas. She does the twenty-minute bus trip up and down four times a day in order to be able to return home for lunch. 'It's cheaper and otherwise I'd have to sit down in Casas from one p.m. to four p.m. when the shop opens.' She would prefer to work as a maid because she finds housework less tiring than waiting for customers to come in to buy ponchos, carpets and souvenirs. But when the job came up her sister insisted she take it because her parents needed the money. She earns 4,500 pesetas a month of which she gives all but 500 pesetas to her mother. She doesn't usually spend that much on herself, but when she needs to buy clothes or something special she asks her mother for the money. She has three girl-friends with whom she always goes out; none of them has a *novio*.

It's dangerous having a *novio* here because there are a lot of foreign girls about. The foreign girls are dangerous, it's frightening. They come for two or three weeks and they don't care about anything. They're shameless. Last summer there were a lot of them who came up from the coast and the things they did in front of everyone at the dances! Things no Tajos girl would do, none I know anyway. Perhaps if they went to Casas Nuevas or Arroyo they might do them but not here. These foreign girls were indecent. What did they do? Well, not indecent indecent but. . . . Yes, they sat out in the patio caressing and all that sort of thing. When I saw the local boys with them, I thought: 'I wouldn't ever have one of them for my *novio*.'

Not that I suppose it'll ever be possible to find a *novio* who hasn't been with a foreign girl. There are kids of thirteen and fourteen who go with them now.

It's the same boys who go with the foreign girls who say they would never want a village girl to carry on like the foreigners. The boys want it both ways – that's why we don't know what to do any more. The girls here are going to have to change. The difference for the foreign girls is that they don't have their fathers around and they're freer for that reason.

And if a girl does have a *novio* it's a boring life. She has to wait at home for him – and as often as not he doesn't tell her whether he's coming. It's different in Casas; there a girl can go out, but not here.

I don't think this is right. It's not right that if the *novia* wants to go to the beach that the *novio* should refuse her. There are many *novios* who won't let their *novias* go, I don't know why; maybe it's because they don't want her to be seen in a swimming costume. So she can't go alone and he won't take her with him; but he goes if he feels like it.

That's another reason I haven't got a *novio*. All this bossing about. If I had one and he said I couldn't go I'd . . . I'd go all the same. Yes, I would. The same with what I wore; I wouldn't let him order me about. Freedom depends on the *novia* really; if he tells her to do something and she refuses that's the way she shows her freedom, isn't it?

Most *novios* don't believe a girl is his *novia* unless he's ordering her about. It's a foolishness. I don't want the woman to boss the man either; I want both to be equal.

I'd accept some things. I don't think it's right for a *novia* to go to the cinema or a dance on her own; she ought to wait for her *novio*. I don't think she should talk to other men either – there the *novio* has the right to forbid her. If he's not going out because he's got a job to do, she shouldn't go out either.

Most of all I'm frightened of having a *novio* with whom I fall out. I don't think I'd fall out if he took me home of an evening and then went down to the coast after a foreigner. He'd be going to get what he can't get from me. As long as it was where no one saw him and it was after he had been with me; as long as no one came and told me – I wouldn't worry. I'd be asleep in my house and he'd be out somewhere and I wouldn't know. It's only if a friend came and said, 'I saw your *novio* in such and such a place with a foreign girl,' that I'd be upset. The trouble in a small village is that everyone knows everything and no one can keep their mouth shut.

I've never thought of leaving the village; my parents wouldn't let me, and in any case I wouldn't want to. I've only once spent a night away from my house. Even if I could go abroad one day to learn English or French I'd always want to come back. I like this village better than any other. Perhaps it's because I've always lived here. When I'm down in the shop in Casas Nuevas I'm always thinking of the time when I can return to Tajos. I have lots of friends down there but they're different. The people I know and have confidence in are here, in the village.

Teresa's only overnight sortie from the village was when she went to Madrid with the midwife's dancing group to appear on television. She liked Madrid but was happy to get back to the village. Participation in the dancing group exempts her, she claims, from having to do her social service. 'It's only when a girl needs a passport or a driving licence that she has to do it because she can't get the papers otherwise.' Teresa doesn't read the newspapers or watch television much. She has seen television news reports on Vietnam but says she has no idea what the war is about or where Vietnam is. 'So many wars, so many people killing each other – it's a shame in the times we live in.'

PEDRO NUÑEZ

Twenty-three

Bricklayer

When I was three my father lost his small-holding. He spent all his savings on trying to cure my younger brother who had gone blind in one eye from a fever. One doctor said the eye should come out, another said it could be saved. My parents sent my brother to stay with an aunt in the village. One day she gave him a toy iron to play with and he dropped it on his eye – the bad one – and he lost his sight in that one for good. How lucky it was he didn't drop it on the other eye!

By then my father had had to sell his farm to a man in the village. Cheap – it was before tourism started. My father became a sharecropper on his own farm.

The new owner used to come down two or three times a week. He'd stand there with his hands crossed looking round. 'Juan, there are two melons missing,' he'd say. He'd counted them all. I can remember this well, it was only ten years ago. I won't say the owner was good or bad, but I'll tell you one thing: whenever we had to take his share up to the village he never once gave us kids so much as a sweet. I looked after the sheep and when they'd been sheared I took the wool to his house – but nothing, he never gave me a thing. Our standard of living went down a lot; one of my older brothers had to go to live with our Aunt Maria at *El Verdegal* to herd the cows.

I didn't go to school until I was eleven – and then only to nightschool with don Eugenio Lopez. I used to feel ashamed coming up to the village with my satchel; the village boys laughed at kids from the country and called them bumpkins. Some of them used to throw stones. Although a lot of country children like me lived close to the village, we only went up a few times a year and we were scared of the village kids.

My eldest brother became a bricklayer and he got me my first job on a foreigner's house as a labourer when I was seventeen. After a year, by watching the bricklayer I was working with and trying my hand during the lunch hour, I knew enough for the contractor to set me to building stone walls. He gave me a peseta an hour more – a rise from seventy to seventy-eight pesetas a day.

But when I asked him for more, because bricklayers were earning 150 pesetas a day, he refused. I left and got another job where I was paid 120 pesetas a day.

It was about then that the owner of our land sold the farm to a Catalan señor. The latter asked my father to look after the land. 'All the crops you plant, all the animals you want to keep are yours,' he said. 'All I want is the place to be well kept.' On top of that he gave my father a small wage of 5,000 pesetas a month. It was as though the farm were my father's again!

Before we only had two bedrooms for the seven of us. The Catalan señor did our house up completely. Five bedrooms, a bathroom, a kitchen he built for us. He put in light and water for nothing and built a new cow-stall and chicken house for my mother a little distance away from our house.

I came back from military service to find all this done. It looked fine. My mother said there was only one thing missing – a washing machine. With my first week's wages I put down the money to buy her one without telling anyone. So she's got that and a TV and a radio and an electric iron and proper cupboards and everything she wants.

All of us, except my mother, are working now and together we bring in about 12,000 pesetas a week. I earn 2,500 pesetas and I give 1,800 pesetas to my mother. Out of that she buys all my clothes and I don't have to bother about anything.

I could have had a job at 4,000 pesetas a week in Palma de Mallorca. A contractor I met while I was doing military service there offered me the job. But I wanted to return home first, and while I was here I found work. Although I'm earning a lot less, everything's looked after for me here. I don't have to worry about my clothes, food, board. That's why I stayed. I'd have a better time there, no doubt. Just to watch all the people in the street is amusing in a big town. Here it's boring. But love comes from contact they say; it's six months since I came out of the army and I've only been to Málaga twice. When I go down to Casas I'm bored. 'Where shall we go?' I say to my friends. 'Where?' And then we come back up here, knowing we'll be just as bored here, but we come back all the same.

Drinking, that's about all there is to do of an evening. Or the cinema. It's the same every evening until Saturday pay-day when there's a bit more life; then it's more drinking. Otherwise there's nothing to do but get washed and changed after work and stand in the square to see what's going on. Still, boring as it is I'd rather stay here. I've been to Barcelona, Valencia, Alicante, Mallorca – and I like Tajos better than any of those.

The women here have become strange. You ask one of them to dance and she says to her friends, 'No, he goes with the foreign girls. . . .' You ask another and she says she's tired, and another and she says she doesn't want to dance. You get fed up. Who do they think they are, these girls? They don't want you to dance with a foreigner? They're jealous or something? When I go to Posadas or Benamalí where I'm not known they'll all dance with me. But not here. It's getting very bad.

Of course, they know I had an English girl for a while. She was only fifteen or sixteen and I used to meet her at night in the garden of her parents' villa and lay her. Foreign girls are easy, they come here for a good time and they'll do anything. Not like Spanish women. Now and again you find a Spanish woman who's done her kilometres and then she's better than any foreigner. But it's rare.

The authorities are trying to make things difficult for the youth. They say the Guardia Civil sergeant has received orders from the Civil Governor that the young can't wear their hair long. A friend of mine was ordered by the sergeant to get his cut recently. I could understand that if he didn't keep it clean and neat but he used to wash it every day. You know – if the sergeant had done that to me I'd have told him I'd taken a vow to the patron saint not to cut my hair for six months. What could he have said then? The trouble with us young is we talk a lot but we don't do anything. Everyone's a bit frightened when it comes down to it.

Small and good-looking, Pedro keeps his own hair immaculately trimmed; he is a snappy dresser, known among the youth for his sharpness of repartee, an important asset in Andalusian life.

At the work level he imagines spending the rest of his life a bricklayer. 'No one bothers me, I earn my 400 or 500 pesetas a day, and I haven't studied enough to do anything else.' Every day the foreman comes from Casas Nuevas to set him the day's tasks because he can't read plans. The foreman has tried to encourage him to learn but he doesn't like to be seen talking to him very much. 'The other men on the site will think I'm talking about them behind their back. That's what I would think if I were they. So if I see the foreman in the street I go in the other direction. I'm the youngest on the site and I have to give orders when the foreman's not there. I'm always very polite to the older men; but I know how everyone thinks here.'

JOSEFA ALARCON *Twenty-one*

Shopgirl

I haven't a *novio*, one hasn't come my way. Hardly any of my friends have one, and if they do the boy is usually from outside the village. The young men here think only of the foreign girls and forget us. They go down to the coast and the young from Posadas come here. Sometimes I go all Sunday evening without being invited to dance. I come away fed up. But the next Sunday I get invited and I forget what happened the week before.

One day I'll get a *novio* and get married. I'm not worried about it. I'll only start worrying if I reach twenty-five or twenty-six and no one comes my way. I hope it'll be before that.

When I marry I want to stay at home. I think that's what most women want, to stay at home and wait for their husbands to come back from work. I'd like my husband to take me out more than just on a Sunday evening. If he said that was the only day we could go out together I suppose I'd have to accept it but I'd try to persuade him differently. It's the man who has to give the orders after all. I don't know who said it, but a woman who bosses her husband about is an ugly sight.

I'd like two or three children; four at the most. I wouldn't want any the first year of marriage. But God will send the number He wants. Maybe it's because I've seen so many children at home – eleven in all, eight girls and three boys. I've seen how hard my mother has had to work. Because nine of my brothers and sisters are younger than me and I had to leave school at thirteen to help in the house. I'd rather stay at home than go out to work but my job helps with the money. I've only been working three months and I give all my 3,500 pesetas a month to my mother. It's very little really.

But I don't have any worries, I'm not bored. After closing the shop at eight I go shopping for my mother; sometimes my girl-friends and I stop for a Coca Cola at *El Portón*. Then I go home until the next day's work. My father and elder brother get angry if I'm out after 10.30. There's not much for the young to do here anyway. The village is dead at ten o'clock. I wish there was a library; well, there is one but when I went once it was closed. I haven't seen it open for months. Or a youth club or something like that.

I spend my time with my girl-friends. Yesterday a whole group of us hired two taxis and spent a few hours in Posadas. All girls; I don't like that very much, it's more fun when there are boys. But where are they? With the foreign girls who are freer than us. I suppose they don't have to ask their parents if they want to go out. It would be nice to have a bit more freedom. . . . But not to go out after supper, no, I don't want that because there's nowhere to go here; I don't need it.

I'd like to travel, go to Portugal, London, Paris. In what country is Paris? I haven't the faintest idea. London? No, I don't know. I wouldn't want to work abroad, oh no. I can't imagine spending my life away from here. I'd always want to come back to my village because this is where I was born.

CRISTOBAL RUIZ　　　　*Twenty-one*

Emigrant worker

Born in León where his Tajeño father had married during the civil war and was working as a coal-miner, Cristóbal spent his early years with relatives in Tajos. When he was ten his parents returned to the village for good and his father took up his old job as fish-vendor. Aged fifteen, Cristóbal left for

Barcelona on his own to find a labouring job, only to discover that 'As a boy I couldn't earn enough to keep alive and
send money to my parents who really needed it'. A year later,
in 1966, he set out for the coal-mines of León. In his three
and a half years as a miner he was seriously injured once and
trapped by rock falls twice – the last time for two days. The
mines were old and deep, badly propped and ventilated. His
elder brother who had joined him left the pits because he had
developed silicosis. Cristóbal thought that sooner or later he
would inevitably go the way of his brother. He decided to
emigrate.

I didn't know where, I didn't care that much. The important
thing was to earn money to be able to send to my parents. I was
the only one of my five brothers who could really help them. I
applied to the *sindicato* for the papers. They arranged my passport and told me I was going to Germany. I signed a contract, but
I didn't know what I'd signed, didn't know what sort of a job I
was going to, didn't know where it was.

It was a special emigrants' train, thirty carriages long and
absolutely packed. There were emigrants from all over Spain.
It took thirty-six hours from León to reach Hanover. There everyone was given a label and an envelope with the name of the town
he was being sent to. The German chief looked at my papers and
indicated a time on his watch; then he pointed at a platform and
I understood I had to take another train. I was scared, everyone
else had gone. I was completely alone.

I got on the train. No one told me anything; I couldn't speak a
word. I kept looking at the envelope and at the names of the
stations. At last I saw it: Soltau, and I got out. I stood on the
platform not knowing what to do, thinking I was lost. Three
men came up to me and one of them started to talk. All I could
do was shrug. They drove me off to a block of flats and gave me
the key to one and showed me the bedroom, bathroom, kitchen.
Then they left me and I ate a bit of food I still had and went to
sleep; I was worn out.

The following morning they came back and took me to the
factory. I saw it was textiles they were making. I signed all sorts of
papers; they gave me 1,000 DM and I came back. I didn't know

how to get any food, but I knew I had to eat. I saw a supermarket – the first I'd ever seen – and went in. The people were just taking things! I was frightened they'd think I was stealing if I did the same. I watched closely what everyone was doing and made up my mind: I took a trolley and put in some potatoes, eggs and oil. I had no idea how much it was going to cost. When I paid and saw it was only four DM I thought, 'Ay! they've given me all that money, what's it for?'

I'd never cooked in my life, not even fried an egg. But it didn't take me long to learn since all I ate was fried potatoes, fried eggs, fried meat. I'd never had a flat to myself before either, and I had to keep it clean. I was a bit ashamed at first having to do woman's work cleaning and shopping, but I soon saw all the men there did that sort of thing. I got used to it – for my good. Now I don't at all care if I'm seen cleaning or washing up; all this is a matter of custom that's all.

They put me to work with a woman, a Pole she was, on a machine; after three weeks I was given my own machine making blanket material sixty metres long by 2·50 metres wide. You couldn't call it work, not after the mines; there was nothing to do but watch the machine carefully to see the material didn't get cut, watch the spools . . . I was very happy about that.

It was a big factory, about 600 workers; we worked three shifts. For the first three months I went from my flat to the factory and from the factory to my flat. The loneliness was terrible; sometimes I cried, I wanted to leave so much. There was no one I could talk to. But I knew I had to hold out. Not only for the money to send to my parents but because I'd emigrated to get out of the mines where I knew what was waiting for me. And also because I wanted to get to know the world and learn something.

My contract was for 3·60 DM an hour but they paid me one DM more right from the start; later it was raised by another mark. I did as much overtime as they wanted. The overtime paid for all the deductions, so I'd end up with 17,000 to 18,000 pesetas a month clear. That was about what I'd been making as a miner. It cost me about the same to live as in Spain: 5,000 to 6,000 pesetas a month, because my flat, which belonged to the factory, cost me only thirty-six DM a month including water, light and heating. Everything over I sent to my parents.

After a time, by listening and asking, I learned a bit of

German. Before going, I'd bought a dictionary but I could only learn single words from it. The people were very patient; they'd repeat sentences until I got the idea. And they were kind; they'd come round to take me out for a beer, they'd invite me to dances, they did everything they could. The Germans like the Spanish, I think. I never felt any discrimination against me personally. Now and again I'd hear someone say something about the Spanish but I'd just keep quiet. I didn't want to get into a fight. But it didn't happen often.

I liked that feeling of equality between people. It's freer than it is here. When I went to a dance, it didn't matter if I asked a girl or a married woman – no one took any notice. I used to be worried; I thought because I'm on the small side no one would want to dance with me; but I never noticed the smallest difference between me and a German. The women didn't refuse me.

I joined a trade union; a companion explained to me what it was all about and I agreed. The union got us a wage rise of one DM an hour. Here the *sindicato* isn't concerned with getting wage rises; it's there if you've got a complaint about dismissal or pay you're owed.

There was solidarity among the workers there too, a lot of *unión*, as there is among the miners in the north here. I like that. At first, when I went to León, it surprised me, because such solidarity is practically unknown here. If a man here says the workers should ask for more pay everyone says, 'Yes! yes!' But at the hour of truth they back down and let him get sacked without a word of protest. In fact the others will probably start to criticize him. Perhaps it's because here there's never been enough work and everyone has had to live off the land; people are more individualistic, thinking only of their own interests because of it.

Among the miners it's not like that. If a man is sacked for no good reason everyone stops work – just like that; it needs no discussion. It's enough for one miner to say the word; the rest comes spontaneously. It gives one a lot of confidence because you know your companions will always stand by you, just as they count on you to stand by them. If you don't, they'll kill you – and I mean it. You try to work when they've downed tools and they'll do you in. . . . That's why they don't like Andalusians in the north; they say they've got no solidarity, and it's true.

I stayed in Germany twenty months in all. I liked it well

enough to want to go back. The workers are better off there than here. They get better money and don't have to work so long hours. A father with four or five children earning 300 pesetas a day as a building labourer here doesn't earn enough – not with the cost of living going sky-high because of tourism. In any case a man can't find work in the village; he has to go down to the coast, take his food with him and pay his bus-fare. As like as not he has to leave before his children are awake and get back only when they're in bed.

But I didn't go back. My parents wanted me to stay here until I went into the army. So I got a job as a building labourer.

I don't like Andalusia, it makes me angry. It's the richest part of Spain and yet it's the region from which most people have to emigrate. Why is that? Because everything is in the hands of only a few people. You don't have to go far from the coast and you'll find plenty of villages that are deserted, where the people have had to emigrate or come to the coast for work.

I don't know anything about politics. I know that Spain is living in part off the money the emigrants send home. The tourists come here with their money and we have to leave to make money. Is that right? I don't know for sure how many emigrants there are; three million, perhaps. But I'm sure that if they all returned none of us would be able to find a job or be able to live.

Spain has a population of thirty-two million. Six or seven million are workers. What are the rest living off then? Off us. If there were more working and less doing nothing – like in Germany – we'd all be better off.

After I've done my military service I'll emigrate perhaps to Australia. I want to learn English. But wherever I go it'll always be with the idea of coming back here for good. As long as I live, I'll always be thinking of the village. Memories of my youth, of the countryside, of my parents who will die here. It would be very hard to know that one couldn't return to the place where they were buried.

JESUS MORENO   *Fifteen*

Bartender

When I was eight I started to go to the sierra gathering pine cones. My father is a building labourer and my parents needed the money. So my two brothers and I went every morning at dawn. By the time I was ten I could carry thirty-five to forty kilos of cones. My brothers the same. We sold the cones to the bakeries to fire their ovens. They paid one peseta a kilo, so most days we made a hundred pesetas. We gave it all to my mother.

I went to school. Sometimes I got back a bit late from the sierra, but I didn't get far behind in my schoolwork. When I was twelve and a half I was offered a job in a bar through a friend. I told my parents and they said I should do what I wanted. I worked in the bar at lunchtime and again after school, from five until one or two the next morning. I got 300 pesetas a month and tips for washing glasses and waiting at the bar; it wasn't much money, but what it was I gave it all to my mother. She needed it because I've got two sisters younger than me. I wanted to give it to her because I don't like keeping money for myself; no more than I need to buy an ice-cream or some sweets.

Going to bed so late I was tired the next morning. My mother felt sorry for me and didn't wake me up. I started missing a lot of school. The week of the exams I only went three times. I failed one subject and that meant repeating the whole year.

I gave up the bar and started going to school again. Soon afterwards *El Portón* opened and I went to see if there was a job. Juan Martín gave me one, the same as in the other bar except the work wasn't as hard because he had two waiters. But the hours were the same. The next summer I failed the exam again.

I kept on with school and *El Portón*; then Juan said he needed me full-time. My father wanted to speak to him to let me stay on at school but Juan said I had to choose between school and the bar. So I left school without completing my eighth year. That was last year when I was fourteen.

I work from eight in the morning until after midnight, with an hour or two off in the afternoon. I earn 1,200 pesetas a month and about 3,000 pesetas in tips. That's not bad – it's better than I could make as a building labourer, though I only get one day a week off and they get Saturday afternoons as well. I give all the money to my mother.

I've been learning English. In the bar I hear a lot of English spoken and I got interested. When I left school Juan wanted me to study an hour a day in a class that the schoolteacher was giving. Juan paid for the lessons, but after three months the teacher went on holiday. When he came back Juan didn't want me to go any more; I don't know why. Perhaps he needed me in the bar. He said I could pick it up from the foreigners. I would have liked to go on studying because I was getting on well; I found it quite easy. But I couldn't.

Maybe now my father has retired we'll go to Barcelona. My brother has gone already. I have aunts there, my mother's sisters. My mother isn't from here; her family comes from Alameda. I'd like to go, I wouldn't mind seeing a bit of the world. I've never been further than Málaga, and I've only been there once.

Anyway, there's nothing to do here. You can't play football or ride a bicycle without having the police on top of you. A few years ago someone gave us a couple of footballs and the police took them away because we were playing in the streets. There's nowhere to play, we haven't got a football field.

On my day off I sometimes ride round a bit on my bicycle. I don't like reading, I never read a newspaper or anything. Not because I can't – I've learned to read and write all right – but it doesn't interest me. Otherwise, when I'm working, I leave the bar to go to bed and I get up in the morning to go back to the bar.

LAW AND ORDER

The Guardia Civil is a para-military rural police force, immediately recognizable in its patent-leather hats and green uniforms. A highly-trained and well-armed force, it patrols – always in pairs – the Spanish countryside where law and order depend largely on it. The force's isolation from the local population is ensured in part by the fact that no *guardia* may serve in the place of his birth and in part by its encampment in barracks in each village and small town. Its local commander, as the reader will know, occupies a position of considerable authority.

Don Francisco Pascual, the tall, dignified Guardia Civil sergeant in Tajos, was standing outside the barracks at the entrance to the village taking the sun; very amiably he agreed to give his views on the village and its youth and to describe the duties of the six-man force he commands.

He began by pointing out that there was no serious crime in Tajos – no murders, no assaults, no brawling; in fact there was very little such crime throughout Spain. One kidnapping, of the German consul in the Basque country, was about the limit of serious crime recently. Spain, he declared, was a peaceful country. . . .

A *guardia* was never off duty. If one of his men were walking through the village and saw something that was an infraction of the law, it would be his duty to denounce it. The municipal police existed to control traffic and to see that the people didn't dump rubbish in unauthorized places and that sort of thing. For any crime, fire or serious event the Guardia Civil would be called for immediately. The major problems that confronted him today were thefts from foreigners' villas in the countryside which were committed by hippies who came to Spain with little money and expected to be able to spend the summer there; and road accidents.

Having served in the north, don Francisco, an Andalusian, was quick to defend his region against the critics, who, he said, claimed an Andalusian would sell himself for a peseta. Andalusians were generous people who wanted to do others favours.

In this respect there were four or five *sinverguenzas* (scoundrels; literally, people without shame) among the village youth who thought they could be on the same level of culture and wealth as the foreigners. There could be no doubt in his mind that the Americans and English were in advance of the Spanish generally in terms of culture and education; but these young men thought they could be their equals. They stuck to any foreigner they saw, he said, and the foreigner who didn't know them might come off the worse for it. They would sell themselves, their families and their country for twenty-five pesetas; they had neither pride nor dignity.

However, don Francisco denied very firmly that he had ever ordered any of these young men, however shameless they might be, to have a haircut. What he had done was to give them the choice of washing their hair and keeping it properly clean or getting it cut. It was a sickening sight, he said, to see a young man with long, dirty hair which he didn't look after properly. A youth who worked all day on a building site, whose hair was covered in dirt from his work and who then went round the village without washing it was disgusting. He told them: hair washed and kept clean or cut. If they chose to have it cut that was their affair. But on his honour he had never ordered anyone simply to have it cut.

On the question of personal authority in the village, he simply smiled and said that his position was one of commander of a force whose task was to maintain public order and respect for property, nothing more.

NOVIOS

Four years ago when the Nilssons left Sweden to retire to a house they had bought in the countryside between Tajos and Casas Nuevas, their seventeen-year-old son, Johan, came with them. He had trained as a mechanic in Sweden, but for a year he did no work, spending most of his time on the coast. Wearying of the life, he decided he wanted to work and his father built him a garage on the outskirts of Tajos. It was and remains the only garage in the municipal district.

Johan is a shy young man with a passion for cars; at first Tajeños appeared reluctant to entrust their vehicles to him, but in the past two years his business has begun to flourish as the people have recognized his skill as a mechanic. Today everyone knows him as Juan *el Sueco*.

Carmelo Moreno is twenty-two and pretty. From the age of nine to seventeen she worked with her sharecropper father in the fields and went to school when she could. She can read and write a bit, enough she says for her needs but not enough to work in an office. In 1967 she got a job in a foreigner's house. 'I preferred that to working the land; I wanted to be like my friends.' One day, two years ago, she was walking up to the village from work when a foreigner stopped his car.

CARMELA MORENO   *Twenty-two*

'Climb in,' he said to my four companions and me, 'I'm going to my son's garage and I'll take you to the village.' All the other girls had *novios* or husbands and didn't want to sit with him; so I got in the front seat. He joked with me about sitting closer to him. Then he said, 'Do you know my son?' and we all said 'yes'. 'Well, I keep telling him every day, get yourself a Spanish girl for a wife – but he doesn't pay any attention.'

So I said, 'Perhaps he doesn't like Spanish girls; why should he marry one?' 'Hum! I hope he marries a Spanish girl. You're very pretty,' he said, looking at me. 'My son hasn't got a *novia*. I'll have a talk with him.'

It was all done as a joke. When we got to the garage he showed us round; then he introduced us to Juan. I'd never spoken to him before. He made me laugh with his long hair and grease all over his face and his yellow overalls.

After that I used to see him standing outside the garage when I walked by. It made me feel ashamed. One day I heard a car behind me and it was him. 'You come with me?' I was a bit surprised and I said, 'Where to?' 'Where you work.' He didn't say any more; he could hardly speak Spanish. At lunchtime, as I was passing the garage, he called to me. I was very nervous as I went over. He asked if I would go to the cinema with him. 'No,' I said. 'Not possible?' 'Not today.' 'Tomorrow possible?' 'Yes, possible.' 'What time?' 'Nine o'clock,' I told him, and to wait for me in the square by the cinema. I was worried someone would see us.

After the cinema I wouldn't let him take me home. I didn't want my father to see me with him. I've always been very frightened and shameful that my father should see me with a boy. I thought he wouldn't like it if I had a *novio*. And even less a foreigner! It would be terrible. The few times after that when I saw Juan of an evening I always left him several streets away from my house. But my cousins knew, and one day they went to my father and said, 'Uncle, you've got a foreigner for a son-in-law, heh-heh!' 'Give up your foolishness,' was all he said in reply.

One evening Juan went to my girl-friend's house down the street. He knew her *novio* who's my cousin. My older sister knew he was there and suddenly she said to me in front of my parents, 'Juan's in Maria's house and he probably hasn't eaten.' I was very upset because I'd told her not to say anything at home.

'Tell him to come and eat, he doesn't want to go hungry,' my father said. 'No, no, he's eaten already.' It wasn't true, but I was very shameful. I went upstairs and when I came down there he was at the table, looking up at the ceiling and making music on the table with his fingers. He was as nervous as me!

Until he came to my house he was only my *pretendiente*. That's how things are in Spain or at least in Tajos. But once he had been in my house, once my father had seen him – then he was my *novio*. To begin with Juan used to say we were friends, but after a while he said we were *novios*. That's how he saw it.

My father never said anything to me; and I've never said anything to him. But he told my mother I could love whom I wanted as long as the man was serious about me.

At the start I couldn't believe Juan would stay with me more than a couple of weeks. The foreigner's life is so different from a Spaniard's. I used to say to him, 'Haven't you got another girl-friend?' 'No, no.' 'But there are plenty of prettier girls in Tajos and with better positions in life than mine.' But he kept saying he'd found something in me he hadn't found in others. 'You're foolish,' I told him. But he stayed with me.

As *novios* we do things the way they're done here. He comes to my house most evenings; my father doesn't want us to be alone, so my mother or sister or girl-friend have got to be with us. It's not because my father doesn't trust Juan; it's because in a small village the people talk a lot. Like any father mine doesn't want the people to speak badly of his children. I agree with that; I'd rather there was someone with us all the time. For my father's sake, only for that.

When the people got to know Juan was my *novio* they said, 'oh, the Swedes are very cold.' And others, 'Tonight he'll be with you and tomorrow night he'll be with someone else.' 'Well, we'll see,' I answered. And the truth is that up to now in two years Juan has done nothing bad for me. The contrary, a lot of good because he has a great deal of shame. My parents like him and his like me, so everyone is happy.

I know it's hard for Juan because he's used to a lot more free-dom. So many things are forbidden, so many things I'm not

allowed to do. I have a lot of respect for my father. The first thing
he always said when I asked if we could go to Casas Nuevas was
'no'. It was only after he got tired of hearing me asking that he'd
say, 'Go then and come back next month.' Of course, if I go anywhere outside the village I have to take my younger sister or a
girl-friend with me.

Because of my father I don't like it if Juan holds my hand or
puts his arm round me where my father might see us. Here in the
village everyone has such bad tongues; my father thinks someone
might say to him, 'Your daughter, look, she carries on as though
she's married already!'

At the beginning I saw Juan sometimes looking very sad and I
thought he felt tied down, thinking of the freedom he could have
if he weren't with me. And I was sad for him because I love him
very much. For me it's not difficult because I'm used to it.

I felt very sorry for him too because he could hardly speak
Spanish to begin with. I still feel sorry because, though he understands everything now, the good and the bad words, we talk very
fast when there's a group of us together and I have to explain two
or three times before he gets the joke. Then I think, 'And what
would happen to me if I had to go abroad?'

He likes to be quiet – most foreigners like silence, don't they?
But I'm a happy person and I'm always singing and talking and
laughing. . . . Sometimes I sing very loud or turn the radio full on,
and he says, 'Don't make so much noise.' 'It's my custom,' I tell
him, 'I feel happier like this.' During the *feria* he'd rather sit
quietly in a bar having a beer than walk up and down with us.
He gets fed up, he doesn't like the *feria* very much. But we – we
walk up and down all the time – 'Uy! *la feria!*' – and make a lot of
noise laughing and joking; he comes too but he does it for me.

He's becoming more and more like a Spanish *novio*, really. At
first he didn't worry too much about anything; the people said it
was all the same to him if I talked or danced with another man. I
thought so too. But it was probably because at the start he was
frightened to say anything in case I got angry. Now he knows me
better he says what he thinks. Not that he worries if I wear
trousers or a short skirt or put on make-up. If I had a *novio* like
that it would be a hell for me. To have a Spanish *novio* who was
always bossing me about would be a real hell. I wouldn't put up
with it. But I don't have to with Juan.

Right from the start I explained our customs, Spanish life, to him. I and my cousin told him he must show respect and not talk about intimate things, only normal things, in front of my parents. Little by little he got used to this and he has never said or done anything he shouldn't in front of them. My parents treat him just the same as they do my sister's *novio*.

I love Juan more and have greater confidence in him than I believed I could ever have in any man. I hope we can stay here when we marry and have a house near his garage. If it was necessary I'd leave the village to be with him; he's more important to me than the *pueblo*. But I'd rather stay here.

I'd like to have two or three children, no more. Life's easier when there are no more than three. Juan and I have discussed it. I've never liked the idea that after marriage it's the husband alone who gives the orders. The way it has been in my home, for example. Juan says he can't stand that; it must be the man and the wife together who decide things. That's what I think, too.

JOHAN NILSSON   *Twenty*

I never thought I'd have a Spanish girl-friend. All I heard from foreigners on the coast when I first came was how difficult it was, so many complications, things you can't do. Well, I know now that everything they said is true!

When I asked her to the cinema that first evening it was just for fun really. I was very surprised when, as I was walking her home and we went down a street I'd never seen before, she suddenly said *adios* and thank you – and disappeared. Just like that!

I asked her cousin, who's a friend, why I couldn't go to her house. He said we'd be *novios* then, and I thought this was a lot of crazy talk. Even after that evening when I was invited to eat I didn't think it was true we were *novios*. I don't think Carmela did either, she thought I was going to get fed up and leave. She was surprised when I didn't; still is, I think. Three or four months afterwards, when I knew her better, I asked for fun once if we were *novios*. 'I don't know,' she said; but after that we thought of ourselves as such.

It was about then that I was able to kiss her – just a peck – for the first time. About once a week, if we're lucky, we're alone for a few minutes when her mother or sister leave the room. Just a minute or two! It makes things very hard. We love each other a lot but we can never really be alone. I can't even take her to my parents' house alone. Carmela says it's because her father doesn't want the people to talk; but I think it's because no girls are allowed out on their own. It's bad really and I believe Carmela regrets it too, but she can't do anything. It's not her fault, and I often feel sorry for her.

But it gets me down. When she won't let me hold her hand in case her father sees us, when she tells me to sit up straight and not too close to her, I sometimes feel it's too much, too difficult. She's always thinking about things we can't do. We've quarrelled a few times and I've walked away – but then I regretted it, knowing she was feeling sad and I was sad too. I love her very much.

I go to her house every evening. A good few evenings I eat there. I've got used to the food now; soup, fried potatoes, fried meat. They don't do anything special for me, although Carmela gives me a knife and fork because I can't manage just with a spoon as they do. It turns my stomach to see a fried egg being broken up on the plate and sopped up with bread. But I suppose it tastes better that way because if I say anything they don't reply.

There's nothing to do in the village except go to the cinema or to a bar. My *novia* likes to go out with her friends. I don't like being with them all that much. They only talk about things going on in the village and laugh at a lot of little things that don't seem very funny. It's boring and I'd rather be with Carmela alone. I think she's coming to prefer that too.

Especially now we can talk about anything together. Talk – but not do the things we talk about!

When I first knew her she didn't know very much – well, about some things like shopping and keeping house she did; but not about anything else. She was completely ignorant of birth control, for example. I told her what we could do if we were in Sweden and she didn't like it because she doesn't think it right that *novios* should sleep together. I tell her it's much better, much freer; I think you're surer of getting the right wife. I'm very sure that Carmela is the right person for me, but if I were in Sweden and there was something I didn't like about her I'd leave. Here it's a lot more difficult.

Other times I think perhaps it's better this way not sleeping together before marriage. Maybe it's more interesting like this. This summer my younger brother came to stay with his sixteen-year-old girl-friend. In a way I envied him his freedom, being able to travel alone with her, being able to sleep with her. He told me that after you've been to bed a few times with the same girl it's not as exciting as the first time, but perhaps he just said that to make me feel good. I don't know. I've never been someone who could talk to a girl easily and I've never had affairs before; I've never been to bed with a girl.

Of course I'd like to go to bed with my *novia*. Sometimes I ask her if she feels the same and she says yes. But it isn't possible.

I suppose I'm getting used to Spanish ways. Not only used to them but becoming more like a Spanish *novio*. I'm jealous of her now; I wouldn't like her to dance with another man, I don't want to see her talking to someone else. There are so many things I can't do that she has to accept some of the things I don't want her to do! Not that I'm as crazy as most of the *novios* who spend all their time bossing their *novias* about. I don't believe in that. But if her blouse is too open I tell her to close it. She can't be completely free with me, so why should she display herself to anyone else? I wouldn't think anything of this if I could go where I wanted with her, but that's not the way it is.

Two or three times a week I take her to eat at *El Portón*. Her father won't let her sit in the room upstairs where the young go, so we stay downstairs. I've never invited her parents to eat because they never go out together. Her mother always stays at home and her father is usually out.

What a closed life they live here! Especially the women once they're married. Except on Sundays when they go out together, the men use their homes just to eat and sleep. They don't seem to have anything in common to talk about; they're like two separate people living under the same roof. My mother and father always have things to say to each other, but here it's so much more limited. The man is the king in the home and that's it. I wouldn't want my married life to be like that; I want to discuss things with my wife, I want there to be equality. . . . Carmela thinks the same but she also thinks it right that the man should decide everything. It must be easy for a Spaniard when he marries! But for a Spanish woman – well, I think she has a much better life marrying a foreigner. For me, too, it'll be simpler because Carmela doesn't expect very much and she'll be easier satisfied.

It's good that we can talk about anything together. But often I think how young Carmela is. I feel much older than her. She's about the same as a sixteen-year-old Swedish girl. Sometimes she gets very excited about some little thing she sees in a souvenir shop on the coast and I feel how little she has seen in life.

I get a bit irritated about it. But then I realize how lucky I am because she's cleverer than the other girls here, she knows how foreigners live and she's more like them because she's always worked for foreigners. She shares my tastes in most things. That's good, because in some of the houses where they're trying to copy the foreigner's style you see some terrible things. Shiny plastic tablecloths on tables that are never used, shiny furniture, fake leather chairs, knick-knacks. . . . I prefer the old village style to that. My *novia*'s house is still like that; just the small wood chairs and the brazier. Her father has repaired it a bit: when I first went there there was a hole in the roof. Someone told me that was why Carmela didn't want me to come to her house. That was silly; I didn't come to see her house, I came to see her!

She says that before we can get married I've got to build a house. All the *novias* demand that because once they're married there won't be money enough to build one. But I tell her I'm not going to do it just because everyone else does. I don't know whether I'm going to spend the rest of my life here; I'm expecting something more than that out of life. Right now she wants to live here – she doesn't want to move even to Casas Nuevas. But when we've been married a few years and I've shown her many things, I don't think she'll want to stay here so much.

My *novia* likes going to church. I ask her what she likes about it. She says it doesn't harm anyone, and she likes me to go with her. I'm nothing, not Protestant or anything. I went for the children's first communion recently and I told her afterwards I'd never go again. The priest went on talking for an hour and a half and I couldn't understand what he was saying. When everyone knelt I stayed standing. Why should I kneel? I don't like these crazy things. But Carmela asked me to kneel; she was embarrassed. So I did. We'll have to get married in church, and I suppose I'll have to become a Catholic. Though I'll never go to church afterwards, I'll do that for her because I love her.

There are so many other things I'd like to do. Just once in a while to be able to take her to Casas Nuevas or Málaga. But it's not possible. The only thing to do is to get the *noviazgo* over and get married.

A few months later, conforming to custom, Johan started to build a house next to his garage. He wasn't sure when they would be able to marry. 'In Sweden I could earn the money I need very quickly. But here I've got to put everything I earn back into the garage. Of course, I could sell my car – I like Carmela better than the car – but it'd take me a long time to save up for another; and we'd need a car if we went on holiday in Sweden. . . .'

VILLAGE SCHOOL

'In education, Andalusia is one of the most backward regions of Spain, with a great shortage of school places. Under a new emergency plan announced today, 112 new state colleges providing places for 71,580 pupils are to be built in Andalusia in addition to the 77,830 places already planned for 1972.'

Sur (Málaga), 17 June 1971

AGUAS DEL SENTIMIENTO
Waters of Emotion

Agua que corres por un sendero malo y cansado,
Water that flows along a poor, tired path,

Agua que te llevas a las hojas de los arboles en otoño.
Water that carries with it the leaves in autumn.

Agua temerosa, que en mi cuerpo formas el anillo de boda,
Timid water, making a wedding-ring of my body,

Tu eres tan bonita, agua, que en ti gozan los peces de vida.
Water, so beautiful that the fish of life delight in you.

Agua, que con tu murmullo alegras el pensamiento.
Water whose murmuring rejoices the mind.

Agua, te sientes satisfecha de que el pájaro
Water, content that the bird

Cansado de tanto volar, se pose en el palito que flota en ti.
Which is tired of flying rests on a twig floating in you.

Agua, me vengo a estas horas contigo, porque junto a ti
Water, I will come with you now because close to you

me duermo como si fuera en brazos de mi madre.
I sleep as though in my mother's arms.

Agua, si yo pudiera acompañarte como las hojas de los arboles
If, like the leaves of the trees, I could follow you

sería tan dichoso como las estrellas en el firmamento.
I would be as fortunate as the stars in heaven.

Agua, que pasas por mi sentimiento desde que brotas de las
montañas
Water, you flow through my senses from your mountain source

Como el sudor del hombre, hasta que te juntas con tu hermana el
mar.
Like the sweat of man, until you mingle with your sister, the sea.

ANTONIO MORENO aged 12

LA CIUDAD Y EL CAMPO
The Town and the Countryside

¡Oh campo en primavera! Las mariposas revolotean en el aire
fresco.
Oh, countryside in spring! The butterflies flutter in the fresh air.

En la ciudad solo hay fábricas echando humo y anhídrio
carbónico.
*In the city there are only factories belching out smoke and carbon
monoxide.*

En el campo hay paz y felicidad.
In the country there is peace and happiness.

En el campo trabajan animales, en la ciudad maquinarias.
*In the countryside there are animals working, in the city only
machines.*

En el campo los pájarillos cantan y el sol alumbra brillantemente
naranjos y limoneros.
*In the country the birds sing and the sun shines brightly on orange
and lemon trees.*

Al sonar el clarín del gallo los trabajadores van al trabajo de
media madrugada.
At cock-crow the workmen leave in the half dawn for their work.

En la ciudad solo hay accidentes.
In the city there are only accidents.

JOSE-MARIA PORRAS aged 11

Don José Lozano, the thirty-two-year-old director of the
village school, shows off his pupils' work with enthusiasm
and pride. For the first time perhaps ever a feeling for nature,
a reconciliation with the land, is evident in these boys' work.
The bitter struggle with the natural environment is over;
confronted with a man-made environment that is replacing
it with 'machines, unhappiness and strife', a nostalgia for
what never was has already set in. . . .

Don José points to the walls of the single-storey classroom,
built under the Primo de Rivera dictatorship, where he
teaches boys from ten to fourteen. They are covered with
drawings from a composition he recently set in which each
boy had to describe his father in words and pictures. Several
drawings show a figure wielding a pick-axe or shovel. 'They
see their fathers exclusively in the role of workers. Look at
that one; he has drawn his father as a puppet, very small.'
The name underneath reads Gil Lopez.

Don José comes from Posadas and has been director two
years. Including himself, there are presently four masters and
four mistresses in Tajos, each responsible for classes combining two years. 'We desperately need at least another six
classrooms and teachers, four for school-age children and
two for a nursery school. In the first year for boys there are
fifty-six pupils and in the second year about the same. With
the growth in the village population, the educational needs

aren't yet being fully met. We need these new classrooms by next year if we are to cope.'

As it is there has been improvisation. The town hall is responsible for finding classrooms and has, as already mentioned, pressed into service the slaughter-house which the municipality was obliged by law to build but never found use for; in addition it has rented a former shop. 'As long as it fulfils the requirements of the Education and Science Ministry's inspectors, any building can be used as a classroom. These two places are by no means ideal, but for want of anything better. . . . I've been told that the town hall has the sites for more classrooms, but I don't really know.'

Passing by the school on hot summer mornings one no longer hears children's voices droning in rote. Those days have gone. Don José lets his class vote on the timetable they want from a number of alternatives he has drawn up; pupils keep track of their own progress on charts which they fill in; don José organizes a 'press conference' at which one of the boys answers the others' questions on a subject they have chosen; there is drawing and modelling and an improvised tennis game in the classroom. . . .

The revolutionary change from the old textbooks and rote has taken place in the past five years. The system was to be further changed in 1972 when children would be allowed to choose what they wanted to study at any one time. The teacher would set certain themes in each subject but the pupils would advance at their own rate. Yearly exams would be replaced by teachers' assessments. In consequence it would be possible for brighter pupils to complete more than one year's course at a time.

Apart from reforming teaching methods, the new law 'will attempt to democratize education generally', don José explains. Fee-paying private schools are to be abolished. 'It's a long-term project which began this year [1971] in the primary schools to the age of ten. This will work its way through the system so that, in the end, secondary and university education will also be non-fee paying. If it isn't totally free, between 25 percent and 50 percent of the costs will be paid by the state. The new law means that general education will reach every corner of the country, and the possibilities of further education will no longer be reserved to the privileged classes.'

At the moment, as far as don José is aware, only one Tajeño is at university. Last year he helped three pupils to scholarships at the secondary school in Posadas. 'If poverty was one of the reasons why so few children in the past went to secondary school, today it's because everyone can get a job here. But also there's a lack of tradition. Parents have thought they were wasting their time trying to push their children on because they would never get to university and a career. They tend to think that the schooling they got is enough for their children.

'In Posadas, for example, there has always been a tradition of education; there are probably as many as forty people at university presently from there. But Posadas is more prosperous; it has a commercial tradition, and people are more oriented to the outside world. . . . Here parents lack information about the possibilities of further education.'

Don José has five or six boys whom he believes could study up to university level and he hopes that they will be able to take advantage of the new law.

School attendance is obligatory and practically 100 percent today. 'But I have two or three boys whose fathers give them permission to work half-day. If they use the rest of their time well in school it doesn't seem bad to me that they should have part-time jobs; they're getting used to working and making a bit of money for themselves.'

Television has had a big impact, particularly on the younger children. 'You notice it immediately in the five- and six-year-olds. Those who watch TV a lot have a much larger vocabulary than those who don't. I can tell almost immediately if a child hasn't got television at home.'

The school has its own television set, a tape recorder, record player, film projector. But don José is short of film, slides, tapes and records. He also wants to set up a carpenter's shop; for all these things he needs parents' and friends' help. He is trying to start an association for everyone who is interested in supporting the school and to help disseminate information about educational possibilities.

Boys and girls, whose classes are segregated, receive lessons in civic and social education. Guide notes provided for teachers give an indication of the themes. For twelve- to fourteen-year-old boys the chapter headings include:

'The unity of national coexistence: Spain (as conquered by the Spanish; Spain as hope and faith in a common task); the doctrine of the Movement as the inspirational source of the fundamental principles of the Spanish state. Political rights: the citizen's rights to elect and be elected to public office; political duties: respect for the person, love of and service to Spain.

'Position of Spain in the present-day world (awake in the pupils the basic attitudes of European man to himself, to nature, to social life). Solidarity and international co-operation (awake attitudes of respect and sympathy towards other people, tolerance towards honest opinions and intolerance towards evil). Avoid prejudice and discrimination.'

DOLORES SEPULVEDA   *Fifty*

Schoolmistress

Doña Dolores comes from Antequera and is a friend of the midwife's. In her home town she was director of the Falange's Women's Social Service Institute, but was unable to continue in her post when the cares of looking after her own children became too great. On her friend's advice she came to fill a vacant teacher's post in Tajos in 1961. 'The great advantage from my point of view was that the house which went with the job was built on to the classroom.' It was her first village school experience.

The first day I found more than forty girls sitting on the benches, on the desks, on the writing table – anywhere they could. It was the youngest class – and it was a disaster. I had to get rid of those who were under six and whose mothers had sent them along just in the hope. . . . That caused me a lot of problems with the people, of course. Then the classroom was in a terrible state. The doors didn't shut; the floor was of old tiles you couldn't sweep and keep clean; my desk fell to pieces every time a child approached. The children were dirty and scruffy, their hair uncombed, their nails filthy – with a few exceptions. I had to set about making new rules and trying to start afresh.

At that time it was a struggle to ensure that the children came to school. The educational and cultural level was very low; the people lived very happily without thought of education. Tajos is a village so in love with itself that the people think they are better than anyone else and don't need to improve! Moreover, the general attitude was that girls didn't need much learning because they were going to stay at home to cook and clean; so mothers brought their young daughters to school to get them out of the house and took their older daughters out of school to help them at home.

Ten years ago – what a change there has been! The standard of living, if not the cultural level, has gone up a lot. There's work now for young girls, and to get a job in a shop they need their school-leaving certificate. The increase in pupils is not only a reflection of an increase in population but one of complete school attendance.

There were three masters and three mistresses when I started, to cope with eight classes of girls and boys. Today we've two more – and hopefully we'll have another two more soon.

As far as work is concerned boys and girls study exactly the same; the major difference in teaching concerns home-making and house-keeping. It is the girl who has to be housewife, who must learn to become fond of her house and make it pleasant for her husband or father; keep it clean, decorate it. All women, whether they're single, married or widowed are housewives after all. . . . They must know how to sew which is a feminine occupation and a good economy: a woman, however rich, who can't sew can never run her household as economically as one who does. Moreover, if she enjoys sewing she'll spend less time gossiping and talking badly behind people's backs.

I like my pupils to be feminine, and I teach them to sew and embroider in the afternoons. I show them how to lay a table and to arrange flowers. I use any suitable occasion to instruct them in these things, to tell them that 'a señorita wouldn't do it this way or that'. I don't have special times for these things except sewing which is part of the curriculum and which we do in the afternoons. I teach them needlework typical not only of Spain but of other countries. At the moment we're embroidering a tablecloth in a Yugoslav pattern.

The girls also get instruction in what we in the Falange call politics but is better described as civic and social education. For example, they're told about the trade union in which their father is enrolled, about the town hall and the municipality, about the mayor's role, the community. It's not politics, you see.*

There are no girls here to my knowledge who have studied for a career. There was one very intelligent boy when I first came and I went all over trying to get people's help for his further education. There was no one in the village who would help so I approached people in Casas Nuevas; finally I found a wealthy woman who was willing to pay for his schooling and he became a teacher. Subsequently he has changed to journalism and will shortly finish his studies in that field. If it hadn't been for me he would have got nowhere.

I know how costly it is to study for a career. I paid for my eldest daughter's education entirely. She did her *bachillerato* in Málaga and is now a beautician. We hope to be able to set her up in her own salon in Casas Nuevas, but meanwhile she helps me a lot teaching, especially sewing and things like that. My second daughter got a scholarship worth 7,000 pesetas – and her boarding-school in Málaga cost more than 30,000 pesetas. The

* Teachers' guide notes for girls from the age of twelve recommend instruction on the overall political structure of the state. 'In preparation, they should be taught to situate Spain historically from the order which collapsed in 1936 to the new order inaugurated in 1939; thus pupils can succinctly understand the reasons which motivated this change – the common task in which all Spaniards were called to participate in order to re-make and exalt their nation.'

rest we had to find. Not to mention clothes, the trips to and from Málaga and all the other things. Now this is beginning to change and there are more scholarships; but in the past from a village like this it was very difficult to get further education.

One of the major problems here is the lack of nursery schools. I deplore the private school a village girl started in a dilapidated house. I don't know why the local authorities permitted it; not only that, but sent their own children to it. Of course, the girl's father is a municipal councillor. Parents were impressed by the huge sums she taught their children; when they started proper school we had to teach them all over again because they had no understanding of what they had been doing.

And playgrounds! We badly need space for the children to play. At the moment we haven't got anywhere adequate to teach gymnastics properly or to play games. A lot has been done in these past ten years but there's a great deal that still has to be done.

I never wanted to become a teacher. I did it only to please my father who wanted me to have a profession, either as a teacher or a pharmacist. Those were his preferences for a woman. Now, late in life, I've discovered my vocation. It gives me great satisfaction to see children I've taught becoming something in life.

Don José's classroom: forty pairs of eyes expectantly watching the foreigner come to be questioned by them. Don José calls them to attention, and explains that the theme is 'life and customs in northern Europe'. When, one day, he enthusiastically invited me to give a 'press conference' to his class, I accepted, not without apprehension, in the hope of discovering through their questions the range of interests among the new generation of Tajeños. I explained my purpose in accepting and don José agreed. I am sorry to say that he lived to regret it; I cannot say the same.

The boys were relaxed, respectful but not in awe of their teacher; alert and full of questions. The 'conference' which was supposed to last half an hour stretched to double that time. In the hour they asked over fifty questions. Excluding the more obvious, the following will indicate their range.

'How are the rulers elected in France? In England? How many years in advance is England over Spain? What is the most important tradition in northern Europe? How is the land worked? What form of government is there in Russia? What is the communist party in northern Europe? Has England taken over many customs from invaders? What are the major industries and the major products of France? Which is the most advanced European country? Which countries are richer than Spain? What are the major sports? Are there bullfights? What form of government is there in Belgium? Where is life more advanced – in northern or southern Europe? What do the people work at mainly in England? Who are the main people in the communist party in England?'

Here don José ordered a break lest the children 'get tired'. During this interval he opened a box on his desk to reveal three fledgelings in a home-made nest which he proceeded carefully to feed with the yolk of an egg. The boys crowded round to watch. The birds had been picked up by the master when they had fallen out of their nest from a tree which was being pruned in front of the school. The care with which he looked after them and the children's interest was the more remarkable when I remembered that, not so far back, such a find might have been the excuse of some instant cruelty on the part of village children. Was not then don José largely responsible for these boys' new-found pleasure and concern for nature?

Already admiring his pupils' interest in the world beyond them, I complimented don José on their advance over the preceding generation. I mentioned in illustration the case of Josefa Alarcon, the shopgirl who had not known of which countries London and Paris were the capitals. He looked at me pityingly. 'There are plenty of foreigners who come here and don't know whether they are in Tajos, Casas Nuevas or Posadas,' he said shortly.

'Is there a city in Europe which can be compared to New York? What countries make up the Common Market? What

are the major wild animals of northern Europe? What is the
climate like? Which country of northern Europe is under-
developed?'

Don José's intense brown eyes behind the metal-framed
glasses became overcast. He raised his hand in deprecatory
imitation of one of the boys and asked: 'Don't you believe
that mechanization and industrialization have caused life to
lose its individual and personal sense, that life has become
standardized in northern Europe, and that in consequence a
great deal has been lost?'

I agreed, suggesting that the youth movement and much
workers' militancy was caused by this sense of depersonalization, of having no control over one's work or
the course of society. The answer appeared not to be the one
he awaited; increasingly I felt him becoming restive.

'What are the main agricultural crops? Is there much livestock? Which country of northern Europe is less developed
than the rest? What are the major customs of England? Is
northern Europe rich in petrol?' ('We will end now,' calls
don José.) A final question comes from the back row: 'Has
northern Europe produced many film stars?'

Don José said a prayer and the class was dismissed. When
the children had gone he turned reproachfully. 'You gave an
unfavourable impression of depreciating Spain in talking
about our country as "under-developed".' Taken aback, I
remarked that this was the very economic category the
Spanish Foreign and Economic Plan ministers had put
forward to an OEEC meeting only a few days before to secure
the economic concessions they felt necessary. The papers had
reported their statements.

'Yes, maybe; but you can't talk to children like that. If
you make out that every country in Europe is economically
richer than Spain you do harm to the children.' In his opinion
I should have counter-posed the beauty of the countryside,
the peace and tranquillity of life in Tajos, the possibility of
individual fulfilment with the pace and depersonalization of
industrialized society; I should have praised Spanish cultural

achievements; I was, he implied finally, like some foreigner who had recently taken photographs of the slaughter-house school in a deliberate attempt to slander the village and Spain. . . .

Nothing I said assuaged his outrage. He left saying that he would have to correct the unfortunate impression I had created among his pupils. A few days later I called on him to ask whether the 'press conference' had indeed had the effects he feared. 'No, no, it's all right,' he said, leaving the impression that his initial fears had been exaggerated. Or was it politeness?

I mention this incident only because I believe it illustrates an important change; don José's reaction was typical of a certain Spanish ambivalence which, on the one hand, likes to state, often in an over-simplified, indeed cynical manner, that 'everything is better abroad'; on the other, recoils with excessive pride into defensiveness about the applicability of 'foreign ways' to Spain.

His pupils seemed devoid of either view. Their questions were pointed, realistic; I do not believe they shared their master's views. I came away encouraged. If, as predicted, Spain by the end of the decade becomes the world's tenth industrial nation, the new generation will need a fair dose of critical realism to deal with the change.

TODAY . . .

'The land is abandoned,' the villagers say, looking down on terraces and fields that only two or three years ago were cultivated. 'No one wants to till the soil any longer.' A typical case is that of old Francisco Avila, the small-holder. When he retired ten years ago, he gave his farm to a sharecropper; three years ago the latter left to work on the coast. Francisco asked his nephew to plough round the trees and collect the olive crop, but he only did a part of what was needed. 'It doesn't pay to farm it with day-labour and I'm too old to do it myself. So there it is. Since last year, in a word, my land has been abandoned.'

Whether they want to or not, there are still several hundred people farming pockets of land hidden among the hills. *El Verdegal* is one of these. When Cristóbal Gonzalez left, Gil Lopez found another sharecropper from the hamlet of Los Peñones to replace him. The man stayed little more than a year. Gil then brought in the son of one of his tenant farmers, Manuel Torres, who sharecrops the farm today.

MANUEL TORRES   *Thirty-two*

Sharecropper

I wasn't sure I wanted to take it on; the farm is too big for one man alone, but Gil insisted, so I came. I brought a milch cow with me as my share, and Gil bought another and a pair of ploughing cows. Gil wanted to turn *El Verdegal* into a cattle-raising farm and that's what I've done.

The terms aren't quite as bad as when Cristóbal Gonzalez had it. Gil provides half the seed and fertilizer but also, when I need it, the extra labour for which he pays. The trouble is you can't get anyone to do a day's work on the land, so he hasn't had to pay many day-wages. The farm could do with a lot more labour than it gets.

I plant only fodder; alfalfa, vetch, barley for cutting green, maize. Some of the smaller terraces I can't get round to planting at all. Otherwise the farm is the same as when Cristóbal had it. Gil hasn't spent any money on it. Look – this is where the milch cows are, in this lean-to with only the door for ventilation. They need a proper yard to be able to move about in because they only get taken out of here to drink. The other cows are in the lean-to attached to the house. Five we've got in all, two of them for ploughing. No one I know of has more around here.

My wife takes the milk up to the village every morning on the donkey to sell it in the shops. It fetches fourteen pesetas a litre. In the evening I go and sell it in private houses. Gil takes about four litres for his own use every day and once a week we settle up. On average the cows give about thirty litres a day.

TB? No, I don't know about that. If a cow is sick I can tell; if it over-eats or something I see straight away and cure it myself. So I don't have to test the milk.

We raise calves and sell them when they're four to five months old and weigh about 150 kilos; they bring in about a hundred pesetas a kilo then.

I've got no savings, nothing at all, except my share of the cows. I don't know what I make a year but I don't suppose it works out at more than a hundred pesetas a day. I could make three times that amount in building. And work less hours, have Saturday afternoon and Sunday and fiestas off. Here I'm busy with the cattle from seven in the morning until nine at night. I have to take them out to graze; I can't leave them because they'll get on to the terraces that are planted with fodder.

I shouldn't have come as a sharecropper – not in the old way where everything is split. I should have come as an *aparcero*, where I'd get two-thirds of the crop instead of half, or as a renter. I haven't made up my mind but I won't stay on in the present conditions. Gil is selling the land where my father rents a plot and has his house. He's offering him 200,000 pesetas to leave. It's not enough; he'll have to pay 500,000 and then we can build a house in the village and I'll go to work as a building labourer to support us all.

. . . AND TOMORROW?

Towards the end of 1971 Marikje and Johnnie, a Belgian couple, came to Tajos. He is a computer engineer and she a barmaid. They heard about the village while holidaying on the coast. After a time they rented a small ground-floor room in a house and turned it into the first foreign-run bar in the village.

'El Flamenco' is fairly luxurious by local tavern standards: bar stools, functioning toilet, ash-trays, hi-fi over which Johnnie blasts out the flamenco to attract local clientele. The latter is sharply divided by age group: men in their 20s and those in their 60s. The middle stratum of married men with young families do not by and large go there. One might hazard the guess that Marikje is the reason. Of generous nature and generous proportions, she is an experienced barmaid, always ready with a wink, a laugh, a touch. She has revolutionized the business of bartending in Tajos – or so, superficially, it seems. . . .

Johnnie: I've done a bit of everything in my time – everything against the law except stealing and queering. I don't like that. I was a gambler for a long time: big-time poker was what I was in. I lost three cars in a couple of months. When I was down to my last 20,000 francs Marikje and I went to Ostend where I had a friend who got us a bar. We built it up fast. We paid twice as much as anyone else to get the best doorman, the best girls in town. We bought champagne – if you can call it that – for eighteen francs a bottle and sold it for 1,000.

When the girls we paid didn't hustle enough my wife showed them how. After a time I didn't like to see her doing that so she told me to let her get on with the bar alone. I went back to gambling.

In the end we gave up the bar and I went into computers, my old business. Big stuff, I built up a firm with fifty people working for me; I was making a good income. One day I woke up and said – 'For what? I'm paying half everything I earn in taxes.' I wouldn't have minded that if it went to build new roads, new schools, even to help the poor. But no, it was going to support people who didn't want to work: hippies and layabouts. So I said, 'What the hell!' I sold it all up and we came down here.

This is the life. I like it here. The bar's going well, it's a success. A barrel of draft lager costs me 235 pesetas and there are thirty litres in a barrel. That's over a hundred glasses. I charge the locals eight pesetas a glass and any foreigner who comes in twelve. That's only fair. I sell a barrel a day – so work it out for yourself.

Marikje: After a while Johnnie told me I shouldn't act the way I did; the people were saying I was a whore. I was just doing what I'd have done at home – women can act more friendly to men there than they can here. I'm a bit more careful now, but still if a man comes to a bar he wants to see a friendly face behind it, doesn't he?

I don't mind putting my arm round a man or whatever, but it doesn't go any further. Sometimes when my husband's not in the mood he has this long face because he gets fed up. You can't be like that if you're keeping a bar. Sure, I get fed up with their jokes: they lack subtlety, they're crude really. I'm always waiting for something funny, and suddenly they've finished and it hasn't come. . . .

Johnnie: They're children, that's what it is, just children. . . .

Marikje: No, that's not it. It's not that they're children. They have a different way of thinking, that's what it is. . . . They treat women differently. They think because I'm a foreigner and friendly they can make me. But when it comes down to it all they do is make me laugh. They'll proposition me but it's always 'Come to Málaga' or somewhere else. They couldn't do it here, in the village, because everyone would get to know. So they have to try somewhere else. That's what makes me laugh.

Johnnie: I don't like it, sometimes they get on my nerves.

Marikje: Ech! You know it's all talk with them. They like it and it brings them in. Nothing ever happens. Here, give me that bill. (She counts the money, checks, double checks. It goes on the adding machine.) I'm the one who has to look after the money, Johnnie doesn't worry about that. . . .

The past here? No, I don't know anything about it; I don't care. As far as I'm concerned the future hasn't started in Tajos yet.

Cost of Living and Wages in Tajos*

	1900	1920	1930	1935	1942 (official)†	1942 (blackmarket)	1952	1962	1972
1 kilo of bread	0·30	0·45	0·60	0·60	2·80 (black bread)	20·00 (white bread)	2·50	5·00	14·00
1 litre of olive oil	0·90	1·75	2·25	2·30	3·50	40·00	6·50	12·00	38·00
1 kilo of dried cod	0·40	1·00	3·00	3·00	5·00	25·00	15·00	35·00	100·00
1 kilo of fresh fish (*jurel*)	0·20	0·40	0·70	0·80	1·25	—	10·00	25·00	65·00
1 pair of man's sandals	0·90	1·50	1·80	2·00	3·00	—	7·00	12·00	35·00
1 pair of man's shoes	8·00	15·00	20·00	20·00	50·00	—	125·00	250·00	450·00
Off-the-peg man's suit	25·00	55·00	90·00	120·00	250·00	—	650·00	900·00	2000·00
Round trip to Málaga	5·00	8·50	10·00	12·00	18·00	—	30·00	40·00	52·00
Basic day-labourer's wage	1·50	2–3·00	3·50	6·00	8·00	—	12·00	35·00	300·00‡

Cost of living and wages in Tajos in pesetas

*Based on oral evidence.
†Rationed food.
‡This is the basic wage of the building labourer. The basic wage of the agricultural labourer is 180 pesetas.

APPENDIX B

The Land, Landowners and Farming

As the reader has seen, for the first sixty years of this century Tajos (as indeed the whole of Spain) remained dependent on agriculture. Control of the land meant control of the major source of wealth and determined not only the economic but social pattern of life. No study of a village, even less a village in Andalusia, where the land problem has, historically, been particularly acute, would be complete without a more detailed examination of the distribution of land, ownership and labour than oral evidence alone provides.

Regrettably, reliable statistics, not only for Tajos but for all Spain, are often hard to come by; and often even harder to draw unqualified conclusions from when they are available. The following, therefore, is necessarily limited; but I believe it does indicate the major areas in which the land question has conditioned village life as related in this book.[1]

THE LAND

The 1947 *cadastre* confirms what is apparent to the eye – the extreme parcelization of the land. A total of 1,193 owners held 8,270 plots, all but fourteen of them under a hundred hectares. The average size of the fourteen was 244 hectares; that of the remaining 8,256 was 1·15 hectares.

The village lands extend over 14,400 hectares and include a wide variety of soil, only 5 percent of which is classified as first grade; this is the deep loam of the *vega* and lower reaches of the river. The bulk (70 percent) of the land is graded as average to poor, with the remaining 25 percent as poor to barren.

Although officially only 1·5 percent of the land is classified as 'unproductive' and incapable of any growth, more than 50 percent of the land has been left uncultivated throughout this century.

Table 1 Land cultivated as percentage of total

1899	34·9
1947	42·3
1962	29·8
1962 Málaga province 48·1	

Even in 1947, when pressure on the land was at its height due to the famine years and a 25 percent increase in the village population from the turn of the century, more than half the land remained uncultivated. Of this approximately 40 percent was pasture, and a further 23 percent the newly afforested sierra. Thus 37 percent – or, more graphically, 20 percent of the total land classified as potentially productive – was left uncultivated.

This untilled land might be expected to consist of the poorer grade soils; in fact 96 percent was first and second grade; while 77 percent of pasture land was classified in the first three grades. Less surprisingly, 68 percent of the land left to pasture or uncultivated belonged to the 3 percent of landowners with holdings of fifty hectares or more.

This phenomenon – marked throughout Andalusia – was even more acute in 1922 when scrub and pasture accounted for 64 percent of all large (over a hundred hectare) holdings; by 1947 the proportion had dropped to 53 percent. The claim by landless labourers that there was plenty of land which could have been cultivated applied to Tajos as much as to other parts of Spain.

IRRIGATION

The importance of water in the sub-tropical climate of Málaga's coastal region (average year-round temperature 18·1° C) has been frequently stressed. Rainfall, as farmers have noted, has increased in the last fifty years.

Table 2 Rainfall: Málaga city average

1915–30	437·1 mm (17·0 in.)
1931–54	455·3 mm (17·7 in.)
1955–64	529·5 mm (20·6 in.)

Were they recorded, slightly lower temperatures and higher rainfall figures would be returned for Tajos. Rainfall is on average concentrated into forty-five days of the year, the bulk of these between December and March. Yearly variations are often very great; seven of the ten years 1955–64 were below the decadal average, though the variations were not usually as extreme as those between 1963 when 814·9 mm (31·7 in.) of rain were recorded and 1964 when only 381·5 mm (14·8 in.) fell.

The irrigation season lasts three to four months, depending on the weather; for the rest of the year the water from the *minas* and springs flows into the sea.

Table 3 Irrigated land as percentage of total productive land

	Total productive land	Productive land cultivated
Tajos 1962	6·3	16·9
Province 1962	4·9	9·2

Though relatively privileged compared to the province as a whole, the large difference in irrigation of cultivated land is in part due to the fact, as we have seen, that a considerably smaller proportion of land was cultivated in Tajos in 1962 than in the province.

In 1962 only eighty-one more hectares were recorded as under irrigation than in 1754.[2] In view of the fact that irrigated land can grow two and often three crops a year (and is thus at least twice as productive as the best dry land), landowners' neglect of irrigation is striking.

Tajos landowners, however, were not untypical of most Andalusian large owners. Malefakis cites the case of landowners in Cadiz province who for forty-two years refused to pay for the necessary conduits to irrigate their farms from a dam built by the state in 1910. The present regime finally undertook the work.

Just under 30 percent of Tajos irrigated land is held in holdings of fifty hectares or more – the medium-large and large farms. And yet the 1947 cadastre recorded only 11 percent of top-grade soil, most of which is in these holdings along the river, as under irrigation.

Dry land, on the other hand, requires fallowing in order to regain its moisture content. 'The higher the proportion of bare fallow in the rotation cycle, the smaller the amount of land effectively at the disposal of the farmer. If an owner of ten hectares can sow his fields only once every two years, he possesses not ten but five hectares of useful soil.'[3] In 1962, 22 percent of Tajos and provincial land was recorded as being fallowed, and thus just over two hectares in every ten were effectively not at the farmer's disposal.

CROPS

In 1754 wheat, barley and maize were the village's three main crops, followed by olives, figs, sweet potatoes and sesame. Two hundred years later, wheat and barley remained the most important annual crops, though olives now accounted for more land than either.

Table 4 Main crop distribution 1968

	olives	cereals	citrus	vines	forage & maize	vegetables
As percentage dry land	49	25	9	6	6	5
Irrigated land	26	24	13	9	12	16

Second crops on irrigated land are not shown; in fact as much land was planted to second crop maize and vegetables as is shown above.

Olives, wheat and barley take up 59 percent of all cultivated land, the same percentage as for the province, although olives represent a slightly higher and cereals a slightly lower proportion of the provincial totals than in Tajos. The importance of cereals, particularly wheat to which three times more Tajos land is planted than barley (while in the province the ratio is under 2:1) is clearly revealed by the proportion of irrigated land devoted in Tajos to these two crops: 24 percent compared to the provincial 7 percent. Wheat yields were the same in Tajos as in the province on average; barley yields lower and maize yields higher.

Table 5 Average crop yields 1948–63 in metric tons per hectare

	Dry land	Irrigated land
Wheat		
Tajos ⎫		
Province ⎭	0·85	1·78
Barley		
Tajos	0·76	1·53
Province	0·93	1·79
Maize		
Tajos		2·69
Province		2·27

A metric ton equals 2,205 lb. Tajos yields are based on oral evidence of small-holders on second and third grade soil.

While irrigated wheat yields were equivalent, dry land yields were between one-half to two-thirds lower than comparable English and US yields. Though maize yielded relatively well, its use in Tajos compared to wheat has traditionally been negligible except at times of wheat shortage.

LANDOWNERSHIP

In 1754 the church and six nobles (2·4 percent of all owners) held 59 percent of privately-owned land in Tajos. Four other non-noble landowners held a further 16 percent. Together these eleven private and corporate owners (3·8 percent) held 75 percent of the land, which included over half the irrigated soil.

The remaining 273 owners (96·2 percent) held 25 percent. However, they were better off than these figures allow. Despite the large owners' domination, small-holders owned an average of 1·2 hectares of irrigated land each – three times the *per capita* amount held by owners of under fifty hectares in 1965. Moreover, commons which could be used by all the villagers for grazing, collecting firewood and hunting game, covered some 2,700 hectares – slightly under half as much land as was in private hands.

And there was room for expansion: over and above the common lands a further 2,400 hectares remained uncultivated for reasons of 'nature or idleness'.

Under the liberal governments of the first half of the nineteenth century church and common lands were put up for sale and noble entailed estates were disentailed. (In Tajos the one entailed estate alone accounted for 15 percent of private land.) These large sales of land did not by and large benefit the mass of the Spanish peasantry. Only those – mainly the middle classes – with accumulated wealth were able to take advantage of the land brought on to the market: most of the contemporary latifundia in Andalusia date from this period, and so too do the peasant uprisings in the south, one of the first of which occurred in Málaga province.

Probably because such a middle class did not exist in Tajos to the same extent as elsewhere, the situation in the village was somewhat attenuated.[4] Total landowners more than doubled by 1863, tripled by 1922 and quadrupled by 1965 compared to the figures of two centuries before. In 1754 8·7 percent of the village population owned land.

Table 6 Landownership 1754–1965

	Percentage increase in owners over previous date	Percentage increase in village population over previous date	Percentage of village population owning land
1863	117	62	11·7
1922	52·5	18·6	15·4
1965	26·3	22·3	15·9

Thus throughout the last two centuries landownership increased at a faster rate than the village population. The initial expansion was made possible in part due to the use of land previously uncultivated.

In 1754 under 200 people lived in the countryside out of a total village population of 3,173. Apart from other considerations it was probably not safe to live far from the village for until the 1830s the coastal zone would have been under threat of raids from the Barbary pirates. By the 1890s, however, one can estimate that over half the village population of 5,700 lived on the land.

But this expansion in ownership was at the cost to the villagers of their commons. In the mid-nineteenth century the landless labourer was dispossessed of the rights he had enjoyed in the eighteenth century. While ownership tripled, and the present-day foundations of a small-holding Tajos peasantry were created, the overall distribution of property, though somewhat less extreme, did not dramatically alter between 1754 and 1922. By the latter date there were forty landowners with holdings of fifty hectares or more; they represented 4·2 percent of owners and held 61·4 percent of the land. The remaining 904 owners (95·8 percent) held 38·5 percent. While 13 percent of the total land had thus shifted from large to small and medium-sized owners, a new class of large owner had virtually been able to maintain the position previously held by the nobility and church. Indeed, proportionately, this new class grew faster than the small and medium landholders.

Between 1922 and 1965, however, an important redistribution of land took place.

Table 7 Landownership 1922–65

	Tajos 1922		Tajos 1965		Málaga 1960
	% of all owners	% of all land	% of all owners	% of all land	% owners only
mini	25·3	0·9	21·1	1·0	46·0
small	56·4	15·9	60·8	21·9	43·8
medium	14·1	21·8	15·0	30·7	7·4
medium-large	2·2	12·5	1·9	13·1	1·5
large	2·0	48·9	1·2	33·3	1·3

mini = up to 1 hectare   medium-large = from 50 to 100 hectares
small = from 1 to 10 hectares   large = over 100 hectares
medium = from 10 to 50 hectares

As the above table shows, small and medium owners now increased at the expense of large owners. Within this latter category there was a 32 percent disinvestment in land and 26.4 percent fewer owners. As the vineyards became less profitable and the old landowners died or moved away, their large holdings were split up among heirs or sold. The break-up of the former Málaga conservative *cacique*'s estate on his death alone accounted for approximately two-thirds of the loss in large holdings. His heirs in 1965 retained only some hundred hectares of the 1,150 hectares he had owned in Tajos; the rest had been sold. Further sales, often by the heirs of former large owners, after the war when rents were fixed and agricultural prices were rising, no doubt accounted for a great part of the remainder. (The role of inheritance in the redistribution of land is examined below.)

Of the 1,858 hectares lost to large holdings, 1,064 hectares went to medium holdings, 714 hectares to small-holdings and only seventy-one hectares and nine hectares respectively to medium-large and mini-holdings.

Although there was certainly a redistribution of land in other than large holdings, we can only examine the net decrease and increase in each of the categories.

Table 8 Increase in land owned by category 1965 as compared to 1922

	Percentage increase of owners	Percentage increase of land
mini	5·4	7·8
small	36·4	37·5
medium	33·8	41·0
medium-large	9·5	4·8

This relatively large increase in small and medium holdings might be expected to have been achieved by reducing the average size of these farms. This, however, was not the case.

Table 9 Average size of land holdings in hectares

	mini	small	medium	medium-large	large
1922	0·48	4·8	19·4	70·5	306·3
1965	0·49	4·9	20·5	67·4	244·2

Taking small-holdings first, it is clear that an important land-holding population was created in this sector over the period.

Except in special cases,[5] it is unlikely that these new small-holdings were directly formed out of previous large holdings, but rather that there was a continual process of parcelization. The very small increase in medium-large holdings (due in fact entirely to inheritance) points to one sector in which holdings were broken up to form smaller units. At the same time the small increase in mini-holdings suggests that there was reconcentration of these tiny plots into more viable agricultural units.

More significantly, it was the medium-sized holdings which benefited most. This ten-to-fifty-hectare category in Tajos conditions provides relatively viable farming. Moreover, holdings of between thirty and fifty hectares showed double the increase of those between ten and thirty hectares. Thus it would appear that a medium-sized landholding peasantry, farming land not previously available to it, had been created. Unfortunately, statistics on how the land was worked do not bear this out.

Table 10 Agricultural units 1962

	Tajos		Province	
	Percentage of all farms	Percentage of all land	Percentage of all farms	Percentage of all land
mini	16·7	0·9	20·2	0·9
small	68·5	24·1	63·7	16·3
medium	12·0	22·9	12·7	18·7
medium-large	1·4	9·2	1·6	9·2
large	1·4	42·9	1·8	54·9

Comparing the above table with Table 7 we see that, when it came to farming, there were only two categories in which farmers and land farmed outnumbered owners and land owned as a proportion of the total: small-holdings and large holdings. Medium-sized holdings showed the biggest proportional *decrease* in land farmed with a 7·8 percent drop that was almost equivalent to the increase in land owned in this category between 1922 and 1965.

The fact that large holdings increased in farming terms while decreasing in ownership is puzzling at first sight. It is explicable by an imbalance in the 1962 census: one-fifth of all Tajos land (which included nearly one-third of all private land) was not recorded in the census. The large farms, being easier to assess, were all recorded; in *absolute* terms nearly as much land was shown farmed as owned. We must assume, therefore, that large holdings are over-represented proportionately in Table 10 at the expense of other categories. (Indeed, were it not so, large farmers would have reasserted control, if not legal ownership, over as much of the land as they owned in 1922; in other circumstances this would be conceivable but in the event it was an improbable assumption.)

Medium and medium-large categories, on the other hand, show staggering falls: in *absolute* terms 50 percent less land farmed than owned and nearly 50 percent fewer farmers than owners. This is particularly striking in the case of the medium-sized sector; the new owners patently neither worked their own land nor even kept it intact, but broke up the land into small-holding units for renters or sharecroppers to work.

This is amply borne out by the increase in small-holdings farmed. Proportionately there were 7·7 percent more farms than owners in this category; and this figure is certainly under-stated. (In absolute terms just over one-fifth less land was recorded farmed than owned in this category.) More significant is the fact that in *only one* of the twenty different hectare categories recorded by the 1962 census was there an *absolute increase* of land farmed over that owned and a greater number of farmers than owners: the three to four hectare range, the area most commonly given by renters and sharecroppers for their farms.

Although the few remaining large landowners provided an exception by continuing to farm the bulk of their land, the new owners followed the pattern which had prevailed in Tajos for at least the past hundred years. Even when their holdings were large enough to have provided them with a living or could have been used in some cases to expand their existing farms into more viable units, they split up their new land into small-holdings. Better to let others work the land for one than to work it oneself appears as a recurrent motif of landownership in Tajos.

This policy has an economic rationale (see below: *Share-cropping and Renting*); it also has had important effects on village life. Without it the pressure on the land of a rising population could not have been met and the proportion of villagers remaining directly attached to the land would not have risen. It gave to the agricultural population its unique composition in which the proportions of small-holders, renters and sharecroppers were very high (see below: *Landlords, tenants and labourers*) and by providing some means of livelihood from the land it no doubt preserved the enclosed character of Tajos which, through emigration after the 1920s, might have otherwise been opened up.

Even this would have been insufficient if, both in ownership and farming, Tajos had not been relatively privileged compared to the province as a whole. A far lower proportion of economically unviable mini-owners and a higher proportion of small-holders – though together less of both than in the province; a larger proportion of land available to small farm units; double the percentage of medium-sized owners and a smaller percentage of large owners farming a smaller proportion of the total land.

This privileged situation still meant that two-thirds of Tajos landowners held land too poor to reach the taxable level of 5,000 pesetas a year; that even in 1947 about one-third of the land in holdings of under fifty hectares was left uncultivated – and was therefore too poor to be thought worth cultivating; and that, although owners of under fifty hectares held 70 percent of all irrigated land, this in fact meant that under one hectare in ten of their land received irrigation. Finally, because of fallowing, as we have seen, one-fifth of the dry lands were of no use to a farmer in a given year.

INHERITANCE

The mechanisms of inheritance accounted in considerable part for the break-up of the large holdings. Given that the law obliges property to be divided among heirs (unless otherwise contractually stipulated, property is jointly held by spouses and the surviving spouse receives one-half and the children the other half of the deceased's property) one would expect all land holdings to be increasingly fragmented. While this is true up to a point, it is much less acute than might be expected.

In 1922 48·7 percent of all owners were heirs and owned 42 percent of the land. By 1965 heirs represented 49·4 percent of all owners and held 44·5 percent of the land.[6] Between the two dates landowning heirs increased by 28·2 percent, non-heirs by 24·5 percent and landholders totally by 26·3 percent.

Table 11 Inheritance 1922–65

| | Percentage increase in land owned in each category by | |
	heirs	non-heirs
mini	2·5	5·3
small	16·5	21·0
medium	20·6	20·4
medium-large	4·8	0
large	−11·3	−20·7

Heirs and non-heirs each accounted for virtually the same amount of the total increase in land owned (heirs: 921 hectares; non-heirs: 936 hectares) though with significant variations in the different categories.

Perhaps the most striking is in the mini-holdings where, given that heirs owned 58 percent of all land in this category in 1922, extreme fragmentation through inheritance might be expected. In fact the change was hardly significant: an increase of one heir (0·74 percent) and 2·9 hectares (2·5 percent). Non-heirs increased their holdings by double the amount, although in terms of the other category increases this too was insignificant.

In small-holdings similarly non-heirs show a greater increase than heirs, indicating again the creation by purchase of a small-holding peasantry. Dividing this category into two sectors one finds, however, changes in the pattern.

Table 12 Small-holding inheritance

	Percentage of heirs	Percentage of land owned by category
1–5 hectares		
1922	40·0	44·4
1965	46·6	50·4
5–10 hectares		
1922	12·6	50·1
1965	11·9	41·2

The above indicates that there was a degree of fragmentation among small-holdings from the larger to the smaller size within the category. But fragmentation did not turn small-holdings into mini-holdings. There is thus a limit to parcelization around the one-hectare mark; when plots become this small the automatic division (or subsequent ownership) of land comes to a halt, with plots being reconcentrated in the hands of one of the heirs or else being sold. (A similar limit to parcelization among non-heirs is also evident.)

At the other end of the scale, in the large holdings, fragmentation is at its highest. Inheritance here plays a larger part than Table 11 indicates;[7] over half the land movement in this category was due to inheritance. Moreover, the land was divided up not into medium-large holdings but into the smaller category of medium holdings. Even here in the category which saw the greatest increase in land owned, the position of heirs and non-heirs remained virtually constant. In 1922 15·1 percent of heirs owned 52·9 percent of this land; thirty years later 16·2 percent of heirs owned 52·1 percent.

Overall, the number of sibling heirs per family and the amount of land owned by each changed very little: 2·9 heirs per family in 1922 compared to 2·7 in 1965; 9·3 hectares per heir compared to 8·9 thirty years later.

With the exception of large holdings and to a certain degree small-holdings, inheritance ultimately appears less important than might have been expected in fragmenting land holdings. And even in large holdings the mechanism of reconcentration of control is always available with one heir farming the land owned by the other heirs.

LANDLORDS, TENANTS AND LABOURERS

The figures on landownership and how the land was actually farmed have already indicated the high proportion of small-holders, renters and sharecroppers in the Tajos countryside. Their full position – and the corresponding one of landowners who work their own land – can now be assessed.

Table 13 Distribution of active male agricultural population 1956

	Percentage of labour-employing entrepreneurs		Percentage of family operators				
	Owners	Tenants	Owners	Renters	Share-croppers	Permanent labourers	Day labourers
Tajos	1·7	0·4	26·2	13·5	16·1	6·4	35·7
Málaga	14·2	7·9	12·5	8·0	2·2	5·4	49·8
Eastern Andalusia	11·9	9·5	15·5	14·4		5·3	43·3

Family operators are defined as those not using non-family labour for more than ninety days a year; permanent labourers are those hired by the same employer for more than 180 days a year.

Eastern Andalusia, following Malefakis from whom the figures are taken, comprises here only the provinces of Málaga and Granada.

While the percentage of *total* owners in Tajos, Málaga and eastern Andalusia shows practically no variation, the percentage of village landowners working their holdings with hired hands is infinitesimal compared to the province or eastern Andalusia. On the other hand the proportion of renters and sharecroppers is three times as high as in the province and more than twice as high as in eastern Andalusia;[8] while the proportion of peasant owners is twice as high as in Málaga.

The percentage of village labourers is correspondingly lower. The *encuesta*, however, did not take into account the members of small-holders' and tenants' families who went out as day-labourers. Six years later, in another *encuesta*, the number of day-labourers was shown to have jumped from 370 to 919. The increase indicates clearly the reserve pool of day-labourers 'available' on the farms when, as in 1962, there was a demand for casual labour in the building trade (where at that time they still remained officially classified in the agrarian population).

Given the very high proportion of family operators in Tajos, it is of interest to know exactly what land was available to them. The 1956 *encuesta* does not answer this question; the 1962 census did provide an answer in terms of farm units but, most regrettably, the National Institute of Statistics (INE) has destroyed all the relevant information at municipal level for the whole of Spain. By reworking the figures over twenty hectares which remain and combining them with the 1956 *encuesta*, the following picture emerges:

Table 14 Family operators and land held

	Percentage of all farmers in 1956	Percentage of all land in 1962	Average size of farm (hectares)
owners	45·2	24·0	6·0
renters	24·0	6·7	3·3
sharecroppers	27·7	7·5	3·1

Compared with tenants and sharecroppers, family-operator owners who formed 45 percent of all farmers and 94 percent of all owners, were relatively well-off. The lot of renters and share-croppers who outnumbered small owners but occupied little more than half as much land is evident from the above.

It must be stressed, however, that while these statistics segregate family operators into three categories, the reality is often more complex. A small-holder may also rent or even sharecrop another plot of land; a renter may own a plot himself or enter into a share-cropping arrangement with another owner; and, though it is unusual for a sharecropper to own any land unless inherited, he may with luck find a plot to rent. For the majority, however, and particularly for the majority of sharecroppers, a living has to be won from a single plot.

SHARECROPPING AND RENTING

Local landlords defend the prevalence of sharecropping by assert-ing that the system provides land and a livelihood for a family which would otherwise not be available to it. This is, of course, true, though it is not an argument often heard among share-croppers themselves.

The 1962 census reported that in Málaga province 4·2 percent of all farm units covering 4 percent of the total land were share-cropped. The proportions in Tajos are considerably less favour-able to the sharecropper, as we have seen: 27·7 percent farming 7·5 percent of the land.

Throughout, the landowners' lack of entrepreneurial spirit

has been remarked on. This, however, should not be taken as a lack of concern with the profit motive. Given the pressure on land, it is arguable that, from the landowners' point of view, it paid to lack entrepreneurial spirit; that, after the vineyard era, it was more profitable for them to sharecrop and rent than to farm themselves. A study of the comparative profitability would have to take into account a number of 'subjective' as well as objective economic factors, such as whether the owner had another occupation which made it unprofitable for him to supervise his land directly. (Tajos absentee owners rented rather than sharecropped as a rule.) Lack of markets or access to markets and the long tradition of leasing land[9] obviously also played their part.

Since the war when rents have not been increasable at will, sharecropping has provided a higher return than renting. Moreover, sharecropping in areas of high crop risk and drought is a form of insurance for the landowners who prefer to share the risk rather than assume it all themselves.[10]

A renter and a sharecropper have given figures from which rough comparisons can be made. In 1927 Manuel Gutierrez paid 500 pesetas rent for his farm which was then producing about 5,000 pesetas income a year. Cristóbal Gonzalez, on a similar size farm and comparable in irrigation, estimates that *El Verdegal* produced then about 6,500 pesetas annual income. Of this, as a sharecropper, half went to the landlord.

In 1965 both estimated their farm's gross income at 100,000 pesetas; Gutierrez was then paying 4,333 pesetas a year rent while Gonzalez paid in produce 50,000 pesetas. Gutierrez admits that his rent was low and that an economic figure would have been closer to 10,000 pesetas a year, making a constant proportion of 10 percent of the farm's income in rent.[11] Gonzalez's payment to the landlord is never less than 50 percent, although the landlord has to pay for half the grain seed, fertilizer and livestock – and, of course, share in the risk of crop failure. Even if the direct costs amounted to half the landlord's income from the farm, which on average is highly unlikely, the annual return to the owner of sharecropped land remains two-and-a-half times as high as on rented land. The rate of exploitation of the sharecropper is thus considerably higher than that of the renter.

Seen from the sharecropper's view, whatever happens he receives no more than 50 percent of what he produces in return for the land and a minimal amount of assistance. The renter, even if he has to pay 25 percent of his gross income in rent, receives 75 percent of his gross product. As Gutierrez put it more simply: in 1927 and in 1971 the profit on a calf raised and sold paid his rent, leaving the rest of the year's produce at his disposal; for Gonzalez, the sale of a calf meant half the profit in cash and no relief from the levy of 50 percent on all the rest of the year's produce.

In one important aspect leasing has a negative result. Neither sharecropper nor renter (though the former possibly less than the latter) has any incentive to improve the land he works; and the landowner, though with the capital to do so, sees no profit in such investment. Irrigation is the most obvious example; but the planting of fruit trees, the opening of lorry access to the farmsteads, the use of mechanical cultivators now seen in abundance in Posadas and Benamalí and even the introduction of new crops or new varieties of traditional crops have been singularly absent. Even with access to loans the small-holder by definition lacks the possibilities of making any dramatic impact on agricultural techniques which, in consequence, have remained at a low level.

THE LAND TODAY

Most of the problems mentioned in this appendix are today being 'resolved' by evasion: the flight from the land. Landownership alone remains important since it is one source of new-made wealth.

How much land is cultivated today? The question is impossible to answer accurately; the *Hermandad* returns for 1971 show a drop of 15 percent compared with 1962 but there is an obvious in-built reluctance to admit to land going out of production. By the most conservative reworking of *Hermandad* figures one arrives at a drop in cultivated land close on 25 percent; the real figure is probably nearer to one-third.

One index, provided by *Hermandad* officials, is of wheat returns. In the post-war years, when wheat had to be sold at state-fixed prices and there was a thriving blackmarket, over 1,000 wheat returns were filed annually with the *Hermandad*; today, when wheat production is subsidized, little more than 120 returns are filed.

FOOTNOTES

1. I used the following sources: Tajos land surveys and *cadastral* returns of 1754, 1899, 1922–46 and 1947–65; the *Hermandad's* 'Encuesta Agropecuaria' of 1956; the first Spanish Agricultural Census, 1962; Málaga statistical handbook; Málaga and local agricultural returns, 1968–71; and local and provincial population census returns. Where there is no possibility of confusion, the sources are identified simply by date. The 1947–65 *cadastre* is referred to under both dates: as far as necessary, I was able to reconstruct 1947 data from it. Except in Table 1, municipal lands, which amount to over one-quarter of the total village land extent and consist of the pine-forested mountains, have been consistently deducted from all tables so as to present a more accurate picture of private land holdings.

2. Irrigation figures vary widely. In 1899 50 percent more land and in 1947 15 percent less land was recorded under irrigation than in 1962. The latter figure, being the only one not involving tax assessments, seems the most likely.

3. Edward E. Malefakis, *Agrarian Reform and Peasant Revolution in Spain* (Yale, 1970).

4. Data for the nineteenth century, when the present pattern of land-ownership was laid down, is sadly lacking. I was able to locate only one reference to the 1863 land returns; but even had these been available they would not have answered the question of individual landowners' holdings, for until the twentieth century the state made global tax assessments on villages and not on individuals.

5. The conservative Málaga *cacique's* land was in part such an exception; farmed by tenants who were given seven years' rent-free occupation to break and terrace new land, many of them were able to purchase their plots from his heirs after his death.

6. Sibling heirs and their land holdings (inclusive of subsequent purchases or sales) identified in the *cadastres* of 1922 and 1965. Inheritance is, however, not confined exclusively to direct heirs and these figures do not account for other than direct inheritance.

7. As stated above, the conservative *cacique's* heirs had sold, before 1965, the land they inherited after 1922; with the exception of a hundred hectares retained by one heir, this land thus appears in the non-heir's list.

8. It is widely admitted, not least by Málaga *Hermandad* officials, that the returns of the *encuesta* are unreliable. Nonetheless they serve to illustrate the relative differences between Tajos, the province and eastern Andalusia.

9. As early as 1863 there were 521 renters and sharecroppers to 618 owners.

10. Sharecropping increases in proportion to the aridity of the land. In Almeria, the driest Spanish province, it covers 23 percent of all farm units (Agricultural Census, 1962). See also R. Tamames, *Estructura Economica de España*, Madrid, 1964.

11. Malefakis estimates that rents in the 1930s equalled one-quarter of gross income as a rule. If this percentage applied on the above calculations, the landowner would have come out no better share-cropping than renting. But since rents have been fixed the ratio of rent to gross income has certainly dropped, making sharecropping more profitable in comparison. As to the question of the landowner's direct costs, a sharecropping contract in the 1930s was legal if the owner provided only one-fifth of the annual production costs.

APPENDIX C

Some Aspects of Social Conditions in Rural Málaga 1960–68

In 1960, according to the national census, 84·2 percent of the rural working population of the province was engaged in agriculture and fishing. The next highest category – 4·5 percent – was formed of white-collar workers in the public and private sector. These were followed by industry (2·9 percent), building (2 percent), commerce (1·9 percent) and transport (1·7 percent).

Education: 26 percent of the rural population was illiterate in 1960. This compares as follows with previous decadal percentages: 1910 – 80 percent illiteracy; 1920 – 74 percent; 1930 – 66 percent; 1940 – 49 percent; 1950 – 43 percent.

Only 400 persons out of the provincial (excluding Málaga city) population of 775,000 in 1960 were in institutes of higher education. Of these only twenty were classified as coming from rural backgrounds.

The 1962 Agricultural Census, which undertook a number of other surveys, reported that in 74 percent of Málaga villages less than 20 percent of school-age children did not attend school because of shortage of places or distance from schools; 22 percent reported that between 20 percent and 50 percent of children did not attend; and 4 percent that more than 50 percent did not attend.

These compared with national averages of 91 percent of rural Spain reporting less than 20 percent school attendance; 8 percent between 20 percent and 50 percent; and 1 percent more than 50 percent.

Social conditions: An official survey of Málaga province in 1968 reported that 99 percent of all agricultural workers had no annual vacation compared to 68 percent of all other workers. Some other figures drawn from the same survey indicate the position of agricultural to non-agricultural workers:

	Percentage of houses without running		Percentage ownership of Television		
	Water	Bath	set	Car	Motorbike
Agricultural	73	98	6	2	6
Non-agricultural	25	81	46	12	10

Agricultural mobility: The degree to which, within agriculture, it was possible to move into a different socio-economic category over two generations was also investigated by the 1968 survey. It produced the following picture:

Percentage who had fathers in same occupation

Labourers	90	8 percent had fathers who had been family-operator small-holders, renters or share-croppers
Family-operators	67	30 percent had labourer fathers
Labour-employing entrepreneurs	74	15 percent had family-operator fathers; 5 percent had labourer fathers

The 1970 census was being taken while the interviews for this book were being conducted. Unfortunately, detailed results have not been published to date. However, the above figures may be of service to the reader in judging the changes that tourism has brought to Tajos in the past few years.

ACKNOWLEDGEMENTS

I am indebted to the staff of the Málaga land registry office (Catastro de Rizqueza Rústica) for locating the 1899 Tajos land survey from whose copperplate I quote in the introduction to The Old. The staff's help throughout with the 1922 Tajos *cadastre* (which happily I reached before it was disposed of) and the 1947–65 *cadastre* – both extensively used, particularly in Appendix B – was invaluable; so too was their kindness in finding space for me while I copied out the more than 2,000 entries. I have also to thank the Ministry of Finance which gave me permission to consult the land registries.

Edward E. Malefakis's *Agrarian Reform and Peasant Revolution in Spain* (Yale University Press, 1970) provided the income calculations in the introduction to The Old. This invaluable book, a monument of patient research and clear analysis, provided me throughout with much background not only on Andalusian agrarian problems but on social matters as well.

In talking to agricultural workers, in particular day-labourers, I was guided by the investigations made by Juan Martinez Alier and reported in *Labourers and Landowners in Southern Spain* (London 1971), an important study of Córdoba agricultural conditions. His book also highlighted the question of class-consciousness among labourers which, as already remarked, is absent from J. A. Pitt-Rivers's otherwise informative *People of the Sierra* (London, Chicago 1961).

For local information from 1915 to 1940 I combed the major Málaga newspapers of the period; though I found only two references to Tajos, this was not the fault of the staff of the

283

newspaper archives in the Málaga town hall who were always most helpful.

In talking to the Men with Ideas I was helped by previous experience writing about another predominantly socialist Málaga mountain village before the war: *In Hiding – The Life of Manuel Cortes* (London, New York, 1972) contains a more detailed account of this experience than was possible here.

Gerald Brenan's *The Face of Spain* (London, 1950) gves the best account of Andalusia during the famine years; it is from this book that the Málaga falangista is quoted in the introduction to The Survivors. On the immediate post-war period and the Franco regime's policies I am particularly indebted to Ricard Soler and his essay *The New Spain* (New Left Review, Nov.–Dec. 1969) which develops in considerable detail the statistics and analyses on which I have only been able to touch.

The land appendix could not have been written without the collaboration of the Málaga office of the National Institute of Statistics (INE) which made available all published land statistics; and of Sr Don Pedro Revilla, head of the INE's agrarian statistical service in Madrid who gave me as much unpublished information on Tajos farming as still remained from the 1962 First Agricultural Census.

I am similarly grateful to the Málaga office of the Hermandad de Labradores y Ganaderos which allowed me access to the results of their surveys; and to the Tajos secretary of the Hermandad who provided me with figures on cultivation for 1968–71.

Finally I have to thank the staff of the Tajos town hall who found and allowed me to work on the hand-written copy of the 1754 survey of the village. This was the forty-question enquiry of the Intendant General of the Kingdom of Granada (in which Tajos then lay) and covered virtually every aspect of village life, as it did for all villages and towns in the Kingdom. No such complete survey of Tajos – evidence of the remarkable energies deployed in the eighteenth century to record and reform national life – appears to have been carried out again until the 1950s.

Among the many books which I have consulted are: Gerald Brenan, *The Spanish Labyrinth* (Cambridge, 1943) and *South From Granada* (London, 1957); Gabriel Jackson, *The Spanish Republic and the Civil War* (Princeton, 1965); Raymond Carr,

Spain 1808–1939 (Oxford, 1966); J. Vicens Vives, *Historia Económica de España* (Barcelona, 1959); A. C. Comin, *Noticia de Andalucia* (Madrid, 1970); and Juan Diaz del Moral, *Historia de las Agitaciones Campesinas Andaluzas* (Madrid, 1929, 1967).

About the Author

Educated in England and the United States, Ronald Fraser has worked as a journalist in Europe and on the *San Francisco Chronicle* and is now on the editorial board of *New Left Review*. The author of two volumes titled *Work,* published in England, and of *In Hiding,* published by Pantheon in 1972, he is working on an oral history of the Spanish Civil War.